Flying the Edge

Other Books by George C. Wilson

Bridge of No Return: The Ordeal of the USS Pueblo
(with F. Carl Schumacher, Jr.)
Army in Anguish (with Haynes Johnson)
Supercarrier
Mud Soldiers

Flying the Edge

Edge

The Making of Navy Test Pilots

George C. Wilson

NAVAL INSTITUTE PRESS
Annapolis, Maryland

Library of Congress Cataloging-in-Publication Data

Wilson, George C., date

    Flying the edge: the making of Navy test pilots/George C. Wilson.

      p. cm.

    Includes index.

    ISBN 1-55750-925-5 (alk. paper)

    1. United States Naval Test Pilot School.   2. Test pilots—United States. I. Title.

VG94.5.N64W55   1992

359.9'83—dc20   92-28515

Printed in the United States of America on acid-free paper ∞

9 8 7 6 5 4 3 2

First printing

To Nathaniel James Wilson, the family fledgling, and James Ricalton Wilson and Carolyn Beckman Wilson, his flight instructors.

Contents

Flying the Edge

Inspiration

Everything conspired to make Navy Lieutenants Donald Boecker and Donald Eaton feel relaxed about their mission this fourteenth day of July 1965. The flying weather was great—clear blue sky flecked with only a few white, benign clouds. Their target was undefended. At least so said the intelligence boys in their brief. Boecker and Eaton were to bomb a bend in a little road inside Laos some sixty miles southwest of Hanoi. Their bomber—the Grumman A-6A Intruder—had plenty of legs to get them from "the boat" to the target and back. No need to refuel on the way in or out. And no North Vietnamese patrol boats had threatened their boat, which was the aircraft carrier USS *Independence.* It was circling in the South China Sea off South Vietnam.

Life had been so peaceful, in fact, that Eaton had successfully lobbied LT Dave Gilbrath, the schedules officer of the VA-75 attack squadron—the Flying Aces—to put them on the afternoon's flight schedule. Otherwise, they would have sat out this day of the young war rather than fly their tenth mission.

When Boecker and Eaton got to their A-6, side number 507, parked on the flight deck, they went over it like doctors giving a quick physical to a healthy patient, looking only for obvious, visible trouble with the bones and arteries of the plane. Then they climbed inside to go through long checklists to make sure the internals of the aircraft were working.

Boecker sat in the pilot's seat on the left side of the fish-globe cockpit. Eaton settled into the right seat, the bombardier-navigator's spot. Their checks completed, Boecker pushed the gray throttle on his left side forward to move the bomber along the steel flight deck. He followed the hand signals of the sailor in the yellow shirt until the plane's nose tow link was fastened to the hook, called a shuttle, sticking up from the catapult.

Boecker pushed the throttles to the firewall to bring the engines to full military power. The bomber strained to break free but was restrained by a holdback fitting that looked like a short, two-headed bolt. It was designed to snap only when yanked apart by the strength of the catapult's flinging of the 25-ton plane down the deck.

After a final check with Eaton, Boecker saluted the catapult officer hunched alongside the roaring bomber, signaling that he was ready to be hurled off the end of the boat.

The cat officer touched the deck with his hand, his signal to a sailor at the edge of the flight deck to push the button that would activate the rotary launch valve and send a gigantic charge of steam into the catapult's throwing arm. The arm slammed forward, yanking the bomber from dead stop to 130 miles per hour in two seconds and breaking the holdback fitting.

Boecker and Eaton felt the familiar thump-thump as the plane's wheels complained about being yanked so roughly along the deck, but a sudden quiet told them the plane was off the cliff and in the open air in front of the boat. They sensed a slowing down in the seconds between the time the bomber ran out of the catapult's energy and the engines took over the job of flying the A-6.

"Good shot!" Eaton told Boecker. A microphone inside his oxygen mask connected his voice to the earphones in Boecker's helmet. Boecker turned the bomber northwest at 450 miles per hour to eat up the 180 miles of sea and land lying between them and the target in the province of Sam Neua in Laos. He flew at 25,000 feet, far above the reach of North Vietnamese AK-47 rifles and 37-mm and 57-mm guns. The Soviets had not yet sent the high-reaching SA-2 Guideline missiles to Hanoi.

Concentrating on the route to their target, Eaton stared down into the black hood that rose from his radar screen and studied the green lines that etched the shape of the approaching North Vietnamese coastline and inland features. He wanted to note exactly where their bomber would cross the beach. He saw they would go "feet dry" a few miles south of Thanh Hoa. Right on course.

Boecker was following another A-6 from the Indy piloted by LCDR Bill Ruby. LT Bill Dunham was Ruby's bombardier-navigator. This was to be a two-plane Barrel Roll attack. Dive on the target, one after the other; pull up; fly back to the boat. Simple.

After they were over land, Ruby radioed that his bombing system was not working properly, ordering Boecker, whose system was operative, to lead the attack. Ruby would follow him down to the target.

Thanks to clear weather and precise navigation, Boecker and Eaton spotted the target while they were still miles from it. They wondered why some unknown targeteer sitting at a safe desk had bothered sending them all this way to bomb such a minor part of the Ho Chi Minh Trail, Hanoi's north–south supply line. Boecker and Eaton could see that the road was little more than a dusty path. There was a bridge over a little stream, but tire tracks on either side of the bridge showed that truck drivers routinely forded the waterway. Knocking out the bridge would not impede the trucks much.

Their five Mark 82, 500-pound bombs would also do little to the road even if they smacked down right in the middle of it. The old bombs had contact fuses in their noses, not the hard casing nor the delayed fuses needed to make an impassable crater by exploding after penetrating the road. The bombs also had obsolete M-990 D-2 electrical fuses in their tails that were supposed to prevent the bombs from exploding too close to the plane.

Boecker rolled the plane over on its back and dove at the bridge at a 50-degree angle. Down, down, down—20,000, 15,000, 10,000 feet. The fliers felt as if they were falling faster than their plane, as if they were afloat in the cockpit rather than strapped down. They knew if they did not keep 3,500 feet between them and the road, shrapnel from their own exploding bombs might knock them out of the sky before they could pull up from their dive.

Boecker pushed the bomb-release button on the left side of the thick control stick between his knees, ejecting the bombs from their hooks on the underside of the bomber.

Kaboom!

They learned later that one of the 500-pound bombs on the right wing of the A-6 had dropped only five feet before exploding, but at the time they suspected antiaircraft fire. The blast pushed the right wing sharply upward and sent shrapnel slicing through the plane. The whirling compressor blades in the right engine were suddenly chewing chunks of steel. The engine growled, groaned, and staggered.

"We've been hit!" Boecker said over the intercom.

The red-colored fire-warning light for the right engine glowered at him from the instrument panel. The master caution light and other warning lights went on all at once.

Boecker looked in the mirror on the right side of the cockpit. The sight was chilling. A Niagara of fuel streamed from the right wing. In seconds it could catch fire and incinerate them. Hydraulics were also losing pressure.

Boecker shut the line carrying fuel into the engine. The fire-warning light stayed on, but the engine stopped struggling and died, leaving the job of keeping the plane aloft to the left engine.

Bill Ruby in the trailing A-6 flew in close to take a look at the stricken plane.

Boecker struggled to gain altitude by pushing the left engine throttle all the way forward. The engine gave all it had and then its fire light shouted the red warning. The thrusting compressor blades slowed and then stopped.

"We're on fire!" Boecker told Eaton. "Left engine's out."

Boecker, twenty-seven, six feet tall, with enough muscle on his 200-pound frame to have played tackle on the Naval Academy's football team, could not budge the flight controls. Bomb fragments had perforated the hydraulic lines that provided the muscle to work the ailerons and other movable surfaces needed to control the plane's flight. There was no control stick on Eaton's side of the airplane. The plane was locked in a 10-degree left bank.

The two aviators found themselves inside an uncontrollable brick hurtling through the sky. In seconds, they knew their brick would fall to the ground, if it did not explode in the air first.

"What's the heading and distance to the beach?" Boecker asked Eaton.

"One hundred thirty-five degrees; 153 miles."

Their engineless brick would not glide that far.

Eaton pulled the knee board from the pocket of his flight suit. He did not want anything to catch on the cockpit if he had to eject himself out of the burning airplane—as now seemed certain. He lowered his seat to improve his ejection posture. His mind flashed back to the instructions on how to sit before ejection. He wanted the odds on his side.

"Hey, Flying Ace!" Ruby radioed from underneath the stricken plane, using VA-75's call sign. "You're on fire! You're going to have to get out! Eject! Eject!"

"I know that," Boecker snapped. "Get away!"

After a few sentences of conversation, Boecker and Eaton agreed that they would be better off ejecting through the canopy rather than trying to jettison it from the damaged bomber. The canopy might get stuck halfway open, providing too little space to squeeze through during the ejection. The top of their high-backed seats had cutting edges that were designed to smash big holes in the plastic canopy. Pulling ejection loops under the seats would trigger the explosive charges needed to rocket the aviators through the canopy, seats and all.

Boecker slapped Eaton's knee. It was the signal to eject.

After struggling upward, the plane was now heading down from 13,000 feet. Their altitude gave Boecker and Eaton time before pulling the ejection handle to recall what they had been instructed to do: keep your arms down and close to your sides; press your head and back into the seat; put the underside of your legs flat against the seat; pull down your helmet visor; reach down and give the yellow and black ejection handle a good yank upward.

Eaton yanked his ejection lever.

Wham!

The charge under his seat exploded against his butt and shot him and the seat through the closed canopy. But the ridged back of the seat had failed to make a big enough hole in the canopy. Eaton's gloved hands jammed against the jagged edge of the small opening. Pain from his cut and bruised hands stabbed him as he hit the open air at 230 miles per hour and began flopping around like a flying rag doll.

With the force of the onrushing air, his lip microphone batted into his lips, splitting them. After leaving the carrier, Eaton had opted to use the lip microphone attached to his helmet rather than to keep wearing his cumbersome oxygen mask with the built-in microphone. The A-6's cabin was pressurized, so the fliers could breathe without wearing masks. As blood streamed from his lips into his mouth, he heard the noise every aviator prays for after ejecting:

Whump! Gotcha!

Those were the sounds of his parachute's opening automatically at 12,000 feet. The yank from the blossoming parachute wrenched his shoulders and ripped his .38-caliber Smith and Wesson revolver from its holster. The revolver swung around on its lanyard and smacked him in the face.

Struggling to ignore the pain, Eaton concentrated on what he had to do before he hit the ground. Almost everything naval aviators are supposed to do is set down step-by-step in thick manuals, with much of the instruction screaming at them in bold type. Whether taking off from a carrier or ejecting from a burning airplane, these mere humans are supposed to remain calm, doing everything they were taught in the right sequence with the deliberate finesse of building an ice-cream parfait one carefully laid layer at a time.

If you find yourself in the sky without an airplane, sermonizes the cold type of the Naval Air Training and Operating Procedures Standardization (NATOPS) manual, do not forget to inflate your life preserver; check your parachute canopy; cut the twisted shrouds with the special cutter in your vest; steer the chute; leave your visor down to keep tree branches from poking your eyes out; unbuckle your chute just as you hit the water or the ground—but not before; flex your knees just before you hit ground or water; prepare to use your pocket radio, but remember that an automatic radio beacon inside the seat pan still attached to you will drown out your signals unless you shut it off; use the day flares in the daylight and the night flares in the dark; relax—but try not to get captured; try to escape if you do get captured. NATOPS says everything except have a nice day if you don't get killed.

Eaton dared to look around as he saw the earth coming at him. It was still light. Villagers and soldiers from miles around could see the big white blossom of his chute. Bad. Eaton saw his A-6 smash into the side of a mountain, break into two giant pieces, and then burn up. He also spotted Boecker drifting to earth below. The heavier Boecker, even though he had ejected second, was going to hit the ground before the five-foot-seven-inch, 138-pound Eaton. Boecker was about a half mile away and would land on the other side of the hill from Eaton.

Suddenly, Eaton sensed an eerie quiet. Then he heard muffled voices, which grew louder and more distinct as he neared the earth. He heard dogs barking and ducks quacking and saw men running toward his landing spot. He knew the Communist Pathet Lao controlled this part of Laos. The men would probably kill him if they caught him. "We're in real trouble," the twenty-eight-year-old Eaton told himself.

After a comparatively painless ejection from the burning bomber, Boecker shared Eaton's dread as he floated to earth so surprisingly fast that he thought he would break his legs or arms when he hit the ground. He was drifting toward the center of a village and could see people pointing up at him. Some of them had rifles and looked like soldiers. He pulled the risers on his chute, trying to angle the canopy so that it would steer him away from the village. It was no use. God or the saint who looks after pilots interceded. A sudden gust of wind pushed against the parachute and carried Boecker away from the village. He landed gently in grass ten feet high. For the moment, he was hidden.

Boecker quickly stripped down for running. He shed his chute, helmet, and harness. He tried to yank out the survival gear packed in the metal container, called a seat pan, that fell to earth with him, but he accidentally set off the bottle of carbon dioxide attached to his life raft. A giant orange blossom started to rise from his hiding place. He gripped the raft's tough fabric and somehow mustered the superhuman strength to rip it open. The raft deflated.

Boecker started running through the high grass. The shouts of his pursuers got louder. He crossed a stream, became mired in a rice paddy, reversed course, climbed onto the hard dike of the paddy, and raced toward the woods on its far side. Gaining the woods, he ran along a trail for a while, then slid into the deep jungle growth alongside it. He tried not to break branches that his pursuers might see, crawling on his hands and knees and sometimes on his stomach to get through the thickest growth. He spotted an animal's den and burrowed into it, pulling brush over the entrance.

A group of men approached. Boecker could hear them beating through the woods systematically to flush him out of his cover. The Laotians knew from finding his parachute, which had caught in a tree, that their quarry could not be far away. This time they walked past. Like a scared animal, Boecker stayed hidden, silent and still.

Twilight and then night came at long last. Boecker decided it was safe to leave his lair. His idea was to search under cover of darkness for a place where a rescue helicopter could spot him in the morning. The jungle where he had been hiding was too thick, and the trees were too tall for a helicopter's horse collar to reach the ground even if would-be rescuers located him. Boecker had to find a more-visible pickup point.

To ease his night travel, Boecker buried most of the items he had taken from the seat pan. He kept a compass, knife, signal mirror, emergency rations, and radio. He pushed northwest until he gained the top of the mountain. The trees were too high there. He descended to an area of thick underbrush, deciding to spend the rest of the night there and hope for rescue in the morning. He lay down in a thicket and tried to sleep, but desperation adrenalin still pumped through him, making all his senses bristle.

Eaton's landing, unlike Boecker's, was on hard ground. His revolver dug into his gut as he smacked down, hurting him for the second time. He felt himself all over and decided the landing had not broken any bones.

"Get up in those mountains," Eaton told himself. Intelligence briefers had said the area two hundred miles west of his position was safe for Americans. He shed chute, helmet, and leg restraints. He started running, but he was too heavy and bulky. He shed his gravity suit and torso harness, then ran toward Boecker's landing spot. He wanted to help his pilot if he were hurt even though they had agreed before that they would separate if they ever got shot down, to make it harder for the enemy to capture both of them.

Eaton was in top physical shape from doing Canadian Air Force fitness exercises religiously on the *Independence,* but as he struggled through the heavy grass, vines, and trees to reach Boecker, the voices of his pursuers got louder. Realizing he could never reach Boecker in time to do him any good, Eaton reversed course and headed east for the nearest cover. He told himself he would circle back toward the west once he had eluded the soldiers. Whenever he reached the brow of a hill, he hurled himself down its slope, mindless of injury in his desperation to get away. He reached a shallow stream and walked in it for a stretch, climbing several feet and then retracing his steps to throw chasing dogs off his trail. He charged ahead this way for an hour, pausing only to gasp for breath and shed more gear. He no longer heard voices.

For the second time he listened to eerie quiet. Afraid to stay put, he pushed on. The sky darkened. He was still free, running on adrenalin supercharged by the same fear that had powered Boecker.

Eaton stopped running at 10 P.M. He was on a hill. Still dangerously close to the village, he could hear its dogs barking. But he needed rest. His hands had swollen, and his stomach and face still hurt from the pistol's banging into them. His throat was parched. He had not stopped to drink from the streams he ran through. He dug a few Charms candies from his survival vest and sucked on them. They generated a little moisture in his dry mouth.

The moon was full. This would have been welcome in his aviator life because its extra light made it easier to land on the carrier at night. Commander's Moon, aviators called it, because older commanders needed more light to see the ship than the younger, sharper-eyed lieutenants. But in Laos the Commander's Moon threatened to spotlight him for the soldiers trying to find and perhaps kill him.

Eaton pondered his plight. He had burned himself out in his dash along the hills and valleys of the jungle. His hands continued to swell, and come morning, he figured his hands would be unable to get him into a rescue collar. And he was not sure how long he could keep running through the jungle in the coming day. He concluded his best odds were to hide some place where a helicopter could land. That way he could jump into its open side door rather than try to hang on to a horse collar as it was cranked up to a hovering helicopter.

Searching his surroundings, he found thick brush near a lone tree he could tell a helicopter pilot to use as a marker to land near. He could not think of anything more to do this night, so he buried himself in the underbrush and waited for first light. Loneliness overwhelmed him. He prayed. Like Boecker, he did not sleep.

During the night Boecker and Eaton heard trucks grinding into the village and troops dismounting. Squads of soldiers fanned out through the hills, looking for the two hated Americans. The downed aviators lay in their hiding places, listening and worrying. Eaton often heard the footsteps of soldiers passing close to him. He once saw the scissor motions of khaki-clad legs passing across the peep hole of his lair. He could have reached out and tackled the man. The soldier walked on.

In the gray light of pre-dawn, Boecker and Eaton heard the reassuring engines of an Air Force C-54 transport plane circling at 10,000 feet over their last-known position. "Victor Control," Eaton called to the plane over his pocket radio. "This is Flying Ace 507. Flying Ace bombardier 507." Eaton was not sure if his call had been received but told himself it must have been.

About 5:30 A.M. Boecker and Eaton heard the distinctive thwack-a-thwack of two Sikorsky UH-34D piston-engine helicopters, which were based in Laos as part of Air America, the airline run by the CIA. Veteran jungle pilot Sam Jordan, they'd learn later, was at the controls of one of the UH-34Ds. They would also learn later that each of their radios was half broken. Boecker's radio could transmit but not receive. Eaton's could receive but not transmit. Eaton listened to Boecker's radio calls in between making ones of his own.

Eaton looked across the valley at the choppers shuttling over what he assumed was Boecker's hiding place. But the helicopter pilots could not seem to find Boecker, flying like hummingbirds unable to find the right flower in which to insert their long bills.

Once during that first search a helicopter flew toward Eaton. He rose from his hiding place and waved, risking being spotted by the Laotian soldiers. The gunner standing in the helicopter's open door waved back at Eaton, but the helicopter kept right on going. The CIA's native gunner had no radio and did not speak English well enough to tell the American rescue pilots what he had just seen.

Shortly after 7 A.M. four A-1 Skyraider propeller-driven planes armed with rockets and 20-mm cannons arrived. Again Boecker called to his would-be rescuers over his pocket radio. Again he heard no response. Was his radio broken? Could it send but not receive? He asked the A-1 pilots to rock their wings if they were receiving his transmissions. They rocked, then flew away. Boecker felt better.

"Where am I from you?" Sam Jordan asked Boecker. Although Boecker could not hear Jordan, he sensed why he was pausing in his search.

"Back here!" Boecker radioed. "I'm at your six." He flashed his pocket mirror at the hovering helicopters. This was dangerous because sometimes door gunners fired down at such winks of light, believing they were coming from enemy rifles. But this time Jordan and his wingman twisted their ungainly machines around and bore down on Boecker.

Pop! Pop! Gunga-gunga. Rifles and machine guns opened up on

the choppers in the hover. Jordan's wingman was hit. Fuel streamed from the helicopter.

"I'm hit," Eaton heard the chopper pilot radio. "I'm losing fuel. I'm going to have to get out of here."

Both helicopters swung away. Jordan escorted his wounded wingman back to the CIA's field at Lima Site 36 near Vientiane. Two of the four A-1 Skyraiders also swung off to see the choppers home.

Without rescue helicopters in sight, Boecker and Eaton worried that their frantic hailing by radio and mirror had revealed their hiding places to their pursuers. When Boecker heard a man approaching, he lay down as flat as he could on his stomach, expecting to feel the jab of a bayonet or the smash of a rifle burst any second. Instead, he saw the man walk within eight feet, stop, and reverse course. The aviator would always wonder whether the hunter had shied from killing him or did not see him in the underbrush.

Eaton figured that it would take at least two hours for the helicopters to refuel and return for another rescue attempt. It was 9:30 A.M. in a rapidly heating day. He decided he would be safe if he climbed the hill and went down its other side, where the gunners who had fired up from the valley at the helicopters could not see him. Perhaps it would be safe for the choppers to land on that side of the mountain if they did return.

Pop!

An unseen Laotian rifleman had fired at one of the two A-1s still circling over the fliers. Eaton told himself he had to load that troublesome .38 revolver if his pursuer was that close. He tried to put shells in the gun but found his swollen hands could hardly manage. The bullets also had so much crud on them that he had to rub them in dirt to make them fit into the pistol's cylinder. With thumb and forefinger, he managed to put four of the roughly cleaned bullets in the chamber.

"If this son of a bitch comes near me, I'm going to shoot him," Eaton resolved.

Eaton heard the high-pitched scream of a diving Skyraider's propeller. The plane boomed 20-mm shells into the valley where the shots had come from. The Skyraider's wingman rolled in next and fired four 5-inch rockets.

With this diversion, Eaton figured he could move safely to the other side of the mountain. Pushing through the thick bush, he stumbled onto a grass flatland with as little cover as a golf-course fairway. He was horrified but committed to this new direction. He ran across the open ground and reached the other side of the mountain with nobody shooting at him.

Shortly before noon, more fixed-wing planes and helicopters arrived. Eaton set off an orange-smoke flare. None of the aircraft saw it. He popped a second flare and hurled it into the air. An Air Force pilot in a Laotian T-28 bomber saw it and bore down on Eaton. He first felt relief and then terror. Perhaps he was about to get strafed rather than rescued by a pilot who thought he was an enemy soldier. Eaton dove to the ground. He looked up after the T-28 had passed over him and saw the flier in the backseat looking back and waving. Jordan followed the path the T-28 had flown. When Eaton stood up from the brush and raised his arms in the cross, signifying he was a friendly, Jordan dove down to the ground. He slowed the helicopter to a walk as he brushed by Eaton, who made a running dive for the open door and landed in a heap on the helicopter's floor. Jordan immediately pulled up on the control stick, raising the chopper up sharply into the sky.

Boecker was still in the bush. He had watched the strafing and shelling of the enemy troops. The attack had exploded ammunition hidden underground, igniting the dry fields and surrounding woods. Boecker worried that the fire might race up to his hiding place in the dry brush. But for the second time nature intervened and saved him. A friendly wind drove the fire away. But Jordan, skittering back and forth over Boecker in his UH-34D, still could not see the downed pilot in the bush.

Boecker set off a smoke flare the next time Jordan flew overhead, but the chopper kept right on going. Boecker decided he could not stay put. He crashed through the deeper jungle, looking for a tree the helicopter pilot could not help seeing. He radioed to his would-be rescuers that he was directly uphill at the tall tree with the big umbrella top. Jordan swung to that spot and saw Boecker.

The down wash from the whirling rotor blades stung his eyes and made it hard to stand, but Boecker saw a horse collar on a steel cable being lowered to him. Then the down wash blew it into the branches of the big tree, halting its descent. The chopper's crew could not position the collar any closer than three feet above Boecker's head and downhill from him.

Boecker backed up the mountain about ten yards, stripped off the rest of his gear, and prepared to make the jump and grab of his life. Miss this version of the brass ring and he was dead. He sprinted down the hill and leaped as high as he could. He thrust his right arm through the collar but could not get his left arm into it. In desperation he locked his left hand over his right wrist and hung on with all his strength.

The crewman looked out the door of the helicopter at Boecker but did not reel him up. Dragging Boecker through tree branches, Jordan backed the helicopter away from the tall tree. He did not want to risk staying in a hover until Boecker was aboard. Gunners in the valley had already hit his wingman and were still firing at the aircraft. The A-1s tried to form a shield of fire by staying between Boecker and the valley. But the A-6 pilot was a great target for any riflemen on the ground, clinging precariously to the rescue collar as he was hauled through the open sky at 60 miles per hour. He could only hang on and hope. He dangled that way until the chopper had climbed to 2,000 feet. Only then did the helicopter slow to a near hover so that the crewmen could reel Boecker up.

Eaton watched anxiously from his spot on the helicopter floor. He could not see the ground because the crew at the door blocked his view. He tried to determine whether Boecker was closer to life or death by watching if the cable continued to reel in. When Eaton at last saw the top of the horse collar, Boecker's head was not in it.

"Oh, shit!" exclaimed Eaton to himself. "They didn't get him."

Then Eaton saw a tree branch. After that came Boecker's arm over the bottom of the collar, then his head and torso, gripped by the helicopter crewmen. They pulled Boecker through the door and onto the floor of the chopper. Eaton skittered across the floor and hugged his pilot and friend. They laughed and cried as they embraced and marveled at their luck in escaping what had seemed certain death.

Back on the carrier *Independence,* CAPT Duke Windsor had assembled a brass band to welcome Boecker and Eaton. Every sailor who was not on duty was standing on deck, cheering, when they walked out of their E-1B Willie Fudd aircraft onto the carrier's flight deck. Boecker and Eaton were the first aviators from the air wing who had been lost during this first Vietnam deployment of the *Indy.* Tears streamed down their faces as they made their way across the flight deck, shaking the hands of their shipmates. "Nice to have you back," said sailor after sailor.

• • •

CDR Leonard Alexander "Swoose" Snead II, skipper of VA-75, gave Boecker and Eaton time to ease their way back into the routine after their rescue. They had five more months of flying before the ship would steam home for Christmas, but it was not too soon to think about their next Navy jobs.

Snead had an idea for Boecker. He told the promising lieutenant with the warming smile, "You ought to apply for TPS."

"What's TPS?" was Boecker's response.

Swoose Snead explained that TPS was shorthand for the United States Naval Test Pilot School within the Naval Air Test Center at Patuxent River, Maryland. It was the place where the Navy made test pilots and then put them to work testing airplanes and weapons. Navy leaders relied on test pilots to tell them whether a new plane lived up to its contract specifications, whether it and the weapons that would go on it were safe, and what effect changes in an airplane had on its performance. This testing was supposed to prevent the kind of accidental explosion that had blown Boecker and Eaton out of the sky over Laos.

Snead knew that Boecker had those special qualities needed to make a successful test pilot, with curiosity, caution, deliberateness, and patience near the top of the list. White-scarfed daredevils need not apply to Test Pilot School. Plenty of aviators wanted to know how to shoot another airplane down. Fewer were curious about what made airplanes do what they do in the sky. Boecker had developed that curiosity while growing up in Naperville, Illinois, a city of forty thousand located on the prairie between Chicago and Aurora. He would spend hours building model airplanes out of bamboo struts, and when Harold White, the editor of the Naperville *Sun*, found out about Boecker's interest, he took the teenager flying in his Piper J-3 Cub. That was it. Boecker had to learn how to fly—and did, earning his private pilot's license at age sixteen. He joined the Air Scouts on the way to becoming an Eagle Scout. In 1955, his senior year of high school, Boecker applied to the Air Force Academy. He did not know the Navy flew airplanes. The Air Force Academy rejected him, so Boecker joined the Naval Reserve; went to the Columbian Preparatory School in Washington, D.C., to improve his academic background; and won an appointment to the U.S. Naval Academy through the Naval Reserve in 1956.

Graduating from the academy in 1960 with a degree in mechanical engineering, he eagerly joined the Navy's flying branch, knowing by this time that the Navy indeed flew planes. He won his wings at Pensacola in February 1962, and he requested and got jets, reporting to Attack Squadron Seventy-Six at Oceana, Virginia, to fly the A-4C Skyhawk light-attack plane. In September 1963 he moved into the left seat of the Navy's newest and smartest bomber, the A-6 Intruder, with attack squadron VA-75. He had no idea—no aviator ever does—when he sailed for Vietnam in 1965 with VA-75 on the *Independence* that he would meet disaster in the sky over Laos and find himself running through the jungle for his life.

The way so many people had gone all out to save their lives had been an inspiration to both Boecker and Eaton. They wanted to pay their country back. Their rescue had hardened their conviction to make the Navy a career.

As Boecker filled out the application forms for Test Pilot School and pondered what it would be like to test airplanes for other aviators rather than fly them in combat himself, he became convinced that Snead was right, that it was time to deepen himself. Dropping bombs was exciting, but there was more to Naval Air than that.

The whole aerospace world was churning in 1966 when Boecker was hoping to go to Test Pilot School. Astronauts were rocketing into space as President Johnson continued the race to the moon started by the slain President Kennedy. And the Vietnam War was proving with searing clarity that the Navy and Air Force had designed their airplanes for a war that would not be fought, a nuclear exchange with the Soviet Union. The Navy's A-4 attack bomber had been designed to carry a nuke, as had the Air Force's B-52 bomber. Both services scrambled to convert these and other aircraft for the ground-support and -interdiction jobs that field commanders in Vietnam were pleading for. The Navy tried to narrow its conventional-bomber gap by rounding up all the flyable A-1 Skyraider piston-engine bombers it could find and sending them to Vietnam, even taking them out of the flight schools.

As for conventional munitions, it was back to the iron bombs of World War II. The Navy and Air Force had relied too heavily on the capabilities of the new "smart" weapons in designing their current planes, so while scientists continued to work on modern bombs and missiles, jets had to be refitted with older, proven systems. The nose of the Air Force F-4 Phantom fighter-bomber, for example, had to be ripped open to install the gear needed for firing guns as well as air-to-air missiles.

Test pilots had to evaluate all these changes before the aircraft went to war. Boecker and the others who had applied to Test Pilot School wanted to get a piece of this high-tech action. They also knew most of the astronauts were test pilots. A diploma from Test Pilot School would help them reach this new frontier in space.

Boecker was accepted to Test Pilot School. His orders directed him to start classes with Class 46 at the Naval Air Test Center, Patuxent River, Maryland, on 24 October 1966. Arriving with a great sense of anticipation, Boecker discovered that not only were there more than a dozen different types of planes and helicopters for the would-be test pilots to fly as part of their training, but there was also a gorgeous golf course that President Eisenhower had found irresistible. If flying was Boecker's professional love, and it was, then golf was his off-duty passion. So the remoteness of Pax River did not bother this twenty-nine-year-old, gung-ho aviator.

Test Pilot School proved a struggle. He had been away from engineering and math for six years, and he had never been an academic whiz. But he struggled through in this precomputer era, working out the problems with a slide rule. He graduated in 1967 and reported to the Attack Branch of the Weapons Systems Test Division at Pax River to put the theory of test piloting into practice. The atmosphere was one of heightened urgency. The scope of the Vietnam War had widened since his time there in 1965. And the war was not going well at all. Field commanders were screaming for more and better of everything, including aircraft and munitions. But the Boeckers of Pax River had to test the ideas and hardware before they could be sent to the fleet, even if the admirals wanted the tests completed yesterday.

Boecker's three years at Pax River raced by. Day after day he evaluated the rebuilt A-7A bomber, which was proving a highly effective day bomber in Vietnam. The Air Force ordered the new D version of the aircraft, and the Navy the E, from Ling-Temco-Vought of Dallas, Texas. Boecker headed a joint Air Force–Navy team of test pilots, who flew to Dallas to conduct the MPE, or military preliminary evaluation, of the A-7D and A-7E aircraft. Then Boecker brought the Navy's A-7E back to Pax River to evaluate it for the Board of Inspection and Survey, a body that advises the Secretary of the Navy about whether a plane on the edge of production is worth buying.

Boecker had never been to St. Mary's County before going to Test Pilot School. Now he was having the time of his life. He loved the friendliness of the local people—it reminded him of the warmth of his native Midwest—and the excitement of flying the edge as a test pilot. The nearness of the golf course and the beauty of the Chesapeake Bay and Patuxent River completed his contentment. He vowed to come back to St. Mary's County, to make it his home when he had run his race in the Navy uniform. He could be assigned to Pax River again during his naval career, but that was unlikely. The Navy is a far-flung and highly mobile enterprise, and you never know where you might end up. But you can hope. Coming home to Pax River some day was Boecker's hope as he left the Naval Air Test Center in October 1969 and resumed his career as a Navy attack pilot.

The Navy, unlike the Air Force, does not believe in allowing its aviators to make a career out of test piloting. The Navy looks upon experienced test pilots as seed corn to be spread around the fleet continuously to grow new ideas and tactics far from test centers like Pax River. Navy leaders contend this revolving-door arrangement keeps the connection between test pilots and the fleet bright and strong. Test pilots recognize that their job is to keep their friends in the fleet, and perhaps themselves when they return to a fleet assignment, from being blown out of the sky by their own bombs, from crashing and burning because the plane they tried to land had flaws that nobody detected before it went to sea.

The fleet is the raison d'être for test pilots. If the United States Navy did not go to sea with airplanes as well as ships, it would not need test pilots on shore. Boecker learned the importance of test pilots firsthand when he ejected over Laos, and he learned at Test Pilot School why some planes are harder and more dangerous to fly than others. The Navy was counting on him to pass his experience on to his fellow aviators. And, to his astonishment and delight, it would give him a big job to do just that.

Class 100 Arrives

The rear admiral sitting in the corner office on the second floor of the headquarters of the Naval Air Test Center at Pax River was waiting for a telephone call to summon him to Test Pilot School two blocks away. He was to welcome the thirty-four nervous members of Class 100. The admiral smiled inwardly as he realized these overachievers were going to be late for their first formal appointment with him because of the terrorist threat.

It was 14 January 1991. The United States had sent Army, Navy, Air Force, and Marine forces to the Persian Gulf in response to Iraq's invasion of Kuwait. War seemed imminent. The intelligence community had warned Pax River and every other military base to be extra careful about whom they allowed to pass through their gates. A terrorist sympathetic to Iraq might well try to blow up an American base, just as someone had destroyed the Marine Corps barracks in Beirut in 1983.

The sailors at the front gate were checking identifications so carefully that traffic was backed up. Among those caught in the slow-moving snake of cars and pickup trucks were many of the members of Class 100. They realized it was not career enhancing to keep an admiral waiting.

The students in the traffic jam had no way of knowing that the admiral, rather than turning crimson with rage, was actually enjoying their predicament. He was a guy who knew something about predicaments. His name was Donald V. Boecker.

Lady Luck had been kind again to Don Boecker. Since yanking him out of the Laotian jungle in 1965, she had steered him through squadron command, several Washington tours, and command of the supply ship USS *Concord*. Although executive assistant to Navy civilian research chief Melvyn R. Paisley, who was convicted of taking bribes from contractors, Boecker was not stained by that scandal. He was promoted to rear admiral and in July 1988 received his dream assignment: command of the Naval Air Test Center, where he had been a working stiff two decades earlier. Now he was boss, not only of Class 100 but of the whole population of about 7,500 men and women working on the 7,000 acres of Pax River.

There was a synergism to Boecker's career. He had done what the visionaries had hoped would be done to prepare people to evaluate Navy aircraft: You fly with the fleet long enough to understand the demands of putting an airplane on a pitching deck at night and dropping bombs from it, but don't stay in the fleet so long that you forget your calculus, aerodynamics, and all that other schooling. Go through Test Pilot School to understand how and why testing aircraft FOR the fleet is different from flying them WITH the fleet. Work as an engineering test pilot for a few years and then leave the testing specialty to enrich other Navy communities with your experience and knowledge. Conclude your Naval Air career in executive positions where you not only know how to separate the wheat from the chaff but have the authority to make sure this threshing is done right.

As Boecker was waiting to hear that all the students of Class 100 had arrived, I was studying the traffic jam outside the gate with detachment. I had spent the night before at the Bachelor Officer's Quarters a few hundred yards inside the base. Having persuaded the Navy's leaders to allow me to see firsthand how it trained its test pilots and engineers, I planned to sit through classes at Test Pilot School, almost all of them unclassified, and get some of the same instruction in the air that future test pilots receive. Only by such an inside look, I had contended, could I write an accurate book about how test pilots are trained, what they are like, and what they really do in this high-tech age once they graduate from Test Pilot School.

To gain approval to fly, I had to pass the same physical examinations and water-survival tests that naval aviators take before they fly over the water. I had qualified once before, in 1983, so that I could deploy with the aircraft carrier USS *John F. Kennedy* to write the book *Supercarrier.* But the rules required that I pass refresher tests in how to eject from an airplane and how to keep from drowning after landing in the water with a parachute over my head. So I went back into the pool in 1991, dressed in helmet, flight boots, flight suit, harness, gravity suit, and radio and assorted hardware to demonstrate that with all that stuff weighing me down I could still use three different strokes to swim seventy-five yards in the pool. Then it was tread water for ten minutes, the hardest part of the qualification for me this time. I had to take the treading-water test twice before I passed it.

It was with a mixture of apprehension and anticipation that I headed for my first meeting with Class 100. The students had been told—warned is more like it—that I was coming. Some of the officers liked the idea of being in a book about modern-day test pilots, but many feared I would write something about them that would hurt their careers. It was going to be touchy going.

As I drove toward Test Pilot School deep within the flatland of the base, I sensed lifelessness. No marching sailors. Few civilians. Once in a while I would see a pedestrian walking from his or her car to a building. But most of the people I saw were inside other cars.

The road leading to the interior of Pax River is Cedar Point Road. Buildings on its right side were mostly one- and two-story rectangles spread far apart on the former farmland. They looked as if Navy Seabees could disassemble them, load them on a flatbed, and cart them away. The only structure with a look of permanence was the old church on the left side of Cedar Point Road.

Farther to the left, in the distance, I could see the silvery-gray hangars with curved roofs. They marked where land met the Patuxent River. The hangars had been built at the river's edge in the 1940s when admirals thought seaplanes had a great future in the Navy. The seaplanes of that era landed on the river, taxied into protected basins, and were hauled up a ramp onto the land. Sailors had to swim out from shore and attach the wheels to some of the seaplanes.

I decided that the base felt lifeless because the big hangars swallowed most of Pax River's population during the workday. And the hangars had been built so far apart during World War II, to minimize the damage from any sneak-bombing attack, that workers had to drive from place to place rather than walk. So it was a base of grass, trees, squat buildings, and cars, cars, cars.

However, there was plenty of evidence inside Pax River's gate to remind everyone that the airplane was king here, and often dangerous. Roads shooting to the left and right from Cedar Point Road were named after those who had died in planes being tested. Among those who have roads named after them are LTJG Richard D. Saufley, Naval Aviator Number 14, who crashed and died on 9 June 1916 while flying an endurance test out of Pensacola; LT George T. Cuddihy, who was killed on 25 November 1929 when the wings came off the airplane he was diving over Anacostia; Third Class Petty Officer John Keating Fogarty, who was killed when a transport crashed at Pax River on 12 April 1944; and LT James Tate, Jr., who was killed the next day—13 April 1944—when the fighter plane he was testing crashed into the Chesapeake Bay.

Further evidence that the airplane rules this domain came when a big red light commanded me and all the other cars on Cedar Point Road to stop for an airplane taxiing across the road on the way to a takeoff runway. I mused that this is probably one of the few bases in the country where carrier planes and automobiles can collide at an intersection.

Test Pilot School is to the left of Cedar Point Road on the banks of an old seaplane basin. I noticed that Test Pilot School is not really a school building at all but two of those old silvery-gray airplane hangars hitched together.

I proceeded to the second level of the school and discovered an alleyway classed up by patches of varnished wood. The wood relieved the gray and green of the walls and asphalt-tile floors and alerted me that I was in the closest thing to flag country or executive row that existed at Test Pilot School. At the end of this hallway I found the conference room where Class 100 was supposed to gather.

Entering that room, which had a rug on the floor and a television set and podium up front, I took one of the straight-backed chairs in the rear and studied the members of Class 100 who were slowly filtering in. I noticed three foreign test pilots, one each from the Canadian Air Force, Italian Air Force, and Royal Air Force. The Canadian government was paying the United States $575,615 to send one of its helicopter pilots through the U.S. Naval Test Pilot School; the Italian government, $677,039. The British student was here on an exchange arrangement, so his instruction required no payment.

The conference room finally filled. I counted eighteen Navy officers, three Army commissioned officers and one Army warrant officer, three Marine Corps officers, the three foreign officers, one Air Force officer, and five civilian engineers. These were the thirty-four students comprising Class 100. There was little talking back and forth. The class was in the measuring phase. CDR Thomas J. Bernsen, director of Test Pilot School, had deftly told me in our get-acquainted session a few days earlier: "You'll notice that everyone in the class knows who is number one"—namely himself or herself. "He's looking around to see who's number two."

"Attention on deck!"

In strode Admiral Boecker, resplendent in dress blues. He walked to the front of the room, took the podium, told everyone to sit down, and surveyed the thirty-four students and this chronicler. He smiled what the women at Pax River had told me was his "killer smile." It lit up his weathered face and reminded the lieutenants in the room that this fifty-three-year-old admiral had been a lieutenant once, too, and still had spirit.

"You're late, and it's only the first day," Boecker began. Then he broke into another smile, this one wide enough to wrinkle the crow's-feet by his eyes, to put the students at ease.

"You'll become so close, you'll be friends for life," Boecker told the class in a warm, confiding manner. "I mean it."

With quiet earnestness, Boecker described the new life the aviators and engineers sitting before him would live in their coming eleven months of Test Pilot School. Their socializing would not be concentrated in the ready room, as it had been for the aviators who had deployed on carriers, nor would it be the 8 A.M. to 4:30 P.M. office environment the engineers had known. He said it would be days and nights of studying together, of flying together, of writing reports together, of eating dinners together and playing with one another's children, of struggling together, of despairing together, of celebrating together. Nobody knew as of that morning whether this bonding would occur. Some of the past classes had bonded tightly, just as Boecker was saying. Others had broken up into cliques. Class 100 would turn out to be a combination of closeness from all the togetherness and conflict from clashing egos and suspiciousness. All this was over the horizon.

He raved about the beauty of the base, the fishing, the boating, the golf. "We have five hundred deer on the base, most of them in my front yard right now." He flashed another smile.

"Unfortunately, you won't see much of that beauty the first eleven months you're here. You'll be very busy. But I encourage your wives to get involved." None of the three women in the class was married, but one was engaged.

"Safety is number one. We have not had a death here in Test Pilot School for many, many years.

"This is going to be the most intensive thing you've done. Each one of you help the other guy out. The astronauts tell us that everything they did here is applicable.

"You are the very best in your squadron, the very best in your services, or you wouldn't be here today."

A few more "attaboys," and then Boecker closed with, "Good luck, and Godspeed."

Commander Bernsen followed the admiral to the podium. A helicopter pilot and native Californian with one of those perpetual tans, Bernsen had gone through Test Pilot School with Class 77 in 1980. He quickly gave some advice to the new class in a low-key, direct, penetrating manner.

"You've never done anything like this before," Bernsen said. "This is a participant kind of learning. We don't teach you—you teach yourselves by learning from other members of your group. It can be a jumbled-up mess. It depends on you, how you manage your time. You can ruin your time here by bringing sleeping bags to work. That's not the right answer. You don't want to walk away from this place with a divorce and with children you don't recognize.

"The biggest problem is time management. Take an evening and take a day as 'my time.' Take Friday for yourself, and pat the kids on Saturday. Trust me. This place will regain equilibrium. On December 13 there will be a graduation ceremony.

"We have twenty-five different fellows on the staff. We're not trying to make you look like me but to be the best you can be. I don't have any preconceived notions about what Class 100 should be. It's up to you to define it.

"This experience is going to change your life. It's like SERE [Survival, Evasion, Resistance, and Escape] School. You'll cherish the experience and never want to do it again. If you fail to enjoy it, it's your fault. Congratulations, and good luck to all of you."

Next came a combination welcome and lecture from CDR Steven "Smiley" Enewold, whose open face and frequent smile confirmed his nickname. His description of his own responsibilities at Test Pilot School was brief: "I'm in loose control of all the flight instructors around here—the quality-assurance guy for the instructors."

He began by explaining what Test Pilot School is all about: "We are here to teach you how to test, not to give you some neat-o things to play with." He compared the school with a triangle, with one leg the flying, the second the classroom work, and the third the writing of reports on the flights these test pilots under instruction, called Tapooies, would fly.

The word "Tapooie" came into use because no one knew what to call the pilots who came to Test Pilot School. They were experienced pilots with big egos who would be offended by the term "student pilot." Yet they had not learned how to be test pilots. So Test Pilots Under Instruction, or Tapooies, was the compromise.

The school has several different kinds of airplanes for the students to fly, Enewold continued, because a "goal of the school is to prepare you to transition from one airplane to another."

He told the students that they would not receive grades. "The goal here is not to spank you but give you the tools required to ... continue on with the course. Probably you will have problems with one area of flying." Rather than grade what the student does as right or wrong, the flight instructor's job is "to instruct you—to turn you into test pilots, not to teach you how to fly.

"Test pilots are not born; they are trained. We're here to train you how to be test pilots. When you graduate from here, you've got a learner's permit to be a test pilot."

Enewold cautioned against pilots' overextending themselves or flying when they were distracted—conditions that would increase the risk of their making mistakes and crashing. "Please come in and say, 'Uncle.'

Just say, 'I will learn a lot more some other day.' If you don't want to fly that day, don't. This is a learning institution."

He warned that there would be "a tremendous buildup" of homework and tests that tell the instructors "how well we're conveying the information to you. . . . Everything we do at the school results in a report sometime. There will be one number one" in the class "and everyone else is number two" when it comes time for the faculty to rank the students at the end of the course in December. The new students already knew that there were plenty of reports around from previous classes that they could copy—contraband called "gouge." Enewold dealt with the temptation head-on: "We don't want you to spend time reading gouge. You're a competitive bunch of guys used to being number one. We haven't washed out anybody for failure to accomplish the work. If you don't quit, you'll make it. Pick out the wimpiest guys on the staff and say, 'If you can make it, I can make it.'

"When you're on break, take the time off. Keep your perspective and your sense of humor," Enewold stressed.

Welcomes, warnings, and advice over, the class members mingled restrainedly in the conference room. It was too early for anyone to emerge as the natural leader of the class, although the oldest student, Marine Maj John J. "Jack" Kirk, thirty-seven, was the designated class leader. With almost every person in the class regarding himself or herself as number one, I realized many would see me as a threat to their ambitions to be an astronaut or Chief of Naval Operations. Director Bernsen had told the students before I arrived, "I've read this guy's books, and he tells what he sees and hears, so remember you're fair game." I suspect his words lowered the already-low temperature of enthusiasm for my presence within Class 100.

This first morning confirmed my belief that it was going to be difficult to establish rapport with many of the students here. It was not going to be like my months on the aircraft carrier *John F. Kennedy* where, after an initial period of suspicion, I was accepted as another crew member who, like everyone else on board, would rather be somewhere else but had a job to do. The first question from one of the Army fliers in Class 100 underscored the point.

"Are you a Communist?"

He was deadly serious. As far as this officer was concerned, I was from *The Washington Post. The Washington Post* printed antimilitary columns by Colman McCarthy. Therefore, everyone from *The Post* had to be a red or at least a pinko. My standard ice-breaking line—"Just remember, no pancake is so flat that it doesn't have two sides"—had no effect on the officer.

After the Persian Gulf War started, the military's hostility toward the press became more evident. Some of the staff officers at TPS, for example, while watching the televised briefings about Desert Storm and listening to some of the stupidest questions I have ever heard reporters ask, shouted at the reporters on the screen: "Give me twenty [push-ups]! Get a job! Get a shave!"

I had been dealing with military hostility toward the press for thirty years. Reporters always want to know more than the admirals and generals want to tell them. It is an adversarial relationship. The writers of the Constitution had decided their new democracy would be better off if its press was free, allowing it to shine light into dark corners and audit the people's government. They did not say reporters had to be pro-military or anti-military, only that they had to be free to write what they saw, heard, learned, or thought. From George Washington onward, few military leaders have welcomed reporters in their midst. They can be meddlesome and troublesome. But they can also be helpful in explaining to citizens, who elect the politicians who determine military budgets, why they need the military and what it is doing with tax dollars.

When I went to Vietnam early in 1968 as a combat correspondent, I was warmly welcomed by rifle battalion commanders and by skippers of warships. They appreciated my willingness to leave the safety of Saigon and hump around the bush and stay overnight on ships. They believed if I saw what troopers and sailors were doing, and wrote about it, the people back home would understand the Vietnam War and support it.

I and other reporters did write what we saw and heard in Vietnam. Many of the stories were negative because what was happening was negative. I was thanked, not condemned, by several field commanders for explaining to the people and government back home about the difficulties of winning a war when the rules of engagement forced units to fight with one hand tied behind their backs. Troopers loved the idea of having a reporter, who might get their names in the paper, tramping along with them. One day I was caught in an ambush with them. Out in the South China Sea, Navy pilots appreciated my visit to the USS *Enterprise* and the resulting stories explaining to civilians what the new, high-tech A-6A bomber, which Boecker and Eaton flew, was doing in the war.

However, when the Vietnam War ended for the United States in 1973 with a humiliating withdrawal, a number of political and military leaders blamed the press for undercutting their efforts. The shorthand became "the press lost the war," not "the tragically flawed policies of Presidents Kennedy, Johnson, and Nixon lost it." I consider this a bad rap against reporters who went into the field to find out what was going on and wrote their findings straight. But many military people who were toddlers at the time of the Tet offensive in 1968 believe the press lost the Vietnam War. Many sailors on the *Kennedy,* for example, who were three years old during the Tet offensive, told me with conviction that the press had lost that war. Therefore, encountering that same attitude among some of the post-Vietnam officers at Pax River came as no surprise, although the venom was stronger than I had anticipated in a few cases.

Despite the hostile environment, I decided to stick with my plan to see how test pilots are made by putting myself in the middle of the effort. I could understand the hostility and guardedness of many of the members of Class 100. My challenge would be to push any ill feelings aside as I studied what was going on around me. Otherwise, I would be seeing and passing on a distorted portrait of some of the best and brightest young men and women America had produced. They were the post-Vietnam generation. Most of them were born a few years before or after President John F. Kennedy was inaugurated in 1961. They had all come to Test Pilot School to pursue excellence, to be better at what they had chosen to do.

One thing I had in common with all the members of Class 100 was love of flying and admiration for men and women who had flown the edge to learn a little more about flying machines. We were all the intellectual descendants and beneficiaries of the aircraft dreamers, designers, builders, engineers, daredevils, and careful testers who had come before us. Not that much before us, actually, considering that ninety years is but a tick on the clock of history. The roots of Class 100 went back to the sands of Kitty Hawk, North Carolina, where on 17 December 1903 Orville Wright became the first pilot to control the flight of a powered vehicle through the air. This made him the first successful test pilot in the realm of powered flight.

During aviation's first days the designers and builders of flying machines had to test their own creations. They quickly saw the wisdom of teaching others how to fly their machines, however. They needed salesmen to demonstrate to the public and to the military that flying airplanes was not the same as committing suicide. Many of these early salesmen became too confident, too soon; flew over the edge; crashed; and died.

While the Wright brothers concentrated on selling their biplanes to the Army, a former bicycle and motorcycle racer named Glenn Hammond Curtiss from Hammondsport, New York, focused on the Navy. Like the Wright brothers, he designed, built, and flight-tested his own aircraft. He hired flying salesmen to help him demonstrate and sell his airplanes. The most famous of Curtiss's demonstration pilots was a civilian named Eugene Burton Ely. With the connivance of the pro-aviation CAPT Washington Irving Chambers, whom the battleship admirals had ostracized because they considered the early flying machines as nothing more than "bundles of sticks," Curtiss asked Ely to try to take off from Navy ships. This would demonstrate to the admirals that the airplane could play a valuable role in the fleet. If nothing else, a plane that could take off and land on a ship would see the enemy fleet before it saw the American one. And even battleship admirals would have to acknowledge that a man up in the air could direct the fire of their guns better than a man down on a ship.

The always-daring Ely was not only willing but eager to try taking off from a ship. On 14 November 1910 he flew a Curtiss biplane with a 50-horsepower engine—a derivative of the engine Curtiss had built for his motorcycles—off a platform built on the bow of the cruiser USS *Birmingham,* which was anchored in Hampton Roads, Virginia. An exultant Chambers capitalized on the historic event by persuading the Under Secretary of the Navy to accept Curtiss's offer to teach a naval officer how to fly the machine that had taken off from a ship. The officer selected to be the Navy's first pilot and first test pilot was named Theodore Gordon "Spuds" Ellyson. He reported to Glenn Curtiss for flying lessons at about the same time that Ely shook up the admirals a second time on 18 January 1911 by landing the Curtiss biplane on the deck of the armored cruiser USS *Pennsylvania,* which was anchored in San Francisco Bay.

Curtiss taught Ellyson how to be not only a pilot but a test pilot. Early planes were so unreliable that the pilots had to listen to every noise and sense every motion to evaluate what was happening to their fragile craft as it flew along. Every flight was a test flight. Every pilot was a test pilot. So Ellyson was not only the Navy's first uniformed pilot but its first uniformed test pilot. Every Navy pilot in Class 100, therefore, was a direct descendant of Spuds Ellyson.

Curtiss drew the designs for his first aircraft and engines on the whitewashed walls of the shop attached to his home in Hammondsport. The day a new janitor whitewashed over the drawings was a traumatic one for Curtiss. But he forgave the janitor and eventually laughed about the setback. As much as he could, Curtiss tested the airplanes and the engines he built for them on the ground before trying them out in the air. Although equipped only with an eighth-grade education, he did detailed calculations about what would happen to the airfoils he designed once they were built onto his planes. Today he would be called an aeronautical engineer without a degree. Every Navy engineer in Class 100 could trace his or her professional lineage back to Curtiss, who designed and built the Navy's first air force.

Boecker mused about the Class 100 descendants of Ellyson and Curtiss as his aide drove him away from Test Pilot School toward his office. "You know," he told her, "these guys are all fired up and tense now. But we'll see a big change in them when we come back for their graduation in eleven months." He predicted the students would be humbler, more serious, more evaluating about everything. He admitted that his own struggle to make it through Test Pilot School had changed him in those ways.

Boecker had grown accustomed to confiding in his aide, LT Paula A. Coughlin, a pert, 5-foot 4-inch helicopter pilot. Unlike many admirals who rode in the backseat of the Navy van like a rajah, Boecker always sat up front with Coughlin and treated her like a fellow officer; sometimes like a daughter; never like a chauffeur.

Right after he had chosen Coughlin for the job as his aide in October 1990, he called her into his office and asked, "Do you think you can tell me when I'm not doing something right?"

Coughlin, who had never been intimidated by anybody or anything in her twenty-nine years, snapped off her reply: "I only hope I can tell you tactfully, [pause] sir."

Speaking her mind and fighting for what she believed was right were at the core of Coughlin's psyche.

In high school in 1980 she had protested against the Virginia Beach school administration for firing a female teacher who gave birth-control advice to a student.

During college summers she was the only female lifeguard on a force of sixty at Virginia Beach. She learned how to rebuff sexual harassment in that job.

By the time she won her Navy helicopter wings, she had learned that in the Navy—as on the beach—a good offense is the best defense. "For a woman, you fly pretty good," an experienced male aviator told her one day. "What did you expect?" scalded Coughlin.

It would be this don't-mess-with-me lifeguard, helicopter pilot, and admiral's aide who would be assaulted by fellow aviators at the Tailhook convention in Las Vegas before the Class 100 school year was out. She would fight back with everything she had. Before she was done, the President of the United States would apologize to her face-to-face; the Secretary of the Navy would resign; her admiral boss, Boecker's successor, would be fired; the Pentagon's most far-reaching sexual-harassment investigation would be launched; and the institution of Naval Air would be rocked from top to bottom.

Without planning it, Coughlin would pick up a torch thrown at her feet and march through the same hostile fire that had raked and ruined CAPT Washington Irving Chambers, the father of Naval Aviation. Coughlin would keep marching because she thought she had a cause bigger than herself—full professional equality for Navy women. In this sense, she would be picking up the revolutionary torch lit by Spuds Ellyson in 1911 when he flight-tested the Navy's first plane over Lake Keuka to change the thinking and culture of the naval establishment of his day.

Lighting the Torch

All Spuds Ellyson had to do to get into the history books this hot evening of 1 July 1911 was fly the rickety biplane up off the lake. Whether he crashed and died afterward or stayed in the sky long enough to complete the test did not matter. Either way, he knew he would make a name for himself. He would be the first Navy pilot testing the first Navy airplane.

The red-headed, twenty-six-year-old Ellyson slid into the open-air pilot's seat on the lower wing and checked out the machine's straightforward controls. Pulling up on the round steering wheel would make the biplane climb. Pushing down on the wheel would make the craft descend. Twisting the wheel right or left would turn the plane in those directions. Rods running down his left and right sides would work air paddles, called ailerons, mounted between the wings. Leaning against the rod to his left would raise the right wing and stop a rolling motion or bank the plane for a left turn. Leaning against the rod next to his right shoulder would lift the left wing. The throttle was a foot pedal.

A 50-horsepower engine sat behind the pilot's wooden perch atop the lower wing, and a water radiator for cooling was attached to the front of the little engine. A big propeller behind the engine pushed the 1,225-pound plane.

Satisfied that he was as ready as he could get, Ellyson pushed down on the foot throttle and lined himself up for the takeoff run. The biplane was floating at the southern end of Lake Keuka near Hammondsport, New York. It was 7:10 P.M., and no wind rippled Keuka's face. This was both good and bad: the 16-foot-long pontoon under the centerline of the aircraft and the floats at the ends of the lower wing would not have to buck any waves, but the biplane would have to generate all of its own lifting airflow by going very fast to break the suction of the lake on the float.

Among those anxiously watching Ellyson's preparations from the shore were two revolutionaries. Glenn Hammond Curtiss and Washington Irving Chambers were the fomenters of a revolution in military thinking, contending that flying machines could add a new dimension to warfare at sea. Each had an immense stake in how this flight went—if it went at all.

Curtiss, thirty-three, had written to Naval Aviation Director Chambers on 27 June 1911, "It is my wish to push the manufacture of aeroplanes, and, if possible, secure a large part of the Navy business." Curtiss urged Chambers to take the train up to Hammondsport to watch Ellyson test the first plane the Navy had ordered.

Chambers, a beleaguered fifty-five-year-old aviation enthusiast, needed little convincing to leave Washington's bureaucratic jungle for the straightforwardness of Hammondsport, where men actually did things. His zeal for airplanes had already made him as unpopular with the Navy establishment as Hyman Rickover's passion for submarines would make him later in the century. The admirals running the Navy of 1911 had marked Chambers for career extinction, banishing him to a basement broom closet of an office—"a good place to catch cold," he wrote—and even denying him secretarial help. The Navy would soon humiliate Chambers further by retiring him.

After Ely had taken off from and landed on Navy ships, Chambers had pushed the Navy into buying a machine that was designated the A-1. Some people called it the Triad because of its triple capability. It had floats for taking off from and landing on the water and wheels for operating from land; hopefully, it could fly through the air as well. Ellyson was about to begin the Navy's first acceptance test—which had to be flown by a Navy pilot—to see whether the A-1 met the Navy's specifications and performed as Curtiss had promised. In the process the young naval officer planned to win international certification as a pilot. Albert F. Zahm, representing the International Federation of Aeronautics—the only body at the time that issued internationally recognized pilot certificates—was with Curtiss and Chambers to see if Ellyson correctly performed the required maneuvers.

Theodore Gordon Ellyson was a determined young man with a fiery temper to match his flaming red hair. Against the wishes of his Old South mother, Ellyson had rejected the idea of attending a respectable southern college and then joining the family in their establishment life in Richmond. His father, Henry Theodore Ellyson, was treasurer of *The Richmond Dispatch*. The young Ellyson shocked his family by announcing that he intended to attend the U.S. Naval Academy in Annapolis and would need their help to obtain an appointment.

Secretly delighted, Ellyson's henpecked father quickly found a politician willing to nominate his son. The young Ellyson was provisionally accepted but needed to go to preparatory school to study for the Academy's entrance examination. He attended Werntz's Annapolis Preparatory School, a three-story brick building on the corner of Prince George Street and Maryland Avenue in Annapolis. It was known as "Bobby Werntz's War College." Ellyson lived in a nearby boarding house with other would-be midshipmen. His enthusiasm for second and third helpings of potatoes earned him the nickname "Spuds."

Spuds Ellyson won admittance to the Academy in 1901, joining the class of 1905. Spuds was fun-loving and serious by turns and thought it worth the risk to jump over the Academy wall after hours to attend a good party. He joined the fleet as all successful graduates did and in 1910 found himself doing boring duty as the prospective commander of a cramped diesel submarine, the USS *Seal*. He heard the Navy was looking for volunteers to learn how to fly. This sounded exciting, so he volunteered in a letter dated 16 December 1910.

Curtiss, as part of his campaign to push the Navy into buying his airplanes, had offered to train one of its officers to fly, free of charge, at his flying school at North Island, San Diego. But Navy Secretary George von L. Meyer saw no future for airplanes and did not take Curtiss up on his offer. Ellyson's application, along with others, stayed buried in the Navy bureaucracy. When Meyer went out of town for the Christmas holidays in 1910, Chambers seized the moment. He convinced Under Secretary Beekman Winthrop, who was serving as Acting

Secretary that week before Christmas, to accept Curtiss's offer and select an officer for training. On 22 December 1910 Winthrop sent this memorandum to the Bureau of Navigation, which oversaw aviation activities:

1. The Bureau will select an officer to undergo instruction as requested in this letter.

2. The selection of this officer should be made with a view to his special physical and professional fitness, having in mind the probability of subsequently detailing him as an instructor in aviation.

3. He should be apt in the study and handling of gas engines, possessed of good nerve and mental balance and be endowed with the adaptability of a seaman.

These were the first specifications ever set down for a naval aviator. Chambers, who wrote the memo for Winthrop, knew from studying Curtiss's airplanes that physical and mental stamina would be key to handling the bouncy craft. Curtiss himself, whose wonderful sense of balance made him an outstanding motorcycle racer and pilot, believed the person at the controls of either a motorcycle or airplane needed to be an extension of the machine. Curtiss had no idea that jet aircraft, hydraulic controls, and computers would make book learning more important than feel, that a different, technocratic breed of aviator than Ellyson and the other colorful fliers of his time was coming along.

Acting Navy Secretary Winthrop's instructions to find an officer to send to Curtiss's flying school created a scramble among personnel detailers on the eve of Christmas weekend. Ellyson's request for flying duty was freshest in their minds. They dug it out of the in basket and sent him these orders, dated 23 December 1910:

You are hereby detached from duty at the Newport News S. B. & D. D. [Ship Building and Dry Dock] Co. Newport News, Va., and from such other duty as may have been assigned to you; will proceed to Los Angeles, Cal., and confer with Mr. Glenn H. Curtis [sic] at his aerodrome at that place for instruction in the art of aviation, and report by letter to the Commandant of the Navy Yard, Mare Island, Cal., for this duty.

[Aviation was so new and foreign to detailers that they did not know how to spell Curtiss's name and believed his flying school was in Los Angeles, where he was attending an air show, rather than North Island.]

You will report your progress at the end of each month, and report any circumstances which in your judgment you may deem of interest to the Navy Department in regard to aviation; you will keep a journal of practical observations such as may be of assistance in the training of the Navy personnel in aviation.

When in your opinion and that of Mr. Curtis you have qualified in practical aviation you will so report to the Navy Department.

Chambers had faith in the young Ellyson but felt compelled to send him a cautionary letter anyway. "I hope you will not feel injured when I remind you," Chambers wrote while Spuds was training with Curtiss, "that you were selected because you were not regarded as a crank but as a well balanced man who would be able to assist in building up a system of aviation training in the Navy. I've no doubt you see the importance of avoiding the hippodrome part of the business and will not do stunts just for the sake of notoriety or to thrill the crowd."

Curtiss knew that he could not sell his airplanes to the Navy unless its young officers demonstrated that they could fly them successfully and safely. He taught Ellyson how to master the planes one step at a time, as these excerpts from the would-be aviator's 1 February 1911 letter home illustrate:

Mr. Curtiss thinks that from twenty to twenty-five runs should be made over the ground before any attempt is made to make the aeroplane leave the ground even in short jumps. And after that, it all depends on the man.

First, before he even allowed us to run the machine over the ground, he made us sit in the seat for about an hour every day and work the different controls and try to think what we would do under different circumstances, such as rising, landing, banking, etc.—after he had explained when and why to do all of these things.

Again, he repeatedly told how we must always test out a machine before going up in it, and made us learn how to set up the machine and make necessary repairs. . . . All instruction will be done with a four cylinder engine installed in a eight cylinder machine. The throttle is so blocked off that it can only be opened half way and hence only enough speed can be obtained to make the aeroplane leave the ground in short jumps. . . .

As a student pilot, Ellyson heeded that advice but still had accidents. During his second instruction period the wooden block Curtiss had jammed under the throttle of the training plane broke loose. Ellyson described what happened next:

> I unconsciously opened the throttle wide. Shortly afterwards I hit a bump, causing me to fall back in the seat, at the same time elevating the front control. And before I realized it, I was fifteen feet in the air. And in making a landing broke one wing of the machine.

> To prevent such slips in the future, metal pins are now used as stops which hold the throttle in the desired place. The first run over the field is made with the throttle barely open and is principally to learn how to steer the machine. When this is accomplished, the throttle is opened a little more, making it necessary to think of the elevators as well as the steering and to some extent remember that the opening of the throttle has to be remembered. The throttle is then given a little more play, and it then becomes necessary to remember to steer, use the throttle, use the elevators, and to some extent the ailerons.

On 5 March 1911 Ellyson wrote to his mother, Lizzie Ellyson:

> Today I made my first real flights. Of course I have jumped off the ground before but only for fifty or a hundred feet. Today I made four flights of about a mile and a half apiece over a straight course. I kept an average height of ten feet and never went higher than twenty-five feet. This was simply straight-away flying, and Mr. Curtiss would not let us attempt to turn or go any higher. In fact, the aeroplane did not have enough power to carry us any higher. . . .

Spuds continued to expand his flying skills, so much so that Curtiss dictated this letter to Navy Secretary Meyer on 12 April 1911:

> Dear Sir:
> I have the honor to report that Lieut. Ellison [sic] is now competent to care for and operate Curtis [sic] aeroplanes and instruct others in the operation of these machines. Mr. Ellison is a hard worker and has acquired considerable knowledge of the art of aviation. He has been especially successful in operating the machine and is easily capable of qualifying for a pilot's license. It is a pleasure for me to recommend Mr. Ellison as a man who will make a success in aviation.
> Yours truly,
> G. H. Curtiss

Curtiss took Ellyson up in the A-1 Triad until the builder felt confident Spuds had so mastered the machine that he could perform the

Navy's acceptance trials without crashing the plane through pilot error. Ellyson's upcoming test of the A-1 this first day of July 1911 would determine not only the future of this one machine but what role, if any, the Navy would give aircraft generally.

Ellyson pushed the foot throttle all the way down. The A-1 picked up speed and soon was streaking across the mirrorlike surface of Lake Keuka. The awkward-looking craft with the box-kite wings strained to break the grip of the water. Curtiss and Chambers suddenly saw daylight under the pontoon. The A-1 was airborne! Ellyson—the Navy's first pilot and first test pilot—had lit the torch for the thousands of pilots who would follow him into the sky to test Navy aircraft.

Ellyson flew figure eights over Lake Keuka, climbing no higher than 300 feet in his fifteen-minute flight. This first acceptance flight went into his logbook as flight number three for the A-1. Curtiss, the contractor, had been at the controls for flights one and two, checking out whether the motor and airframe were balanced before the Navy's own pilot took over the testing. Having the contractor's test pilots fly their own planes first was to become the traditional way of evaluating Navy aircraft. Ellyson made a second solo test flight—number four for the A-1—that lasted twelve minutes.

"Lt. Ellyson tried for pilot's license in A-1," the aviator wrote in his logbook for 1 July 1911, "but did not qualify as the judges later decided that he had not been given proper instructions."

RADM George van Deurs, himself an early naval aviator, elaborated on that brief explanation in his book *Anchors in the Sky.* After Ellyson had completed his second flight in the A-1 that evening, Zahm explained:

> "Sorry Lieutenant. I can't certify you for a license on those landings. Your engine must be stopped before you touch down."
>
> Spuds' face flushed. "This is a hell of a time to say that. Why didn't you tell me before? You said stop beside the marker. I did. You never said I should kill the engine."
>
> Spuds' face got redder, his voice louder as the scientist insisted that a dead engine was the rule. Zahm may have felt an explosion coming. "Possibly my instructions were unclear on that point. Let's try it again in the morning. The light's too far gone now."
>
> "At daylight then," Spuds said, his ears still red. . . .

As it turned out, Ellyson did not get airborne again in the A-1 until twilight of the next day. He flew two solo flights, satisfying Zahm's requirements. Long after those first flights over Lake Keuka, the Navy designed a system for certifying its would-be aviators. Not until 1 February 1915 would Theodore Gordon "Spuds" Ellyson receive from the Navy the certificate stating that he, "having fulfilled the conditions prescribed by the United States Navy Department, has qualified as a Naval Aviator and is hereby appointed a Navy Air Pilot." A less-official-sounding certificate calling him "Air Pilot No. 1" was dated 1 January 1914.

The day after Ellyson earned his international pilot's license, the Navy's first aviator tried to fly Chambers from Hammondsport to Penn Yan at the northern end of Lake Keuka, where the Navy's aviation director could catch a train to Washington. Once again it was a windless evening, and the A-1's 50-horsepower engine did not have the strength to lift the 170-pound pilot and 155-pound passenger off the lake. So Ellyson taxied the A-1 with its distinguished passenger the twenty-two miles to Penn Yan. The trip so buoyed Chambers that he sent his friends pictures showing himself and Ellyson in the A-1. Across the face of the photo he wrote, "Taking the airs on Lake Keuka."

"The return trip to Hammondsport," wrote Ellyson in his logbook, "was made [through the air in the A-1] by Lt. Ellyson alone. Stopped at Keuka after dark for oil. It was very dark when Hammondsport was reached, and as there was no light as an aid, the distance from the water was very misleading. The first attempt to land was a failure, the machine striking the water and rising again. On second attempt a normal landing was made." He had just become the first Navy pilot to fly over water at night, to land on the water at night, and to make the first stall landing.

Ellyson continued to test the A-1 during the summer of 1911 until the Navy formally accepted it as an airplane that it intended to order in quantity. Curtiss had designed a 75-horsepower engine for the A-1, but it was always having more problems than the 50-horsepower engine he often used as a substitute—and upon which he had had to rely for Ellyson's first acceptance flight. Ellyson also tested the second hydroaeroplane the Navy had ordered from Curtiss, the A-2, which the Navy accepted as well.

Aviation director Chambers was determined to grow a Navy air force. Ellyson was the first seed to sprout, and Chambers ordered the Navy's first aviator to teach other officers how to fly. Ellyson—the Navy's first uniformed pilot and test pilot—had no choice but to become the Navy's first flight instructor. He decided to teach his students how to fly the same way Curtiss had taught him.

The first officer the Navy sent to Hammondsport to learn how to fly from Ellyson was a twenty-six-year-old lieutenant junior grade from Rome, Georgia, and the U.S. Naval Academy's class of 1906. His name was John Henry Towers—and he was fiercely, if quietly, proud of it. He stood five feet ten inches tall and weighed 150 pounds, and his erect bearing and even features had inspired his classmates to call him "Handsome Jack." He was as introverted, serious, and abstemious as Ellyson was extroverted, carefree, and indulgent. But the two young officers seemed to get on well at Hammondsport, even though Towers had assumed he would learn flying from the great master, Glenn Curtiss.

Shortly after Towers's arrival on 27 June 1911, Ellyson checked his student into Mrs. Lulu Mott's boarding house, where most of Curtiss's flying students lodged, and then took him to meet Curtiss himself. Towers wrote that he expected to meet "a dynamic sort of man with goggles on his forehead, wearing a cap backward, dashing about and followed by throngs." He continued,

> I couldn't believe it when I met this modest, retiring man in an ordinary business suit. He didn't wear any uniform and was a very reticent sort of a fellow . . . who looked as though he had never been on anything faster in his whole life than a tricycle. I was rather diffident myself, and that, coupled with my upset mental picture of him, did not put me completely at ease.
>
> He did his best to make me feel at home, taking me around the shop and explaining what was going on, particularly in the way of improvements in design. As I hardly knew one end of an aeroplane from the other, this did not help matters much.
>
> I asked him if he would let me see the plans and specifications for those two Navy airplanes he was building. The contract specifications were absurdly simple. They covered about four lines. The plans were something else, and he took me to see them. He had sketched them himself with a carpenter's pencil on the white-washed wall of the shop.

Those were the only plans, and that's what they were using to build those [first two Navy] airplanes! The men would come in and look, and go back, and that's the way they worked!

Not long after, Ellyson gave Towers his first flying lesson on the field beside Lake Keuka called Kingsley Flats. Wrote Towers of his initiation to powered flight:

> We pulled Lizzie out of the barn, and Spuds whittled a little wedge and put it under the throttle. Then with rocks under the wheels, he pulled the propeller through, and the engine started. He made what was called a grass-cutting run hopping up the field, [got out of the plane,] lifted Lizzie up by hand [to turn it around for the return run down the field,] and came back. . . .

Then Spuds guided Towers into the plane and explained to him how to steer it. After that, Towers was to mimic the run that Ellyson had just completed. In Towers's words:

> [I] was afraid to step on the throttle, but equally afraid not to, so I pushed it down as far as it would go. The plane bumped across the field like a scared rabbit. When I was about half way up the field, a little zephyr came along, and the next thing I knew I was twenty feet in the air and headed for those trees [at the end of the straightaway track].
>
> I didn't stay there very long. Before I even had time to think, the left wing dropped, and we hit the ground with quite a thud. I tried to roll myself into a ball like a tumble bug, but the plane also rolled completely over, and Lizzie and I went into a beautiful cartwheel. I ended up rolling the plane up into a mass of bamboo, wire and linen, [tore some ankle ligaments,] and got all bruised up.

Towers healed and continued his flying lessons. The early planes were so unreliable, however, that even the most experienced aviators could suddenly lose control of them. On 21 August 1911, for example, Ellyson and Towers were flying the A-1 about 200 feet above Lake Keuka when the engine quit with no warning coughs or chugs. Ellyson told Towers to hang on to the plane until just before it hit the water and then dive off it. Wrote Towers:

> We glided down to sit on the water, and when we hit in a landing which would have been very good on land, I was shot out of my seat

like the man comes out of Ringling's circus gun and straight through the front elevator. The shock of landing threw Ellyson forward, and he went under water with the plane which promptly turned over.

We got to the surface at about the same time, neither of us hurt except that the front elevator, pretty strongly built, had taken a few pieces off me as I went through. The water was pretty cold, and as everyone had been at the field watching the take-off, there were no boats ready. I swam in the lake every day and was used to the cold water. Not so Spuds. We were in up to our necks, holding on to the floating plane, and his teeth were chattering.

A young fellow paddled out in a canoe and said he had telephoned the field, and could he help in any way? Spuds said, "Yes! Bring us some whiskey!" And he returned in a few minutes with a half-pint of Bourbon. I hardly drank, and Spuds was feeling the cold more than I was, so I told him to keep it all.

Eventually the rescue boat arrived and took us back. They had built a big fire on the beach to warm us up, but we hadn't stood before it more than a minute before Spuds toppled over. He fell face first right into the fire. The combination of that near-freezing water, the liquor and the heat right on top of it was just too much for anyone.

Eighty years later, standing on that same beach where an excited Ellyson had climbed into the A-1 floatplane for its first acceptance flight and where he had fallen drenched and exhausted into the fire, I had no trouble visualizing those scenes. As the pictures from the early 1900s reveal, the twisty lake, which the Indians called Keuka, meaning Crooked Lake, and the lovely village of Hammondsport have not changed all that much since Curtiss's day. There is still enough unoccupied flatland behind the lakefront for a skillful pilot to land on in a slow biplane. The stone wall at the end of the old straightaway where students did their grass-cutting training is still there. No doubt a fair number were terrified of slamming into that wall, and probably did.

Leaving the site of the Curtiss's lakeside flying camp, I drove the half mile to the Glenn H. Curtiss Museum in the heart of Hammondsport. Curtiss finished his last year of school, eighth grade, in the stone and brick building housing the museum in 1991. His grades showed him to be a wizard in math but just average in other subjects.

Tony Doherty, seventy-four, a former Spitfire pilot for the Canadian Air Force, is director of the museum. His father was William E. "Gink"

Doherty, who was a colleague of Ellyson and Towers and one of Curtiss's first test pilots. Tony was full of praise for Curtiss's accomplishments.

"All you have to do is look at pictures of different planes through the years and see the developments. There isn't a great deal of difference between the Wright Brothers 1903 Flyer and the last one they made. You see they sold out early. [Orville Wright sold the Wright Company to a group of New York investors in 1915 after waging and winning a bitter patent-infringement suit against Curtiss.]

"Curtiss kept developing things. If you look at an airplane today, you can't see anything except that it flies through the air that dates back to the Wrights.

"But if you look at the ailerons, retractable gear, the elevators in the back—these are all things that Curtiss pioneered. He also did most of his own testing. So he was the Navy's first civilian test pilot."

Curtiss was born on 21 May 1878 in the Methodist parsonage that stood on Orchard Street. It is a quiet, leafy byway—the kind of street where you probably do not have to lock your doors at night. Two generations of the Curtiss family lived in the parsonage. The Reverend Claudius Curtiss, a well-traveled preacher, and Ruth Bramble Curtiss, a sturdy farm woman, were the older couple. Frank Richmond Curtiss, a harness maker who drank too much, and Lua Andrews Curtiss, the ebullient church organist who also painted, sang, and trotted around town on a horse, were the younger folks. Lua Curtiss decided to name her son after the glen at the edge of town where she loved to go to paint, and after the founder of Hammondsport, Lazarus Hammond. Historical accounts of life inside the parsonage suggest a home of warmth, music, prayers, big dinners with many guests, and a tolerance of individual and collective foibles. Money was always tight.

When Glenn Hammond Curtiss was still an infant, the two generations of Curtisses pooled their resources and bought a big white house with green shutters on the heights of Hammondsport known as Castle Hill. Sadly, the lovely house no longer stands, just some of its stonework. An ugly, yellowish-tan brick school has been built near where the old Curtiss homestead once stood on Castle Hill. When I entered the school's front door, I expected to see some information and memorabilia about the man who had made so much history on these heights. But the educational bureaucracy as of 1991 allowed only a brief look back at Curtiss. His picture hung over the drinking fountain in the entryway, and a plaque read,

GLENN H. CURTISS

Born Hammondsport 1878

Early maker of motorcycle and airplane engines—

flew successfully airplanes and hydroplanes here 1908–1911

State Education Department 1957

Records verify that Ellyson and Towers were among those who enjoyed the beauty and warmth of the Curtiss home atop Castle Hill. But the Navy did not allow its pioneering aviators to linger in Hammondsport beyond the summer of 1911. They were ordered to establish a Navy flying school at Greenbury Point across the Severn River from the Naval Academy in Annapolis.

Ellyson and Towers began flying from an old cornfield on the point in September 1911, only to discover one October afternoon that the hangar built for the A-1 was directly in line with the rifle range used by the midshipmen on Wednesdays and Fridays. While seated together in the A-1 in the doorway of the hangar, Towers and Ellyson "heard something strike the radiator directly behind us. Turning quickly, we saw water spouting from a hole in the metal . . . caused by a bullet which had passed directly between us," Towers wrote.

Naval Aviation director Chambers, who was in charge of the flying school, directed Ellyson and Towers to test the endurance of the A-1 by trying to fly it from Annapolis to Hampton Roads, Virginia, a distance of 147 miles. The logbook of that early odyssey over the Chesapeake Bay by Ellyson and Towers dramatizes how test piloting was an ordeal of takeoff, breakdown, land, repair, takeoff, breakdown, land, and repair. Each step was freighted with unknowns, dangers, frustrations, discomforts, and delays. Here are excerpts from the log of the first endurance flight attempted by the first Navy test pilots in the first Navy airplane:

[11 October 1911] Started on flight to Old Point Comfort, Va. At 12:30 P.M. landed and ran on beach 30 miles below Annapolis on West

Shore 8 miles below Chesapeake Beach. Safety wire on after end of gasoline tank broken and one bolt out of after hanger on same. Underway at 1:00 P.M. Lt. Towers driving from right seat. At 1:20 P.M. landed on water off Cedar Pt., and ran on beach. Bracket on carburetor adjuster broken. Underway at 1:30 P.M. Lt. Ellyson driving. Landed at 2:05 P.M. at Smith's Point, Va., owing to #3, #4, #7 and #8 crank bearings burnt out. Total distance 79 miles in 85 minutes. Disassembled the machine and placed it on the U.S.S. Bailey which had been summoned by wireless, and returned to Annapolis, Md.

[25 October 1911] The objective point of this flight was Fort Monroe, Va., and the purpose of the flight was to determine and eradicate the weak points of the machine, to determine the physical strain caused by a long trip, and to thoroughly test the shift control.

Lt. Towers occupied the right seat which can be disconnected from the controls, and several times during the trip he was able to tighten water connections and make minor repairs, doing away with the necessity of landing. Once he stopped a bad water leak by climbing partly out of his seat to the engine section and tightening the water manifold.

Lt. Ellyson and Towers drove alternately for fixed periods, thus preventing fatigue.

Landed at 2:17 P.M. at Milford Haven, Va., having covered 112 miles in 122 minutes. The landing was made through a 6 foot surf with a 20 mile wind astern, and was made because the engine ran hot due to loss of water from the radiator. The radiator was leaking in the honeycombing at the lower right hand corner. The water connection at the upper right hand corner had broken due to vibration, and there were leaks around the packing nuts on the water manifold. It was impossible to rise from the rough water in the Bay, so the machine was towed into Milford Haven where the water was smooth. The leakers were temporarily repaired, radiator filled, and five gallons of gasoline added. The metal pipe connecting the auxiliary oil tank to the oil case was found to be broken in two places, so the auxiliary tank was unrigged and shipped to Fort Monroe, Va.

Underway from Milford Haven, Va., at 4 P.M., and landed at Buckroe Beach, Va., at 4:25 P.M., having covered 35 miles in 25 minutes. This speed was due to an estimated 35 mile wind off the port quarter. Landed through an 8 foot surf with the wind astern. The landing was made owing to the engine missing which was due to a broken magneto connection and to a radiator leak grounding magneto. Split the bottom of the bow of the main pontoon in running through the surf at such high speed.

[26 October 1911] Temporarily repaired the radiator and magneto lead, took on 5 gallons of gasoline, and patched bottom of boat with tar and canvas.

The surf was too high to launch the machine from the Bay, so it was hauled into a small inlet. There was less than 700 feet of smooth water before reaching the breakers.

At 12:50 P.M., Lt. Towers got underway and landed at Fort Monroe at 12:55 P.M.

[27 October 1911] The spare boat [pontoon that went under the centerline of the plane] and radiator were received from Annapolis, Md., and the machine was tried out that afternoon. Gasoline and oil had been supplied by the U. S. Army, but the gasoline was of such low gravity that the machine did not develop enough power to fly with two people, and it was necessary to send to Newport News, Va., for high gravity gasoline.

[29 October 1911] Underway from Fort Monroe, Va., at 10:20 A.M. Landed at the mouth of the York River[,] Monroe, Va., at 10:40 A.M. having covered 21 miles in 20 minutes. The landing was caused by the radiator steaming, and the engine was stopped about three miles from shore, being towed in by a motor boat.

Upon examination found that the water pump shaft had sheared and the radiator was leaking badly, due to a crack caused by vibration. Patched the radiator and made a new shaft for the pump. At the same time wired for spare pump. This pump did not fit so old pump was installed.

Underway at 2:00 P.M. Landed at Fleettown, Va., at 2:45 P.M., having covered 49 miles. Upon examination the radiator was found to be steaming but this was thought to be due to loss of water as the pump shaft was found intact. Took on one gallon of oil, filled the radiator. Underway at 3:30 P.M. Stopped at 3:42 P.M. having gone eight miles. The radiator was again steaming, and it was found that the pin holding the rotor to the water pump shaft had sheared, due to the fact that the rotor was binding on the pump casing. It was found that the pin was of soft brass instead of steel. Put in steel pin and made a sleeve bushing so that the rotor could not bind against the pump casing.

[2 November 1911] Underway at 6:45 A.M. and landed at 7:10 A.M. near Point No Point, Md., having covered 28 miles. The landing was made on account of breaking of carburetor brace. The vibration was so great after the brace carried away that it was feared that the intake manifold would be broken if it was not repaired.

[3 November 1911] Underway at 3:20 P.M. and arrived at Annapolis, Md., at 4:40 P.M. having covered 66 miles. The weather was intensely cold and both Lt. Ellyson and Lt. Towers suffered severely.

When December winds buffeted Greenbury Point and ice choked the Severn River, Ellyson and Towers gratefully broke off their instructing and test flying to head west by train for Curtiss's sunny flying establishment at North Island. They were accompanied by one experienced aviator, LT John Rodgers; newly accepted student pilot ENS Victor D. Herbster; four mechanics; and a fox terrier that had adopted Towers.

Ellyson and Towers started off the year 1912 by learning how to fly the Wright Brothers' B-1, along with continuing to test Curtiss's machines. They both preferred Curtiss's ailerons to the Wrights' wing-warping arrangement for controlling roll. But Towers found that the Curtiss elevator mounted right in front of the pilot was always in the way. "One morning I decided to leave it off and see what would happen. Nothing at all happened. In fact, the plane controlled even better without it, so they were then and there abandoned for both sea planes and land planes," he explained.

Towers wrote about many of the accidents he witnessed at North Island. "Every flight was an event" in the Wright B-1, which he said was "notoriously underpowered" and would nose over "on the slightest provocation [because of its two big floats]. . . ."

We always stood on the beach and watched for the inevitable crash of one kind or another. . . . On one occasion Rodgers was flying close to the water with a stop watch strapped close to his wrist timing the speed [of the B-1]. He got too close to the water, the floats touched and the plane turned a complete somersault. Rodgers swam all the way to shore, a distance of some 300 yards, holding his left arm out of the water [to keep his watch dry]. Then one of us enlightened him: "Great work, John! The water wasn't over waist deep all the way!"

On 14 March 1912 Ellyson took up the A-2 OWL (over water and land) plane, the second aircraft the Navy had purchased from Curtiss, to see if the winds over North Island were too tricky for student flying. Towers wrote Chambers a report on what happened:

He went down [the practice straightaway at low altitude] all right, but got badly tossed about.

He had gotten about a third of the way back when he took a sudden drop, recovered, then a second one caused him to shoot straight into the ground at an angle of about 45 degrees and from a height of about twenty-five feet. It was so sudden that he did not have time to do anything and there was not enough room to recover anyway.

The machine plowed an awful hole in the field, then turned over.

As near as I could tell from conditions, Ellyson was thrown from his seat through the forward controls to the ground, striking on his helmet, then over and striking on his back and hips. The machine sort of scooped him up when it turned over.

I fortunately had my motorcycle there, and when I got to the wreck he was lying half in the wreck, the lower part of his body on the top engine section and his head and shoulders just a few inches from the radiator. The helmet and his face were completely covered with earth and the first thing he said when he began to regain consciousness—which was three or four minutes after I got there—was that he couldn't see, which was no wonder for his eye sockets were completely filled.

I got some water from the radiator and washed them out and went over him and found that apparently no bones were broken and then got him out of the wires which were cutting him.

He then fainted again, and about that time the others came up. So I went after a doctor and some whisky. . . .

Ellyson recovered, but he would have a kinked neck for the rest of his life. Citing his own accident, Ellyson persuaded Navy superiors to conduct all training flights over water in the belief that this would reduce injuries to the students when planes crashed—as they often did.

Ellyson, Naval Aviator Number One, peered into his crystal ball and made some right and wrong predictions about the airplane's future in the Navy. In a chapter in a 1912 book entitled *The Curtiss Aviation Book,* Ellyson wrote the following:

In my opinion the aeroplane will be used by the Navy solely for scouting purposes, and not as an offensive weapon as seems to be the popular impression. This impression is probably enhanced by the recent newspaper reports of the damage inflicted upon the Turks in Tripoli by bombs dropped from Italian aeroplanes. Even could an explosive weighing as much as one thousand pounds be carried and suddenly dropped without upsetting the stability of the aeroplane, and were it possible to drop this on a ship from a height of three thousand feet, which is the lowest altitude that would ensure safety from the ship's gun fire, but little damage would be done. The modern battle-ship is subdivided into many water-tight compartments, and the worst that would be done would be to pierce one of these, and destroy those in that one compartment, without seriously crippling the gunfire or maneuvering qualities of the ship. In only one way do I see that the aeroplane can be used as an offensive weapon, and that is when on blockade duty, with the idea of capturing the port, ships out of range of the land batteries could send out [flying] machines with fire bombs and perhaps set fire to the port. . . .

In my opinion, the ideal aeroplane for naval use should have the following characteristics: the greatest possible speed, while carrying two people and fuel supply for at least four hours' flight (not under sixty miles an hour speed, as this has already been accomplished), and, at the same time, capability of being handled in a thirty-mile wind. There are many machines for which this quality is claimed, but few that have really proved it. Double control so that either person can operate the machine. Ability to be launched from shipboard, without first low-ering into the water, as on many occasions the wind at sea will be suit-able for flying whereas the sea will be too rough to rise from. Ability to land on rough water. The engine to be fitted with a self-starter. Also that the engine be muffled and the machine fitted with a sling for hoist-ing on board ship by means of a crane, and so constructed that it can be easily taken apart for stowage and quickly assembled. A searchlight for making landings at night and an efficient wireless apparatus should also form part of the equipment.

I did not make one of the requirements that the aeroplane be able to rise from the water, for in actual service it could always be launched from the ship. . . . In the near future I predict that the aeroplane adopted for naval purposes will operate from a ship as a base, and the great part of the instructional work will be done in the hydroaeroplane on account of the large factor of safety.

On 12 November 1912 Ellyson advanced his prediction of ships becoming aircraft bases by serving as the test pilot when a Curtiss AH-3 pusher plane was successfully catapulted off a barge anchored at the Washington, D.C., Navy Yard. Once again Curtiss and Chambers were on hand to watch him make history.

Three days later—on 15 November 1912—Ellyson eloped with

Helen Mildred Lewis Glenn of Atlanta. They were married in the rectory of Christ Church in Alexandria, Virginia, telling their parents about it after the knot was tied.

Ellyson left flying in 1913 to serve as a line officer on a succession of surface ships. Chambers had confided to Curtiss that he had become concerned about Ellyson's preoccupation with achieving firsts and records and preferred Towers's more systematic approach to flying. Ellyson's children said their father felt every naval officer should remember his first responsibility was to the fleet—that he should not be allowed to make a career out of one specialty like aviation. Perhaps Chambers's concern and Ellyson's philosophy converged, enabling Naval Aviator Number One to make a graceful exit from aviation in 1913 while Towers continued flying. Whatever his reasons for leaving flying, Ellyson went on to distinguish himself in the surface fleet, winning the Navy Cross during World War I "for distinguished service as assistant for operations to the commander, Submarine Chaser Detachment One. He was largely responsible for the development of successful submarine chaser tactics and doctrine."

Ellyson remained in the surface Navy after the war, commanding several ships, but he went back to Naval Air in 1921, serving as executive officer of the Naval Air Station at Hampton Roads, Virginia, until October of that year, when he joined the newly formed Bureau of Aeronautics. He headed the plans division at the Bureau until 1922 when he went to Brazil as the aviation member of the U.S. mission.

He returned to the Bureau in 1925, and the following year was ordered to Quincy, Massachusetts, to help convert the battle cruiser USS *Lexington* to the Navy's second aircraft carrier and serve as her first executive officer. She was commissioned in Quincy on 14 December 1927. Ellyson expected to be promoted to captain and intended to request command of the Lex. But on the evening of 26 February 1928, while the ship was anchored in Hampton Roads and Spuds Ellyson was celebrating the eve of his forty-third birthday, he received a fateful telegram from his wife, who was living with the family in Annapolis. The ear infection their eleven-year-old daughter, Mimi, was suffering had gotten so much worse that she was to undergo a mastoid operation on Monday morning at the Navy hospital in Annapolis. Could he come there? Earlier he had received permission from CAPT Albert W. Marshall, skipper of the *Lexington,* to use the carrier's amphibious plane if

Mimi's condition turned grave. Ellyson decided that Sunday night that the time had come to fly to his daughter's side. When the ship's OL-7 amphib would not start, he requested and received permission from CDR Albert C. Read, commander of the Hampton Naval Air Station, to use one of the base's OL-7s.

Once inside the second OL-7, LT Rogers Ransehousen, who was sitting in the pilot's seat, got the amphib's Liberty "V" engine roaring. LCDR Hugo Schmidt took the right copilot's seat, and Ellyson sat in the observer's seat. The three took off from Willoughby Bay at 1:58 A.M. on 27 February 1928. They had planned to follow the ship-channel lights to Annapolis but apparently got lost. When the plane crashed into the Chesapeake Bay near Cape Charles, Virginia, in the predawn dark, all three were killed.

The death of the legendary Ellyson had an ugly side. Rumors sprang up that Ellyson had been drunk, that he had used his commander's rank to force subordinates to undertake the dangerous flight in the dark, that pilot Ransehousen and copilot Schmidt had also been drunk. The Naval Court of Inquiry that investigated the crash reported that "the evidence adduced leaves no doubt in the mind of any of the members of the court that all three occupants of the plane were in full possession of their normal faculties and that these malicious rumors have no basis in fact." Nevertheless, Mrs. Schmidt blamed Ellyson for her husband's death and remained hostile to Mrs. Ellyson for the rest of her life.

Helen Glenn Ellyson showed the grit of the true aviator's wife by hosting a big cocktail party at the family's little yellow house at 11 Maryland Avenue, Annapolis, shortly after Ellyson's body had been found, to make the point that life must go on. She wore a long cocktail dress, laughed with her guests, and had a quick reply when friends asked where she had gotten the beautiful orchid she was wearing: "Gordon sent it to me."

After the party Mrs. Ellyson ordered Navy wings to be carved on her husband's tombstone, starting a tradition among aviators' widows. Mrs. Ellyson died in 1972 at the age of eighty-seven.

"I always felt guilty that Daddy died coming to see me and I lived," Mildred "Mimi" Ellyson Court told me in 1991 when I called on her at the family farm in Harwood, Maryland, south of Annapolis. Her eyes shone with her mother's legendary fire. Aged seventy-four, she is married to retired Navy Captain John M. Court.

"He was a wonderful, wonderful father," Mimi Court recalled.

Towers had a longer career as a test pilot than Ellyson, but he had his narrowest escape on 20 June 1913 while flying as a passenger, not a pilot, in the troublesome Wright B-2. ENS William D. Billingsley was piloting the plane on a routine flight out of Annapolis when they ran into a rainsquall on the return leg. They were flying at 1,625 feet when a gust lifted up the B-2's tail, throwing the plane into a dive. In this day before mandatory seat belts Billingsley was thrown from the plane, falling at least 1,500 feet and dying after slamming into the Chesapeake Bay. He was Naval Aviation's first fatality. Towers, too, was hurled from his unbelted seat but grabbed a beam as he was shooting past it, somehow holding on despite the violent motion of the plane.

"The strain on my arms and fingers was awful," he wrote afterward.

I tried to kick the steering gear back into working order, but I could not make it go. . . . The machine began to dive straight down. . . .

The machine seemed to take quick darts, shifts of direction, now and then. I don't know how I ever held on. At first, my instinct, or whatever it was, told me to let go. I had more fear of the machine's falling on me than I had of hitting the water. Then I recovered presence of mind enough to believe that I was going to certain death anyway. Falling from that height, if I fell by myself, I might never come to the surface. . . .

Just as I decided to hold on, the machine checked suddenly with a vicious twist, slacking its speed somewhat, and turning almost bottom up in a complete somersault. This twist tore away the grip I had with my right hand, although I held on with every ounce of strength I had [with my left]. . . .

The muscular strain of keeping my grasp of the upright tore one of my ribs from the breastbone. . . . The machine must have been going off on a . . . more slowly descending slant, like a piece of cardboard that is spun into the air. . . . I suppose I was about 800 feet above the water when the machine took this first long dash sidewise. . . . It was the only thing that saved my life, for otherwise I should have gone down almost as fast as Billingsley. . . .

After the machine turned upside down it shot down at least 400 feet, not straight, but at an angle of about 50 degrees. Then it flattened against the air resistance. It was poised for a fraction of a second, stopping partly and turning. Then it started down again on another dash in the opposite direction. It was about 400 feet high when it began the last dive. This time it took a sharper angle.

I was still holding with my left hand, unable to get a better grip. The machine was still upside down. The motor was now in a position to strike the water ahead of me instead of crashing down on me. It was the best place for me—another strange piece of luck—because there were no heavy weights above me except the beams of the plane. . . .

Then came the crash.

Towers lost consciousness at impact, came to with his head above the water, lashed his good arm to the plane's pontoon with his handkerchief, and held on for his life once again. He heard the crash boat coming toward him in the mist. The crew of the boat did not see him, but his adopted dog either saw or smelled its master floating out there in the mist and began barking fiercely just as the rescue boat turned away from Towers. The two crewmen headed back toward Towers and pulled the exhausted aviator aboard. He had been in the water for forty-five minutes. Billingsley's body floated to the surface a week later.

Towers recovered to continue a brilliant career that made him one of the giants of Naval Aviation. While Curtiss, Ely, Chambers, and Ellyson were the first to secure a beachhead within the Navy for aviation, Towers greatly expanded it. Ellyson, the Navy's first test pilot and Naval Aviator Number One, scored many of the early firsts in demonstrating what the airplane could do as a machine. Towers, the Navy's second test pilot and Naval Aviator Number Three, scored many of the early firsts in demonstrating what the airplane could do as a weapon. In 1914, for example, Towers commanded a contingent of aircraft that flew scouting missions from Veracruz to keep track of two warring Mexican armies. The information the scout pilots gave to the American admirals on the scene wiped away much of the skepticism about whether airplanes could help the fleet in wartime. After the Veracruz deployment Navy Secretary Josephus Daniels said, "Airplanes are now considered one of the arms of the fleet the same as battleships, destroyers, submarines and cruisers."

Next came the wide use of aircraft in World War I. This blew away the old question of whether airplanes could do more than scout and help win battles. New questions arose, including what kind and how many aircraft should the Navy buy? Underlying those questions was an equally important one: How could the Navy determine whether a plane could do what its builders claimed? The admirals realized they needed pilots trained to evaluate the good and bad in the aircraft being offered to them in the post–World War I era. No longer could they expect one pilot with no special training to fly, teach, and evaluate as Ellyson had done. The Navy needed a new breed of fliers—ones who were technically educated and meticulously and mercilessly honest. The Navy, in short, was looking for a flying truth squad.

Mapping a New Course

Number 6878 was a lucky plane. That was the PN-9A flying boat in which CDR John Rodgers had set a world record from 31 August to 1 September 1925 by flying 1,841.12 statute miles from San Francisco to an emergency landing in the Pacific Ocean 460 miles short of Hawaii. The flying boat had stayed intact after its forced landing at sea. Fashioning a sail from the wing fabric, Rodgers and his crew sailed the plane for 450 miles before being taken under tow by the submarine *R-4* only 10 miles short of Kauai Island. All five men aboard the PN-9 survived.

On 31 March 1927 LTJG William T. Rassieur and his crew would not be so lucky. But Rassieur would live long enough to commission a test center designed to make planes safer for the pilots who came after him.

The Caribbean Sea that day was so full of big swells that CDR Felix Stump had his unit's torpedo seaplanes hoisted off the sea and tied down on the deck of the tender USS *Aroostook* lying in the lee of tiny Navassa Island. But the larger flying boats, Rassieur's PN-9 and the newer and more powerful PN-10, were ordered to complete the day's flying.

CDR Robert W. Cabannis, skipper of the *Aroostook*, "decided he wanted to spend the last day of the annual fleet problem in the air,"

Rassieur recalled years afterward, "and I felt some pride in that he chose my plane.

"Commander Cabannis, first to board, took the left pilot's seat. I said, 'Commander Cabannis, would you mind taking the right seat? I always fly from the left seat.'

"'Gladly,' he replied.

"PN-10 Number 7028 took off ahead of me and was airborne some 100 yards before the end of the island," which was blocking a strong crosswind from the Windward Passage between Jamaica and Haiti.

"I commenced takeoff. Once on the step [skimming along on the hull, the last part of the plane to leave the water] we gained flight speed over the uncomfortable swells until we reached the end of the island. The 27-knot wind shear factor hit flush on our starboard.

"I had just pulled off the water when a swell rose up and hit the tail. A crew member saw the wave knock off the horizontal stabilizer. We crashed back down on the water.

"The impact wrenched the right engine out of its nacelle. The right engine was mounted rearward of the right pilot's seat. It hit Commander Cabannis with such force that it killed him instantly.

"Fire erupted when the 50-gallon reserve tank behind the pilots' seats ruptured, pouring gasoline over the adjacent storage batteries. Fortunately, the main tanks full of gas did not explode. They withstood the crash.

"I was momentarily knocked unconscious by the impact. When I came to, I realized I was trapped in the flames that enveloped the wreckage of the crushed cockpit and bow compartment of the seaplane. I could not break free in several tries. I made one final effort to extricate myself from the wreckage. I exploded through the burning debris and found myself in the sea.

"I could not see. I had no life preserver. I felt some floating wreckage and hung on to it. I heard the rescue boat and felt someone pull me aboard. Then I passed out again."

Passing out had been merciful. Rassieur was so horribly burned in the face that his friends could not recognize him. His hands and arms, especially his wrists, were deeply burned. No one knew whether "Ras" Rassieur would live, far less continue a Navy career that had held such bright promise.

The "golden years" of Naval Aviation were just dawning. Three

Curtiss flying boats—NC-1, NC-3, and NC-4—had crossed the Atlantic in 1919, demonstrating that planes could have global reach. World War I had convinced the most hidebound admiral that if he did not have planes to knock down the enemy's aircraft, his ships would be sunk. Jack Towers, by 1927 the Navy's senior aviator, was skipper of the Navy's first aircraft carrier, the USS *Langley,* a converted coal carrier. Spuds Ellyson was slated to become executive officer of the USS *Lexington,* the second aircraft carrier. Within a few months a slim flier named Charles Lindbergh intended to fly alone across the Atlantic. The Navy needed hundreds of new planes, and it would also need young pilots like Rassieur to follow the lead of Ellyson and Towers in testing all the unknown aircraft to determine which ones were worth buying for the fleet.

But on the evening of 31 March 1927 it looked as if "Ras" would miss his big chance for the second time in less than ten years. He had joined the Navy in 1918 in hopes of flying in World War I, but the war had ended before he could get into it. So he pursued his boyhood dream of going to the Naval Academy, graduating with the class of 1923. He won his wings in 1926 and was a rising star in the Naval Air community. Then came the crash. Friends who saw him shortly afterward felt sure he would never fly again if he lived at all. His luck seemed to have run out sixteen days after his twenty-seventh birthday.

Lady Luck, after her AWOL from Navassa Island, revisited Ras Rassieur, first by helping him heal and second by putting him on a course that would make him the first commander of the world's most advanced flight-testing facility. But neither Lady Luck nor Ras could have reached those heights if it had not been for a little-known naval reservist who had picked up the revolutionary torch the Navy establishment had yanked out of the hands of Washington Irving Chambers.

Edward W. Rounds, a Naval Reserve pilot who had been a flight instructor during World War I and a test pilot for the Navy Bureau of Construction and Repair in 1918, was this torchbearer. A 1917 graduate of Massachusetts Institute of Technology, Rounds despaired about how little thought went into assessing the airplanes that the world's contractors were pressing the Navy to buy. He had looked at that process from both the Navy's and the contractors' ends of the telescope, for he had resigned his regular Navy commission in 1923 to become the chief aircraft designer for Wright Aeronautical Corp. Returning to the Navy

Bureau of Aeronautics in 1926, he dared tell his bosses that they were like farmers buying pigs in pokes when it came to purchasing airplanes. More important, Rounds wrote down his criticisms, suggested reforms, and sent the whole package to RADM William A. Moffett, chief of the Bureau of Aeronautics.

At the time of Rassieur's crash, Moffett was transforming Rounds's ideas into a whole new way of evaluating aircraft. The Rounds-Moffett initiative would not only give birth to a new, systematic approach to evaluating aircraft but lay the foundation for a huge testing complex that the scarred Rassieur would command later in his naval career. Rounds's memo of 23 August 1926 contained the guts of the Rounds-Moffett initiative: "The basis for the choice of individual models rest largely on performance. . . . one of the greatest handicaps in design work is the lack of reliable data concerning the performance of Naval airplanes. . . . In nearly every case, the actual performance [as determined in the air through flight-testing] has been below that calculated" by engineers on the ground. Somebody is wrong, Rounds contended, at great peril to the Navy, to the nation, and to the pilots who would fly the planes the Navy was buying for the 1930s and beyond.

Rounds urged the Bureau of Aeronautics to establish two new groups under its umbrella. One group at Bureau headquarters would write instructions detailing how a plane was to be tested in the air. The second group at the Anacostia Naval Air Station on the outskirts of Washington, D.C., would do the actual flying and write down what happened to the plane during each of the specified tests. The two groups would analyze the data and resolve any discrepancies in their findings with more tests in the air or calculations on the ground, or both.

Before notifying the plane maker that the product fulfilled the performance requirements of the sales contract, the Bureau, Rounds recommended, should send a two-man truth squad aloft to wring out the airplane.

> [These] acceptance trials should be conducted by two pilots, one from the Bureau test section and one from Anacostia test section. This will to a great extent obviate the uncertainty which has existed in the data obtained, and will ensure the running of trials in the proper manner by competent personnel. . . .

It should perhaps be emphasized that the duties of the test sections are to measure the performance of the airplane and to act in an advisory capacity on points concerned with performance. Final decision as to suitability of any airplane for any purpose should be vested in a board or its equivalent composed of those concerned in the Bureau [of Aeronautics] and such others from the operating units as may be desired.

In other words, Rounds wanted a firebreak dug between the testers and everybody else, particularly the manufacturers and government decision makers. Under Rounds's recommended code of ethics for test pilots, the testers were to get the facts, period. Other people would decide what to do with them, if anything.

On 14 December 1926 Admiral Moffett informed the commander of the Anacostia Naval Air Station that the Bureau of Aeronautics would form a Flight Test Section, which would begin operating on 1 January 1927. Moffett asked the Anacostia commander to establish a separate Flight Test Section at Anacostia

as soon as possible. . . . The Bureau recommends that the Flight Test Section at Anacostia be definitely charged with the following duties: (a) conducting flight tests of airplanes and accessories as may be requested by the Bureau; (b) maintenance of airplanes under test; (c) maintenance of flight test equipment; (d) interpretation of results in conjunction with the Test Section of the Bureau. . . . By interpretation of results of tests is meant the formation of opinions and conclusions regarding the suitability of the airplane for any purpose, taking into consideration all features such as performance, maintenance, physical dimensions, ease of control, comfort, appearance, etc. It is intended that both test sections be coordinated to the greatest possible degree. In general, it will be the function of the Anacostia Test Section to conduct flight tests, and the function of the Bureau Test Section to take care of any technical details involved.

Moffett appointed Rounds, the architect of this new testing structure, to head the Flight Test Section at the Bureau of Aeronautics. Anacostia also took Moffett's request seriously, putting its hottest pilot, LT George T. Cuddihy, in charge of the new Flight Test Section. In that capacity, Cuddihy discovered how to bring aircraft out of spins. He was killed on 25 November 1929 at Anacostia when the plane he was testing came apart in an almost vertical dive from 10,000 feet.

As the aircraft of the 1930s became more sophisticated, they required specialized testing beyond what could be done at Anacostia. After performance tests at Anacostia, planes were sent to Dahlgren, Virginia, to test their dive-bombing capabilities; to Hampton, Virginia, to examine their handling in rough water; to the Washington Navy Yard to study their performance on the catapult; and to the Naval Aircraft Factory in Philadelphia to test their suitability for aircraft-carrier operations.

The inefficiency of passing planes around like medicine balls generated the Navy's search for a location where all the testing could be done. The center would need water for the seaplanes and flying boats and thousands of acres of land for runways, hangars, catapults, gunnery ranges, barracks, a hospital, and a chapel. The population of the surrounding area would need to be sparse so that people would not be crowded against the runways, but the center had to be within easy reach of Washington's policy makers.

With the outbreak of World War II in Europe providing a sense of urgency, RADM John H. Towers—the same Towers who flew with Ellyson and commanded the Navy's first aircraft carrier, the USS *Langley*—on 10 September 1941 named a board to find a site for "a proposed Navy Flight Test Center." Towers had risen to Chief of the Bureau of Aeronautics by 1941. On 6 November 1941—just one month before the Japanese brought the United States into World War II by bombing Pearl Harbor—the Towers board recommended the "immediate purchase or condemnation of a tract of land embracing about 2,400 acres on Cedar Point, Maryland, bounded as follows: Patuxent River from Cedar Point to Hog Point to Fishing Point to Millstone Landing; Chesapeake Bay from Cedar Point to Pine Hill Run; and from the bay shore line along Pine Hill back to Millstone Landing on the Patuxent River."

On 22 December 1941 Towers asked Navy Secretary Frank Knox to approve the location and directed the Navy Bureau of Yards and Docks to acquire the site then known as Cedar Point. Through condemnation, the Navy wound up with 6,400 acres at Cedar Point for $712,282. Navy contractors broke ground on 4 April 1942 for what was at first called Cedar Point, Maryland, Naval Air Station. Secretary Knox worried that the new base would be confused with the Marines' Cherry Point, North Carolina, installation, so on 4 June 1942 he changed the name of the new base to the United States Naval Air Station, Patuxent River, Maryland. Its nickname soon became Pax River. Eddie Rounds, who had risen to the rank of commander in the Naval Reserve, was named officer-in-charge of the Experimental Flight Test Center within the base for the summer of 1942—brief recognition for his vision that had brought the test center into being.

The men on the bulldozers did not know that they were on the former home of the Mattapient Indians nor that they were ending a way of life that had thrived in the feudal kingdom of Cedar Point ever since the Indians had been ejected. Britain's Leonard Calvert had landed in the region in 1634 with a party of colonists, who settled at St. Mary's and eventually spread northward to farm at Cedar Point.

A fifteen-year-old boy who had played and worked on one of Cedar Point's biggest farms watched, with a mixture of fascination and dread, as the machinery scraped away the face of the farmland and pushed through many of the buildings. The Navy was taking over his own home on the beautiful plantation called Susquehanna. The boy was James Maguire Mattingly, Jr., the son of the manager of Susquehanna Farms.

James Maguire Mattingly, Sr., had moved his family from Leonard-town to Cedar Point in 1928 to take the job of managing Susquehanna Farms. The farmers he supervised lived free in houses on the farm's 2,000 acres and received $1.25 for a 6 A.M. to 6 P.M. day plus fresh produce in the summer and a barrel of flour and a pig in the winter. When the Navy arrived in 1942 to take over the land, fifty-four men, women, and children were living at Susquehanna Farms. The livestock included three hundred highly prized polled Herefords, one hundred horses and mules, one hundred sheep, and scores of hogs.

Years afterward Mattingly recalled how he and his young friends on Susquehanna often spent their hot summer afternoons: "We'd get a watermelon from the patch, set it in the pump house to cool while we went swimming in the river, and then eat the melon afterward on the beach. The Patuxent River was so clear when I was growing up that you could see bottom at the end of our pier where the water was 12 feet deep."

Other afternoons the teen-aged Mattingly would ride the family plow horse, Nancy, up to Millison's general store in Pearson, which was in the middle of the property the Navy had obtained. The Millisons kept sodas in the iced metal box in a cool, dark corner of the store.

Summer evenings there were always enough kids and adults on hand for games of softball. And there were plenty of fish to catch, especially hardheads, in the river. The Mattinglys had a power boat for excursions up the river and out on the Chesapeake Bay.

Come winter, the big pond on Susquehanna Farms froze, making an ideal skating rink. If it snowed, there were sleighs in the barn and plenty of horses to pull them. Once in a while a sleigh would take Mattingly to Little Flower parochial school, which was run by the Sisters of St. Joseph in Great Mills, three miles west of the farm. Usually, though, he caught the school bus at Pearson.

Many of the people who had lived for generations on the lands around Cedar Point reacted to the Navy's invasion with sorrow, anger, and resignation. Shouts of, "Don't you know there's a war on?" drowned out any protests. The Mattingly boy would marvel after he grew up at the grace of his mother, Helen Barrett Mattingly, who made sandwiches and provided beds for the engineers and workers who were taking away her home and forcing her family to sell the animals they all loved so much. "The day finally came when Mom and Dad had to auction off the farm's machinery and livestock," Mattingly recalled. "That was the day Mother and Daddy cried."

The elder Mattingly grieved along with his neighbors but argued that the Navy's presence would assure their children of a brighter future. The Navy would provide jobs and training in highly marketable skills, giving the boys and girls of Cedar Point the chance to do something besides farm. Mattingly also met with Navy leaders and counseled them about how to win the cooperation and friendship of the community rather than its enmity.

Leonardtown was the nearest big town to Cedar Point, and its citizens saw evidence all around them of the boom the Navy had brought to sleepy, God-fearing St. Mary's County. Farmers, clerks, housewives, day laborers, con men, gamblers, prostitutes—they all streamed through Leonardtown on their way south to the frontier town the Navy had created. A lanky teenager named Ed Stokel joined the stream when his Leonardtown high school let out for the summer of 1942. LT Dick Mann, already a legend at Cedar Point for his patience and tact in getting the base built, hired Stokel. The innocent seventeen-year-old's job was to walk around inside the fence and count the workers so that Mann could determine if the contractors were charging the Navy for no-shows. This roving job showed Stokel both the bright and dark sides of the boom.

Stokel found the can-do spirit breathtaking, exhilarating, inspiring, awesome.

No railroad? Hell, we'll just build one to the nearest terminal. Down went track from Cedar Point to Brandywine, Maryland. Forty miles for $1.7 million.

Road too narrow for trucks? Widen the son of a bitch. The road running from Cedar Point to Waldorf was widened, straightened, and repaved.

Need a school for the Navy kids coming to Cedar Point? Build one, name it after Navy Secretary Frank Knox, and turn it over to St. Mary's County.

Want a hangar where that creek is? Fill in the creek. A hangar designated as Building 301 was built that way. One morning the Navy found one of its heavy planes hanging by its wings over a cavity inside the hangar where the creek used to run.

The dark side of constructing Pax River may have been awful to some, but it was sure fun for young Stokel to watch.

With teen-aged fascination he stared as dozens of men of all ages hurled dice and flipped cards on blankets spread out on the floors of the tar-paper shacks that dotted the base. He laughed when Pinkerton guards at the front gate finally stopped the cement truck that never had its mixer rotating. A guard lifted the lid of the mixer and discovered cases of whiskey stacked inside. Workers could not buy liquor inside the base and were not supposed to drink it there, either, so sales had been brisk and profitable. And Ed Stokel hooted when he heard about the guards' finding a prostitute rolled up in a rug inside a fast-buck artist's car. She was going to sell her favors to the army of workers inside the gate of the barren, sexless base.

William G. Carter of Washington, D.C., had the contract for feeding the motley force of seven thousand workers. The war had taken the cream of young men, so Carter and the other contractors had to hire almost anyone who could breathe.

"It was a rough camp," Carter wrote.

The criminals, gamblers and sharpies who were on the run learned that it took the FBI approximately 30 days to report back [to the Navy] on identities, which gave [criminals with records] at least three weeks at

Patuxent to earn a little money, steal it, win it gambling, get well fed, get the wrinkles out of their bellies and give them a week's start going north, south or west before the FBI came looking for them.

As a consequence, we had approximately 25 of our slightly over 100 employees getting afraid and leaving each week after Saturday's pay day. This necessitated our establishment of an employment office on the Bowery in New York where, each Saturday, we hired the needed 25 or 30 replacement bodies, put them on a bus to D. C. late Sunday, met them at the bus depot with a truck, took them to Patuxent. In order to prepare breakfasts and lunches [on the following Monday] we were forced to take them over the fence or under the fence [because the new hires did not have the identification badges the guards demanded for entry to the base.]

It worked. We didn't miss serving a meal or having a bed ready. At the peak we were feeding about 7,500 and bedding about 3,000 at Patuxent. One thing that helped us tremendously was the finding and hiring of those two Austrian bakers—Max Dick and Julius Kali, the best I ever saw. Their pies, Danish, tarts, cakes and doughnuts were so good that they were a stabilizing and quieting influence, not only to the contractors' personnel but to the Navy personnel as well. . . .

Due to the scarcity of beef, some beef wholesalers were insisting that purchasers buy a pound of very fatty sausage for each pound of beef. We were forced to turn to the black market. We purchased a closed van truck; purchased live steers from a very wealthy and prosperous farmer of Montgomery County, Maryland; transported those steers to Waldorf; had them slaughtered and hung in a cooler for a week; picked them up and took them to the [Naval Air] Station where the meat was butchered in serving portions. . . . The Ship's Service approached us asking that we supply Ship's Service with the hamburger that he could not buy. We did. . . .

In August 1942, when Patuxent was a maelstrom of full-throttle construction, CDR Ras Rassieur was a staff officer in the tightly controlled Navy Command Center at Pearl Harbor. In the fifteen years since his accident he had regained his handsome appearance and career momentum. Only scar tissue on his arms and lips reminded people of his ordeal off Navassa Island. More recently he had been through another harrowing ordeal, the Japanese attack on Pearl Harbor, and he had been awarded the Bronze Star and Purple Heart for his heroics as executive officer of the USS *Curtiss*.

Rassieur was itching for something more exciting than his staff job when CAPT Logan Ramsey, chief staff officer for Patrol Wing Two at Pearl, telephoned on 21 August 1942 to inform him of his new assignment.

"Some place named Patuxent River," Ramsey disclosed.

"Logan," Rassieur said incredulously, "I've never heard of the place."

"Neither have I," Ramsey replied. "The orders read 'hereby detached,' so they must want you right now."

Rassieur found himself at the entrance gate of Patuxent River in September 1942 with orders to serve as prospective commander of the base not yet commissioned. He wrote down his recollections of those first hours:

> There were Pinkerton guards unimpressively waving a long line of traffic through at 10 to 15 miles per hour. It was worth your life to stop. My first impression was a bare, sprawling open space; a frontier setting. Billowing dust clouds, scrapers, bulldozers, dump trucks moving with uncontrolled cross traffic in all directions along the main entrance road. You proceeded at your own peril.

CAPT William Gates, Rassieur's escort, showed the future commander his domain, at the last taking him past trees and bushes screening the prospective commander's living quarters. "You'll agree, the quarters are adequate," Gates said wryly.

The forty-two-year-old Commander Rassieur and his wife, Ruby-Irene "Honey" Holsapple, gazed at one of the loveliest mansions in the world. They could not believe they would be living in it. A U-shaped driveway swept past the rear entrance of the classic, two-story, white colonial built in 1722 by Maryland Governor Charles Calvert. Four chimneys, two at each end of the roof punctuated with three dormers, spoke of spacious rooms heated by fireplaces. In front of the mansion a green lawn wider than a golf fairway sloped invitingly down to the Patuxent River. Named Mattapany after the Indian tribe that had camped on the ground, the home had just been refurbished and was literally fit for a king. Ras and Honey were to have the happiest hours of their lives living and entertaining at Mattapany on the Patuxent.

Rassieur assumed command of Pax River on 21 September 1942, although he was still technically only the "prospective" commander because the base had not yet been commissioned as a living Navy establishment. The labor turnover, a shortage of housing, transportation bottlenecks, poor weather, a scarcity of material, gas rationing, and a thousand other problems combined to delay the completion of Pax River.

A marine security detachment under the command of Maj Harry E. Leland reported to the base on 20 October 1942 and immediately started to impose law and order on the rough and tumble project. Replacing the Pinkerton guards, marines fanned through the base to check identity cards. With rifles and fixed bayonets, they made surprise raids on barracks and cars to recover mattresses, blankets, silverware, tools, building materials, and other items that the workers had stolen from the government. Years later Rassieur looked back on those raids with amusement and admiration:

"I recall the day at high noon when the whistle blew and the contractor's work force found themselves surrounded at the housing facilities, cafeteria, and canteen by marines—bayonets fixed.

"'Nobody move!' Major Leland ordered.

"They didn't. Everyone was halted in their tracks for identification or arrest. This was the first step in driving the professional gamblers and thieves from the camp.

"Then there came the day the first car search was conducted. Orders were issued to search every car leaving the station at close of working hours. As soon as the first car in the mile-long line was searched, cars waiting in line started to unload. There were so many whiskey bottles, brass knuckles, revolvers, blankets, sheets, pillowcases, flatware thrown into the ditches alongside the road it took two days to collect it. Over five hundred blankets were recovered, and there was no estimate of amount of equipment and tools that were recovered."

As 1942 ended, Pax River's airplane runways had been laid; seaplane basins had been dredged; and homes, hangars, and office buildings had been built. The electricity, water, and sewer systems were working; and roads connected the testing centers that had been built far apart so that they would not all go up at once if bombed. Rassieur dared set 1 April 1943 as the date for commissioning this first centralized facility for testing Navy airplanes.

RADM John S. McCain, Chief of the Bureau of Aeronautics in 1943, worried that Pax River would go beyond its mission of wringing out aircraft once the base and its eager leaders came to life. He tried to nip kingdom building in the bud with this memorandum dated 27 January 1943:

The intent of the Bureau of Aeronautics in seeking the establishment of the experimental portion of the NAS Patuxent River is to provide aircraft, equipment, personnel, a physical location of proper size and scope and necessary facilities for the testing of experimental and development materiel under the cognizance of this Bureau. This testing embraces the flight test of experimental planes and equipment; the tactical test and development section; and the ground testing of any equipment or materiel coming under the cognizance of the Bureau. . . .

It is not intended that the NAS Patuxent River shall be used for the design and development of aircraft and equipment, but rather that aircraft and equipment developed elsewhere be flown, tested and criticized at this station. . . .

The Bureau particularly desires to avoid the accumulation at the Naval Air Station, Patuxent River, of personnel and ground facilities which depend upon research, design or development to justify their continuing existence. It is hoped that the observance of this general policy will permit NAS Patuxent River to apply its experimental efforts to the testing aspects of the materiel with which it deals rather than with the development of the materiel itself, which can normally be more effectively obtained elsewhere. . . .

By mid-morning, 1 April 1943 had mellowed into a good day for flying—clear air with only a few clouds and a manageable wind—as well as for officially bringing Naval Air Station Patuxent River to life through a commissioning ceremony.

The New York Times that Thursday morning carried a story about Navy Secretary Knox's telling newly commissioned ensigns in New York City that it was up to the United States to win the sea battles of World War II "because we have the greatest fleet." Another story a column away was headlined, "Heaviest Weight of Bombs in History Rained on Hitler's Europe During March." The data in that story showed that the "flying kites" of Chambers's day had indeed evolved into a primary weapon, as he had predicted. The Navy's consolidation of testing teams at Pax River was supposed to make ships and planes an even more lethal combination.

"Today marks a step of unusual importance in the history of Naval Aviation," Navy Aeronautics Chief McCain said from the flag-draped platform as he began sketching out the mission he envisioned for Pax River.

Our service has commissioned many naval air stations, but never one with such far reaching importance as the Naval Air Station, Patuxent River.

It is the function of this station to test and criticize, from an operating point of view, all changes and improvement in the material that goes in the air. . . . A great responsibility is put into your hands, for growth and change is still the very life of any air service which hopes to survive.

The whole country is aroused to the need for quantity in our weapons. But I look to Patuxent River to carry a large part of the burden of insuring that quality, imagination and resourcefulness are all included in our future equipment and in its typical use.

The Bureau of Aeronautics is vitally interested in the results you obtain. It will always want those results in a hurry, but they must be accurate, thoughtful and reliable. The course of the war will show whether you are right or wrong, and you cannot afford to be wrong.

You are starting out on the basis that if you produce high quality, timely results, you will be left as free as possible to work in your own way with your numerous and changing problems.

You have the chance to make a great reputation, and I am confident that you will do so. . . .

Two more brief speeches—one from RADM Ferdinand L. Reichmuth, commandant of the Potomac River Command, and the other from Representative Lansdale Geselin Sasscer, Mr. Democrat of Maryland, who had lobbied to have the base located in St. Mary's County— and it was time for CDR William T. Rassieur, the first skipper of Pax River, to put the base in business symbolically. "Ras" Rassieur believed in the maxim that the best speech has a good beginning and a good ending very close together. He spoke only briefly of how honored he was to assume command and then stood straight and stiff to conclude the ceremony by reading his orders.

By August 1943 most of the scattered aircraft-testing units had moved to Pax River, including Anacostia's Flight Test and Radio Test and Norfolk's Armament Test teams. The testing was grouped into the following specialized units and placed under the distant supervision of the base commander, who was still trying to get the installation built:

Flight Test, for conducting tests for the two separate, Washington-based bureaucracies of the Bureau of Aeronautics and the Board of Inspection and Survey;

Service Test, for determining which parts would break first by wearing out airplanes;

Radio Test, for improving plane-to-plane and plane-to-ground communications;

Armament Test, for testing out the guns and bombs put on airplanes;

Tactical Test, for developing the tactics to reduce the vulnerability of U.S. warplanes, sometimes by flying captured German and Japanese aircraft.

Rassieur's command lasted nine months after Pax River's commissioning. CAPT Aaron "Putt" Storrs relieved him on 11 January 1944.

Back to School

The civilian test pilot made his fateful remark right after he had checked out several naval officers in Lockheed's Lodestar transport plane at the Flight Test Section at Anacostia. It was early 1943, and Flight Test was still packing up for its June move to Pax River.

"I'd like to get into uniform," the test pilot told CDR Paul H. Ramsey, head of Flight Test. "What the hell, we're in a war."

"You'd really like to get into the Navy?" Ramsey pressed.

"Very much," said the civilian flier, who had been conducting high-altitude tests in Lockheed's P-38 Lightning fighter, the "forked-tail devil" used extensively by the Army Air Corps during World War II. The Navy was far behind the Army in high-altitude warplanes in 1943.

"You're just what we've been looking for," enthused Ramsey. "We want somebody with high-speed, high-altitude experience."

Three days later the civilian test pilot was in uniform. He was now LTJG Najeeb E. Halaby, United States Naval Reserve. After a brief detour to Corpus Christi, Texas, to learn how to fly the Navy way in the Stearman "Yellow Peril" biplane, Halaby reported to Pax River in September 1943 to start his new life as chief flight instructor at Flight Test.

"It was a sea of mud," Halaby recalled. The view outside the fence was no more inspiring, especially for a rich California boy with a taste for high living. "Jeeb" Halaby had inherited a Pierce Arrow roadster from his wealthy grandfather while still a teenager and had roared around on a Harley-Davidson motorcycle during his college years at Stanford University.

At this new Navy base in the boonies of St. Mary's County, there was not much else to do besides work. So Halaby dug in to his job of teaching veteran combat pilots, several of them heroes, how to change their way of flying.

The Navy sent to Pax River men who were good at maneuvering an airplane to shoot the enemy out of the sky. "The pilots who came to Pax river were all the way from aces like [Marine Corps Maj] Marion Carl to an enlisted AP pilot whose name was Don Runyon," Halaby recalled. "Some of the combat pilots were pissed off that they had been assigned to Flight Test. They wanted to be back in combat.

"Of all those hotshot pilots from the fleet, the guy who really applied himself to learn how to test was Marion Carl. He was a very serious guy.

"Runyon literally had a high-school education, but he was self taught and a fabulous pilot. I tried to help him get into the theory of flight and the aerodynamics of stability, control, handling qualities and all that. He was eager to learn because he had never had a good education while I had had four years at Stanford and three years at Yale Law School."

Marine Capt Jack T. Daugherty and Navy LTJG Robert F. Gabrelcik were among the first combat pilots ordered to Pax River to test airplanes. They underscored Halaby's memory of hotshot pilots who did not know anything about testing airplanes.

"Hell," recalled Daugherty, "we didn't know anything about what made airplanes fly. We just flew 'em—flew the hell out of them."

"I was in Service Test," Gabrelcik said. "Our job was to fly an airplane until something broke. The idea was to find out what parts wore out first so they would know how many of which ones to put on the ships for the airplanes.

"I remember flying down to this field at Banana River, Florida, in 1945 and blowing a tire on landing. I had the tire changed and left the old one down there. I got back and filed the report. They said, 'Get your butt back in the airplane and bring back that tire. That's part of the test.' So I had to fly all the way back to pick up the tire."

Halaby said another problem he encountered when he started teaching in 1943 was that many Navy pilots treated the engineers and other civilians at Pax River "like dirt." Many of the fleet pilots "were Annapolis graduates and very aware of that heritage." This attitude undercut the Navy's attempt to harness their skills together to evaluate the dozens of airplanes that Navy leaders wanted tested.

The former Lockheed test pilot, despite his low rank, resorted to teaching the fleet pilots the basics of flight testing one student at a time. It was slow going. The thin and sometimes nonexistent technical backgrounds of the World War II pilots, coupled with the shortage of instruments to record what was happening to the test airplane, kept the Navy's new technical center from living up to its potential.

"To calibrate your airspeed on the test airplane," Halaby said, "you flew alongside an airplane with a trailing pitot head. The most primitive thing."

World War II had already given birth to new generations of aircraft in several countries, but there was little data about them. Yet Navy leaders in Washington directed the new Test Center at Pax River to tell them what these high-performance planes could and could not do, including the captured German Focke Wulf 190 and Messerschmitt 262 jet.

"The big thing was articulating the good qualities of an airplane in terms that were precise and standard. From the fleet pilots, you'd get descriptions like this: 'That's a hell of a good flying airplane,' or 'That thing rolls like a son of a bitch.'

"That was fine. The fact that it went aboard a carrier beautifully— that was fine. But the real need was to articulate those generalities into specifics of why or why not the Navy should accept the airplane. Navy test pilots were in the acceptance business. We didn't build any airplanes. We were acceptance pilots."

Halaby said he and others at Flight Test were determined to go beyond generalities and "carve out some yardsticks" for measuring acceptable and unacceptable performance. "We tried to set standards for the rate of roll, for example," specifying how much roll was acceptable at various speeds.

"My main contribution was perhaps in going from the primitive to the more instrumented theory; from the feel to the standards; take it from 'It feels good' to 'It is instrumented good.' We tried to move from subjective to the objective. And we got a lot of help from the men at the National Advisory Committee for Aeronautics. If I contributed, it was in that area."

Although Halaby and the others put in long hours to develop a modern testing program, they also worked hard to maintain their distant social contacts. In Halaby's case, a British exchange pilot named Donald Callingham provided the bridge from barren Pax River to swinging Manhattan. The British admiralty had assigned a Widgeon, an amphibious plane, to Callingham at Pax River. Halaby reminisced, "That was the most marvelous boondoggle of all. He had a girl up in New York, and so did I. The Widgeon was a perfect way to get to New York and land right in the East River. You couldn't get caught for breaking any flight regulations because you weren't in a Navy aircraft; you were in a Royal Navy aircraft. So Callingham and I hit it off."

Jeeb Halaby left the Navy and Pax River in 1946 and began a distinguished civilian career in both government and business. His posts included administrator of the Federal Aviation Administration and board chairman of Pan American Airways. When interviewed in January 1992, he voiced a complaint about the popular image of test pilots that I have tried to keep in mind as I write about them:

"In a way, Chuck Yeager has so dramatized, so spectacularized, so commercialized test-flying that I kind of resent it. There are an awful lot of people who did a lot more test-flying with a lot more results than Chuck did. But that symbol of his supersonic flight being the breakthrough to end all breakthroughs has done one of two things: It either has exaggerated the role of the test pilot—which I think is the case with Yeager—or has underplayed this guy who has to slug out day after day the characteristics of, say, the V-22 [the Marine Corps's Osprey tiltrotor transport] or something like that. Our whole media attention on a spectacular event, the first supersonic event, tends to draw away from the professional, day-after-day hard work of test-flying.

"On balance, test pilots have done a hell of a good job over the years. Almost all of them have been conscientious. There are not many bullshitters in test-flying. I think they have been calculatingly courageous.

"'Slim' Lindbergh is the perfect example of the calculating pilot. He had every inch of that *Spirit of St. Louis,* every pound, every inch of view, every periscope worked out. In that sense, he was a test pilot as well as a daring aviator.

"If you could contribute in this book to the understanding of the careful, professional, calculating, intellectually and physically courageous side of test-flying, rather than its spectacular single-event qualities, that would be very useful."

"So you're Sherby," said CAPT Aaron P. "Putt" Storrs in his opening salvo against the new officer standing before his desk on the Fourth of July 1944. Storrs, a flier on the Navy's Sea Hawks stunt team, had relieved Rassieur as skipper of Pax River in January 1944.

An apprehensive CDR Sydney S. Sherby admitted to his name and saw his hopes for making captain sinking fast.

"You're a damn AEDO [Aeronautical Engineering Duty Officer], aren't you?"

"Yes, sir," Sherby replied, realizing that some pilots had no use for AEDOs who worked on the ground at desks rather than flew.

"What the hell are you doing here? We got no use for any damn AEDO here."

"Well, sir," Sherby struggled. "I was told to set up and operate a Class-B O-and-R [Overhaul and Repair] shop to do mod [modification] work, repairs, and instrumentation for the test units."

"Hell no!" Storrs roared. "We got nothing like that in our plans. I don't know what to do with you." Storrs paused, obviously enjoying Sherby's discomfort. "Wait a minute. Do you know Paul Ramsey?"

"Yes, sir!" Sherby answered as hope flooded into him with the mention of the name of an old friend.

"Well, I'll call Paul. He's my Director of Tests. He may know something about you."

Storrs punched some buttons on his desk phone and immediately had Commander Ramsey's ear.

"Hey, Paul. I got a damn AEDO by the name of Sherby here. Do you know anything about him?" Pause. "Yeah." Pause. "What does he want with him?" Pause. "Yeah? OK. I'll send him down."

Turning to Sherby, Storrs with a twinkle in his eye belying his meanness asked, "Do you know Tom Booth?"

"Yes, sir!" Sherby answered with relief. CDR C. T. "Tommy" Booth had been Sherby's shipmate in the VF-4 fighter squadron on the aircraft carrier USS *Ranger*. Booth had become head of the Flight Test Section on 8 May 1944. His former boss, CDR Paul H. Ramsey, had been promoted to Director of Tests, the overseer of tests conducted by five separate sections: Flight, Armament, Electronics, Service, and Tactical.

"Well, Tom wants you down at Flight Test. What the hell for I don't know. Anyhow, go on down to Paul's office and he'll take you over to see Tom."

"Thank you, sir!" a much-relieved Sherby said as he gratefully exited.

Ramsey's greeting was as warm as Storrs's had been cold.

"Thank God you're here," Ramsey told Sherby. "Tom's got a real problem, and he's counting on you to solve it."

Once inside Tom Booth's office, the new head of Flight Test quickly explained his problem and how he was counting on Sherby to solve it:

"Here we are with a magnificent new plant, a group of first-rate pilots and engineers, two hangars filled with new high-performance aircraft, and no one here really knows how to test them. We are technically bankrupt. We are not doing the quality job we should be doing. We cannot write competent reports on the aircraft we're given to test.

"Now, here's your job, and why you are here. I want this place put on a sound, modern, technical basis with pilots who know what to do when they fly, and engineers who know how to get good data and how to analyze it and prepare good, accurate reports. I have established a new officer billet of Chief Project Engineer. That's you. The old Chief Engineer is gone. You have the ball. You do whatever you think is necessary, and I'll back you all the way. Just keep me informed. The need is urgent! So get busy!"

Sherby—a 1936 Naval Academy graduate who had received his master's degree in aeronautical engineering at Massachusetts Institute of Technology in June 1944 and thus was up-to-date academically—spent the rest of July planning his attack. He ranked third in the Flight Test bureaucracy, right behind Director Booth and his deputy, Marine LtCol Des Canavan, whose title was Assistant Flight Test Officer.

Sherby had visited the National Advisory Committee for Aeronautics (NACA) while working on his master's degree at MIT and remembered how advanced their experts were in aeronautics. He telephoned Mel Gough, director of the Flight Research Division, and explained the big gaps in Pax River's capabilities for evaluating the aircraft that were piling up in the hangars.

"Syd, come on down here and we'll give you everything we have," Gough replied.

Syd Sherby and his deputies, sometimes including flight instructor Halaby, started making pilgrimages to NACA at the Langley Memorial Aeronautical Laboratory in Hampton, Virginia. For the Navy testers of 1944, it was like discovering the Mecca of modern aeronautics. Experts like Gough and his deputy Herbert Hoover in NACA's flight-research division knew all about the high-speed, high-performance aircraft manufactured during World War II.

Sherby also found that Robert R. Gilruth and William H. Philips, who headed the stability and flight-control division, had a pleasant surprise for the Navy's test pilots. "Bill Philips had just completed a remarkable paper," Sherby recalled, "entitled 'The Appreciation and Prediction of Flying Qualities.' This work gave us the tools and methods to fly an airplane, take data, and relate all of its characteristics to design and wind-tunnel data. It took all of the guesswork out of stability and control testing. We could, for example, cut the time for the determination of center-of-gravity limits to about a third."

Sherby said that Hartle Soule, director of NACA's performance division, "gave us all their latest test programs and data-reduction methods." Experts at NACA's instrumentation and hydrodynamics branches were equally helpful, sharing their knowledge and loading up the visitors from the Naval Air Test Center with papers on their findings.

Tommy Booth was elated with Sherby's quick incorporation of this new knowledge into flight-testing at Pax River. However, Booth was transferred to a new job before he could see the full fruits of his drive for excellence, leaving the top job at Flight Test on 2 January 1945. He was succeeded on 1 February 1945 by CDR Carl E. Giese, a former test pilot at Anacostia. LCDR Thomas F. Connolly became Giese's deputy.

By the time Giese and Connolly took over Flight Test, "the only thing that had not been done" with all the papers, methodology, and data obtained from the wise men of Langley "was to determine exactly the best way to introduce it to our personnel and put it into practice," Sherby recalled. On 21 February 1945 Giese named Sherby and Lieutenant Commanders Edward M. Owen and H. E. McNeely to address that question. Only two days later Sherby, who had been pondering the matter for twenty months, submitted a plan under the heading "Suggested Procedure for the Establishment of a Proposed Course of Instruction for Navy Flight Test Pilots." He suggested a ten-week course of instruction and flying, with his old friends Gough, chief test pilot at NACA, and Gilruth, the stability and control expert, among the guest lecturers.

Sherby's plan was adopted, and he became schoolmaster for this course. The first class of fourteen test pilots and engineers convened on 12 March and graduated on 30 May 1945. Captain Storrs, who had given Sherby the wire-brush treatment when he reported to Pax River, now praised Sherby and his school, handing the diplomas and slide rules to the first graduates.

Storrs left as Pax River commander on 15 June 1945, the day before the testing and housekeeping functions were separated. From 16 June 1945 onward the top officer at Pax River was the commander of the Naval Air Test Center. The housekeeper of the base—the skipper of the naval air station—reported to NATC. CAPT James D. Barner became the first commander of NATC on 11 August 1945. CAPT Frederick M. "Trap" Trapnell, a legendary test pilot at Anacostia, became Barner's deputy and coordinator of all the testing done on the base, not just at Flight Test.

"I had never met Trap," Sherby recalled. "I went to introduce myself. I took with me a draft copy of the new 'Flight Test Manual, Part Two, Stability and Control,' which Tom Connolly and I had prepared.

"About three days later he called and asked me to come to see him. He had been through about the first quarter of the book. He had meticulously printed notes all over the book. I was horrified when I saw how much he marked up. A bit sharply he asked how we dared put his name as a reviewer when he hadn't even seen it and we hadn't asked him. I explained that we knew he was coming, had intended to have him review it, and had included his name in order to have it as near correct copy. He finally accepted that. Then he started in on his comments: 'Why this? Why that? What did this equation mean? Why is this symbol used? Where did you get this terminology?' I carefully explained each little point. He then said he would go on with it and would call after he had done some more.

"This went on for the next two weeks. Each time there was the same great number of meticulous notes in red pencil and the detailed questions. To say that I was apprehensive and distraught was the understatement of all times. If I had to make all the changes that he had questions about, I would just have to start all over.

"At the end of the last session, when we had just finished going over his last comments, he said to me, 'Syd, I owe you a great apology. I have made you give me a complete course in stability and control aerodynamics in the most difficult manner. This has all been new to me. You have had to do it by answering my comments without any preparation. I want to thank you for the education. I think the book is great, and I would not suggest you change one thing. This kind of information has been needed for a long time.'

"He held out his hand. This was the beginning of a lifelong friendship and wonderful working relationship. The man had uncanny engineering instincts. He did not have graduate engineering training. You could show him an equation or a bit of technical logic. If he said it looked OK, it invariably was OK. If he said he didn't know why but it seemed like something was wrong, it proved to be that he had sensed a problem, and that he was right. This proved to be valuable more than once. He was a superb pilot, one of the very best ever. He could take a plane out for evaluation and could qualitatively tell you everything you could determine from instrumented data analysis."

Barner and Trapnell, who sometimes sat through Sherby's classes, became enthusiastic backers of the school and pressed Navy leaders to open it to test pilots and engineers beyond those assigned to the Flight Test unit.

"One of the fallouts of the training" provided at the new school "was the knowledge that our pilots took back to the fleet with them," Sherby said. "It was beginning to show up in improved fleet operations." Barner and Trapnell "both looked at the school as a sort of postgraduate flying school as well as just one to train test pilots."

On 1 May 1947 Trapnell recommended to the Chief of Naval Operations that Sherby's course become a permanent school that thirty pilots and engineers would attend for six months. RADM Apollo Soucek, another legendary test pilot who in 1929 had set a world record by climbing to 40,000 feet in an open-cockpit Wright Apache airplane, succeeded Barner and took up his torch for the school.

Trapnell drafted a blueprint for what he called a Test Pilot Training

Division. The Navy adopted Trapnell's blueprint on 19 January 1948 by issuing Aviation Plan Number 65. The plan called for a nine-month course given to thirty students, thirteen of them Navy aviators, five Marine Corps aviators, and no more than twelve from other communities, including civilian contractor pilots.

The purpose of the school was "to develop a technical and analytical understanding of basic theory and test procedures" through a combination of classroom work and flight training, Plan 65 said. On 4 March 1948 Skipper Soucek issued the order that formally established the Test Pilot Training Division, which would become known as TPT, as part of his command. Sherby became director of the division in April. The five small classes Sherby and others had taught in 1945, 1946, 1947, and 1948 were lumped together as Class 0. Rear Admiral Soucek on 6 July 1948 welcomed the twenty-one students comprising Class One of TPT. Class 1 lasted six months, not the originally envisioned nine months, and graduated on 21 December. CDR Thomas F. Connolly relieved Sherby as the first director of the school on 31 December.

Most of the test pilots and engineers who graduated from TPT stayed at Pax River to conduct flight-testing at Armament Test, Electronic Test, Flight Test, Service Test, or Tactical Test. The pilots usually returned to the fleet after serving about two years in one of those specialty branches, eventually called directorates.

The flight instruction for future test pilots was dangerous, the test-flying they did after graduation was dangerous, life in the air all around Pax River was dangerous, whether you were at the controls or in the backseat working the radios and reading the instruments. Pilots made mistakes, weather went sour, machines broke. There were crashes and tragedy along with tedium and joy at the Naval Air Test Center, which only a few years earlier had been peaceful farmland where the most common cause of death was old age.

But the training and testing went on.

There were two types of flight tests—acceptance tests and experimental tests.

The acceptance tests were done on aircraft the Navy had ordered from a private contractor but had not yet approved for volume production. Ellyson's 1 July 1911 flight in the A-1 was the first acceptance test. Samples of the aircraft, called test models, were sent from the factory to

Pax River for evaluation. The contractor's own test pilots had already flown the airplanes and written down for the Navy what they could do. The Navy's test pilots then took the planes and flew them at the edges of their performance envelopes to see if the contractor's claims were true. The Navy's test pilots made exhaustive evaluations of the planes' flaws, either for the Bureau of Aeronautics or for the Navy's Board of Inspection and Survey, which reported to the Secretary of the Navy. Each test pilot wrote down his findings, and these reports went up the chain of command to the Navy's decision makers who determined whether an airplane should be accepted and put into production. The preproduction tests were called service-acceptance trials.

If the airplane passed muster and went into production, the test pilots at Pax River were also asked to test planes selected at random from the production line. This was to make sure the production models were being built as the Navy had specified. These were called production-inspection trials.

The Bureau of Aeronautics was the agency that usually requested the experimental tests, which would determine how adding fuel tanks or installing different bomb racks or engines would affect a plane's performance and handling qualities. Often the Bureau was in a hurry to learn the result of somebody's tinkering with an aircraft. The tinkering makes a known airplane unknown, and often dangerous.

From World War II onward, aircraft designers and builders from all over the world have raced one another to make airplanes do more and more. Electronics have been miniaturized to fit inside aircraft. Gadgetry has extended the capabilities of the eyes, ears, hands, and feet of the humans inside the planes. Radar now sees the target long before the pilot's own eyes. A hum in the ears indicates when an air-to-air missile is in killing range of the enemy plane. Hands on the stick no longer feel the pressure of the wind on the wings or tail. A mechanical pilot in the form of hydraulics and computers absorbs that sensation. This mechanical pilot passes along some of the actual pressure it is feeling to the control stick so that the human pilot can believe that he or she is still flying the plane. Missiles were invented that ride radio beams into enemy radar sets on the ground or aircraft in the air. Weapons makers perfected bombs that ride light beams down to their targets or see their way down to them with television.

While loading up aircraft with these "systems," airplane manufacturers also designed sleeker airframes and more powerful engines, so the airplane and all the new systems go faster. One airplane can now do hundreds of more things than the rickety A-1 that Ellyson and Towers flew in the early 1900s. But these new systems, airframes, and engines are also hundreds of times more complicated. They cannot be mastered during a half hour spin around North Island or Lake Keuka with a latter-day Glenn Curtiss or even via six months of studying under Syd Sherby. The pilots and engineers of the 1980s and 1990s have to know far more engineering and science than their predecessors. They have to go more vertical than horizontal in their learning. The Navy has insisted on this. Aviators have been forced to narrow their focus, to concentrate on technology, to be more disciplined in their ground preparations and in the way they actually fly. Aviators have become more technocratic, less free-spirited, perhaps less fun or interesting to anyone who wants to talk about something besides airplanes and aircraft systems.

Test pilots have been pushed to the top of this narrowing pyramid. They knew what was happening to them, often disparaging themselves as "geeks" and "nerds" who were paying a high price to get ahead in the military of the 1990s. But the thirty-four members of Class 100 whom RADM Don Boecker welcomed to the U.S. Naval Test Pilot School on 14 January 1991 were willing to pay that price. It is time to get to know this new breed better.

Class 100—
Who They Are

Wes "Otto" Nielsen was distressed. But not so much that he could not share his distress with his colleagues from Class 100 gathered in the study area of the Test Pilot School hangar.

"Here we were on our time, drinking beer," said the F/A-18 pilot fresh from the fleet and now in Pax River trying to become a test pilot, "and we were geeking. Worse than that, we were enjoying it!"

Instead of moving their hands around to show how one pilot got the drop on the other in mock aerial combat, Lieutenant Nielsen related how he and his fellow aviators found themselves talking about the aerodynamics of airplanes—why they behave as they do—rather than about how they fly. They were talking engineering, not flying, and they were both happy and unhappy about how their immersion in the scientific side of flying at Test Pilot School was affecting them.

John J. "JJ" McCue, Jr., an aerodynamics instructor at TPS, would have been pleased if he had heard Otto's lament. Sitting through his and other teachers' classes at TPS, I assumed that the main thrust of the whole academic effort was to force the students to examine the why of aircraft behavior, not how to make it behave by working the plane's stick and rudder pedals.

"They know how to fly," JJ began when I asked him if my assumption was right. "Flying is second nature to them. We're trying to give them the understanding they need for the testing. In other words, how are airplanes designed? How do you test them? We get into building a math model for the aircraft. What are the important variables, as you look at weight or altitude or rotor speed or airspeed?

"If you get a real appreciation for what the equation is, what the important variables are, and how they influence [the performance of the airplane], then you can come back and say, 'Now, do we need to come back and control all three or four of these variables [to find out what's happening to the airplane]? Is one more dominant? Can we blow the others off?'

"The philosophy is this: The more understanding that you can get, the better you can test the aircraft."

Sure, I interjected, but these students are not going to remember all those long formulas you keep putting on the blackboard. They have forgotten them before, and they will forget them again. So why go through them day after day?

"I don't want you as a student to memorize the derivation," JJ replied. "Understand it at the time I do it. If you have a question, sing out. But you've seen me thump on the board to say from that development there are a couple of things you do need to know as a tester. Use the theory to guide the testing.

"If you do the cookbook approach and say, 'I'll just do items one, two, three, four, and five,' what happens if somebody throws you something new? If you're just a cookbook tester and don't understand what some of the problems are and some of the assumptions are, and then somebody gives you something new, you have no idea what to do.

"So the idea is that if you understand the background and assumptions that were made, you can take the old test and adapt it to the new aircraft."

I understood and applauded that philosophy for turning fliers into testers. But sitting in the classroom and listening to JJ and the others lecture, watching the students struggle at their computers over the homework, I quickly decided that TPS is not for everyone. As an English major, I found the courses just as tedious as the engineering courses I had tried to master, usually unsuccessfully, while going to Georgia Tech in my ancient past as a Navy aviation cadet in the V-5 program. Then and now I wanted to fly, not study formulas and hear why wings and rotors bent a certain way when subjected to various forces. But nobody in TPS was a liberal-arts major, and they would have no doubt been bored with the "bull" courses I enjoyed, like English literature.

So who fits in at Test Pilot School? Men and women with engineering backgrounds who want to know the why of mechanical and electronic behavior and are willing to do lots of drudgery at the computer and elsewhere to find out. The students in Class 100 were highly motivated, often driven; patriotic; politically conservative; technologically oriented, computer adept; narrowly focused; cautious; systematic, conscientious; self-assured or, in some cases, openly egomaniacal. Navy specifications for test pilots and engineers virtually required them to be engineers first and fliers second. The five civilian engineers in the class seemed to be the most enthusiastic fliers, probably because Navy flying was new to them.

Of the twenty-nine U.S. and foreign officers in Class 100, twenty-three were married. They typically went home to supper with their wives and children, watched some television, sat before the computer to do homework, went to bed, and got up early to prepare for another day of studying and flying, which began at 8 A.M. Weekends they shopped with their families at suburban malls and often went to another student's suburban house for drinks and dinner. In other words, they worked and lived like the middle-class suburbanites the officers of the modern-day American military have become. A flying naval aviator with the rank of lieutenant was paid $62,172 per year in 1991, which includes $650 per month in flight pay; up to $12,000 per year as a bonus for every year beyond the initial obligated tour, up to the fourteenth year of commissioned flying service; and housing and food allowances. A sailor with ten years service with the rank of first-class petty officer received $25,536.

Some of the members of Class 100, especially the singles, certainly went pub crawling. One bachelor aviator in search of female companions often cruised, for example, through the Green Door tavern near St. Mary's College as well as Captain Seaweed's, The Pier, and the Tiki Bar on Solomons Island across from Pax River. Others favored quaffing a Bass ale at the St. James Pub north of the gate or hitting the bars in Washington, D.C., two hours north of the base. But most of this new breed of flier ate healthily, drank sparingly if at all, lifted weights, jogged, and stayed home most of the time.

The Roost restaurant and bar just outside the front gate dramatized the contrast between the aviators who earned their wings during World War II, Korea, and Vietnam and those at Pax River in the 1990s. The earlier aviators drank, hooted, sang, and hollered at The Roost. Tarnished brass plates hammered onto the wooden bar still mark where the most regular of the regulars stood to tell their flying stories and sing a little. Almost no one from Class 100 went into The Roost, far less stood at the bar long enough to earn a brass nameplate.

"You've got to remember," one of the few swingers in Class 100 told me, "most of these guys are geeks."

One of the most respected flight instructors at TPS confided to me that he thought it tragic that many of the officers striving to be test pilots become so driven by their ambition that they ignore their spouses and children: "They're like pumpkin seeds squeezed between fingers at regular intervals to move along the career path. They ignore the really important relationships as they go along. By the time they realize what they've missed, it will be too late."

On the other hand, military leaders have insisted upon molding their best and brightest into narrowly focused, highly educated technocrats who can master the multimillion-dollar, high-tech weapons without breaking them. With one aircraft carrier costing more than four billion dollars and one bomber up to two billion dollars, the admirals and generals no longer want the colorful Mr. or Ms. Personalities who fool around, no matter how brave and talented they might be. If this makes for duller aviators, for geeks, goes the military's management philosophy for the 1990s, so be it: war is too technologically sophisticated for the technologically unsophisticated.

Understanding this evolution in thinking at the top of the military, I was not surprised to find the Test Pilot School aviators less colorful and engaging than those I had become such close friends with while at sea for seven and a half months on the aircraft carrier USS *John F. Kennedy* in 1983 and 1984. The constant needling and repartee of the *Kennedy's* ready rooms were muted inside the walls of TPS. And at TPS, posters of helicopters and airplanes had replaced the pinups of models like Farrah Fawcett that I had found on the *Kennedy*. As Otto observed, the conversation on and off duty among the students was almost always about airplanes. I never heard them discuss any of the topics atop the rest of the nation's agenda, such as crime and homelessness. I saw many of these future test pilots as high hurdlers running along the track and gathering themselves to clear the next hurdle, and the next, and the next. They knew they might trip and fall if they looked too far to the left or right as they ran along. I admired their dedication and tried to keep out of their way and not distract them during their race toward graduation.

In trying to describe the collective personality of the officers in Class 100—the civilians in the class were less driven, less obsessed with winning the race—I am trying to be accurate, not pass judgment. All thirty-four students were pursuing excellence. To go beyond the generalized picture, here are thumbnail portraits of every member of Class 100, men and women who typified the best and brightest in America's all-volunteer military of 1991—the year the downsizing of the armed forces began. (Students' ages are as of 14 January 1991, when Class 100 convened; the towns are birthplaces.)

Navy Lieutenant Robert D. "Bullet" Allen, twenty-nine. Peoria, Illinois. Married. Southeast Oklahoma State. F-14 fighter pilot. One of six children in what he jokingly called "a big Irish family." Banged around the Southwest as a commercial pilot before joining the Navy in 1984. Liked flying far more than studying about it, especially dogfighting. Would have been happy flying with Ely in 1911 or barnstorming in the 1920s with the World War I aviators in a Curtiss Jenny. His wife, Cynthia Hazell, was a TWA pilot.

Navy Lieutenant Charles S. "Scott" Anderson, twenty-nine. Honolulu, Hawaii. Married. U.S. Naval Academy. P-3 antisubmarine-warfare pilot. His father, CAPT Carl Anderson, advised, "Only one way to go—submarines." Scott decided to hunt for them instead. "It's the microwave dinners," Anderson joked because this is what the P-3 crew eat during their twelve-hour patrols over the ocean. An upbeat aviator who saw TPS as a launching pad to getting into space as an astronaut.

Army Captain Roger A. Arnzen, thirty-two. Cottonwood, Idaho. Married. U.S. Military Academy. Helicopter pilot. Grew up as one of eleven children on a 2,000-acre ranch. Became convinced that "farmers are always dirt poor." Fell in love with helicopters. Commanded a company in 1st Battalion of 6th Cavalry Regiment of

2nd Armored Division at Fort Hood. TPS seen as a way to stay in the cockpit and avoid a desk job in the Army's Aviation Systems Command in St. Louis. I found Arnzen rancher-quiet, solid.

Army Captain Arthur T. "AT" Ball, thirty-one. Davenport, Iowa. Married. U.S. Military Academy; master's from Georgia Tech. Helicopter pilot. Over-achieved early, making $150 per day as a fifteen-year-old running his own Uptop Roofing Co., spray-painting houses, cutting down trees for pulp. Senior-class president at Nacogdoches, Texas, high school. Loved helicopters because "I don't think there's anything that can compare to flying down low. It's quite a rush." Politically conservative, he asked me if I were a Communist because I was from the press.

Navy Lieutenant Ramon A. "Babaloo" Collazo, twenty-eight. Single. U.S. Naval Academy. Mission commander supervising crew in the back of the E-2C Hawkeye command-and-control aircraft. Emigrated from the little village of Santurce, Puerto Rico, at age nine to Glen Burnie, Maryland. Only five feet four inches tall, he proved to be an outstanding infielder. Studied the stars from boyhood onward; hoped graduating from TPS would improve his chances of rocketing into space.

Italian Air Force Captain Sergio "Sergetto" Comitini, twenty-seven. Married. Italian Air Force Academy. Tornado fighter-bomber pilot. Born in Cagliari, Italy, to retired Brigadier General Paolo Comitini of the Italian Air Force and Rosa Indini Comitini, an elementary-school teacher, Sergetto grew up on air force bases, where planes became as familiar to the boy as trees. "This was my life. But my father never pushed me. It was really the dream of my life to fly the Tornado." Came to TPS to see "what else I can do."

Navy Lieutenant Robert L. "Beamer" Curbeam, Jr., twenty-eight. Baltimore, Maryland. Married. U.S. Naval Academy; Navy Postgraduate School. F-14 radar intercept officer. The only black in Class 100, Beamer was the most natural and tolerant member of a minority that I had ever encountered in three decades of covering the American military. He also wrote the best reports in the class. Regarded TPS as a new challenge.

Civilian engineer Gregory D. Dungan, thirty. Clute, Texas. Mar-

ried. Georgia Tech. Earned private pilot's license while a junior
Boca Raton, Florida, high school. Entered the Air Force after hi
school to save money for college. Joined Strike Directorate at Pa
River as a flight engineer in 1987. Believed going through TPS
would increase his credibility as a flight engineer plus put him "
closest I'll ever get to a squadron environment."

Navy Lieutenant Nancy "Nofun" Dykhoff, twenty-six. Park
burg, West Virginia. Single [married Navy Lieutenant Scott Fec
later in the school year]. U.S. Naval Academy. Naval flight offic
EA-7C electronic-warfare airplane. Four brothers hardened her
the rough and tumble of men's sports. Went to Annapolis becau
"I wanted to do something different." Believes women aviators
should go into combat because "if the men are being shot at, gu
we should be shot at."

Navy Lieutenant Commander Steven R. Eastburg, thirty-on
Oakland, California. Married. U.S. Naval Academy; Navy Postg
uate School. Tactical commander in the S-3 antisubmarine aircra
Son of Paul H. Eastburg, an agricultural chemist and World Wa
Navy veteran, and Barbara J. Rodgers, a laboratory technician,
Steve had broad intellectual curiosity. Intensely interested in the
whole Navy's future, not just his own. Specialized in unmanned
weaponry. Precise in everything he did and said.

Canadian Air Force Captain Robert T. Erdos, twenty-seven.
Toronto, Canada. Married. Royal Military College of Canada.
Search-and-rescue helicopter pilot. Son of Joseph and Magda W
Erdos, both survivors of the Holocaust. Grew up suspicious of n
tary organizations, even the Boy Scouts. Earned glider's license a
age sixteen, private pilot's license at seventeen, commercial licen
at eighteen. Became my best friend in the class, partly because he
was deeply interested in what I did as a reporter and why.

Navy Lieutenant Thomas J. "Fitz" Fitzgerald IV, twenty-seve
Washington, D.C. Single. Catholic University of America. SH-3 F
helicopter pilot. Son of Thomas J. Fitzgerald III, treasurer of The
Nature Conservancy, and Kathleen Farrall, staffer with the Easte
Seals Society for Disabled Children. Joined the Navy in 1985
because "I didn't want to go out and get a desk job. I could alwa

do that later on." TPS appealed because "I like looking at the way things work."

Civilian engineer Kathleen Y. "KT" Fleming, thirty. Norfolk, Virginia. Single. University of Maryland; master's from Florida Institute of Technology. Her father, Bruce S. Fleming, was a Navy helicopter test pilot who graduated from TPS with Class 29 in 1961. "Before I came here I couldn't tell you anything about the operational side of flying. For an engineer, TPS is really tremendous. You get hands-on experience. So if you're discussing stick force, you can say, 'Oh yeah. This means this in the cockpit.' Flying enables you to say, 'Oh, that's what these guys have been bitching about.'"

Navy Lieutenant Christopher L. "Spanky" Frasse, twenty-eight. Oceanside, New York. Married. U.S. Naval Academy; master's from Catholic University of America. E-6A pilot and mission commander. His father, John Frasse, is a Nassau County police officer and was a Navy tail gunner during World War II. Spanky played ice hockey, soccer, and lacrosse in high school. Won Class 100's first physical-fitness competition. Believed TPS would "broaden career possibilities, civilian or military."

Navy Lieutenant William C. "Boomer" Hamilton, Jr., thirty-four. Anastre, Alabama. Married. Auburn University. F/A-18 pilot. His father owned several aircraft and inspired Boomer to learn to fly at an early age. Termed himself "Joe Average" at Anastre High School. "Second-string athlete; B student; almost a wallflower." Earned his private pilot's license at age nineteen. Flew Auburn coaches from place to place to help pay his way through college. After flying F/A-18s off carriers, saw TPS as a new kind of challenge.

Royal Air Force Squadron Leader Laurence Stanley "The Gov" Hilditch, thirty-six. London, England. Married. Queens University, Belfast; Royal Air Force College. Fighter-bomber pilot. Son of Stanley Campbell Hilditch, a Baptist minister serving prisons, and Florence Halliday, a nurse. A brilliant student, Hilditch said, "I never wanted to do anything else but fly." Soloed at age fifteen; won a flying scholarship from the Royal Air Force at age sixteen. Wanted to

go to TPS to learn more about "how and why the beastie does what it does."

Navy Lieutenant Jeffery D. "JD" Hood, twenty-nine. Albuquerque, New Mexico. Tulane University. SH-60 Seahawk helicopter pilot. His physics teacher at Albuquerque Academy, Charles "Skip" Porter, a former lieutenant commander, inspired "JD" to join the Navy in 1983. "I always wanted to fly." Believed TPS would provide "the chance to fly more things. I wanted to get out and broaden myself. You get in a fleet squadron, and you get real narrow. TPS broadens you out again."

Marine Major John J. "Spade" Kirk, thirty-seven. Groton, Connecticut. Married. U.S. Naval Academy. F/A-18 pilot. Class 100's leader. Played football at West Springfield, Virginia, high school; graduated in 1971; enlisted in the Marine Corps. Selected from enlisted ranks for Annapolis, graduating in 1976. Considered TPS "a new adventure." Was a taciturn, dedicated marine. His wife, Ann, ran the wives' club, which turned out to be a frequently fractious group.

Navy Lieutenant Glen A. "Popeye" Knaust, twenty-eight. Newburgh, New York. Married. University of Florida. Helicopter pilot. Son of Alan S. Knaust, owner of a food market, and Sheila Raab, accounting clerk. Played football and ran track at Largo, Florida, high school; graduated in 1980; joined Air Force ROTC at the University of Florida. Entered the Navy in 1985 to fly jets but was assigned to helicopters. Saw TPS as a way "to tie in flying with my degree and fly some other types of aircraft."

Navy Lieutenant Paul F. "Morty" Linnell, twenty-nine. Newburyport, Massachusetts. Single. Notre Dame University. F-14 radar intercept officer. His father, Charles W. Linnell, was a carpenter. Morty worked as a grave digger while attending St. John's Catholic Preparatory School in Danvers, Massachusetts, inspiring his nickname. "We were a poor family. Only way to go to college was join the military." Became Class 100's amusing, acerbic, complaining cynic. Included "to end world hunger" when I asked him for a list of reasons for coming to TPS.

Navy Lieutenant Darryl J. "Spike" Long, twenty-eight. Red Bluff, California. Single. Santa Clara University. E-2C Hawkeye pilot. Spike matched Spuds Ellyson, Naval Aviator Number One, closer than anyone else in Class 100. Both were daring and fun loving with a serious determination underneath. Spike had Ellyson's "go for it" attitude, even to inviting President Bush to be Class 100's graduation speaker. Bush declined. Spike strongly supported my book project.

Civilian engineer Andrew C. "Andy" Maack, twenty-six. Belleville, Illinois. Married. Parks College University. Joined the Strike Directorate at Pax River in August 1985 to gain responsibility early in his career. Was the lead civilian engineer on the rewinging of the A-6 bomber; solved the bomb-loading problems generated by the stiffer plastic wing that replaced the metal one. Won the John E. Burdette Award in 1991 "for outstanding managerial" performance. His affability and brilliance quickly bridged the traditional gap between pilots and engineers.

Marine Captain Marcus G. "Nino" Mannella, twenty-nine. Columbus, Ohio. Purdue University. Single (married Crystal Michelson, a school teacher, during the school year). Helicopter pilot. Exhibited Midwestern friendliness and idealism, making him the best-natured member of Class 100. He was in love with both the Marine Corps and his new wife and did not mind showing it. He told me that as a test pilot he hoped to have "a profound impact on the future of aviation in the Marine Corps."

Army Chief Warrant Officer Third Class David S. Mari, thirty. Indiana, Pennsylvania. Married. Embry Riddle University. Helicopter pilot. Joined the Army as a private to save money for college; fell in love with flying. Wanted to be a medical-evacuation helicopter pilot because "I always wanted that hero thing." The Army assigned him to Cobra gunships, not medevac helicopters. Advanced to warrant officer; joined Task Force 160 Night Stalkers, a shadowy antiterrorist outfit. Participated in the Panama invasion.

Air Force Captain William M. "Fish" Mason, twenty-eight. Lockbourne AFB, Ohio. Married. U.S. Air Force Academy; master's from New Mexico State University. F-15 fighter pilot. Son of the late Air Force Maj Robert S. Mason. Captained the swim team at Eau Gallie High School, Melbourne, Florida. Graduated with honors from the Academy, where "I had one date in four years." Impressed me as the straightest of arrows. Took over the children and household chores one day each week so that his wife could "go do anything she wants to do."

Marine Captain Stephen C. "Mac" McCulley, thirty-four. St. Louis, Missouri. Married. University of Missouri. Helicopter pilot. Mac epitomized the study discipline at TPS. He often sat at his home computer with plugs in his ears and earphones over them so that he could concentrate on his homework while his children played all around him. Came to TPS "to learn more about an aircraft. Hopefully I can have an impact" on what the marines buy. "When I was in the fleet, I saw this garbage come out and asked, 'Why did we get this thing?'"

Navy Lieutenant Lori J. "Wrench" Melling, thirty. Hammond, Indiana. Single. Michigan State; Navy Postgraduate School. A-7 pilot. Became fascinated with automobiles at an early age and even rebuilt them herself. Planned to be a designer or engineer at an auto company until a friend took her flying. Earned degrees in mechanical engineering and theoretical applied mechanics. Joined the Navy in 1983 with the hope of becoming a fighter pilot on an aircraft carrier and/or an astronaut.

Navy Lieutenant Steven "Ski" Modzelewski, thirty-one. New Brunswick, New Jersey. Married. Rutgers University; Navy Postgraduate School. Helicopter pilot. Ski told me, "I'm perfectly happy with helos. Being down low, you actually get the feeling of flight. You've got the bird, and you're part of it." He studied nights and weekends at TPS. I worried about his overdoing it as I watched deep, black circles develop under his eyes. Regarded TPS as a "broadening experience."

Navy Lieutenant Wesley S. "Otto" Nielsen, twenty-nine. San Jose, California. Married. Jacksonville, Florida, University. F/A-18 pilot. His father, Einer D. Nielsen, was a former Navy fighter pilot who taught electrical engineering at San Jose State College and "filled me up with stories. Took me to Blue Angel air shows." A leader in a class filled with leaders, Wes played the leading role in the "You'll Be Sorry" skit and kept his ready-room humor. Went to

TPS because "I wanted to be part of the leading edge of technology; see a different part of the Navy."

Navy Lieutenant Erford E. "Erf" Porter III, twenty-eight. Philadelphia, Pennsylvania. Married. Muhlenburg College. P-3 tactical command officer. Sang, danced, played baritone horn, and became an Eagle Scout while growing up; played football, captained the wrestling team, ran track at Greenwich, Connecticut, high school. "I love being a P-3 TACCO. It's a great game of cat and mouse. It's three dimensional—more like a chess game." Erf was a low-key, considerate officer whom pilots loved to have handling the electronic systems in the back.

Navy Lieutenant Ralph I. "Iggy" Portnoy, twenty-eight. Groton, Connecticut. Single. U.S. Naval Academy. A-6 pilot. Son of Navy CAPT Howard R. Portnoy, a diesel submariner, and Paula J. Fox, a health-club executive. "I've always kind of been interested in flying; always liked airplanes." Saw TPS as an "opportunity to fly different kinds of airplanes, an opportunity which is almost nonexistent in the fleet. . . . I wanted to push myself further."

Civilian engineer Jeffrey L. Rusher, twenty-nine. Charlotte, North Carolina. Single. North Carolina State. Joined the Force Warfare Directorate at Pax River in 1985. Saw TPS as "a great opportunity to get more diversified. I felt there would be some very cocky people here—I was intimidated. But there have been no problems. I was afraid the instructors would be biased against civilians." TPS "has opened new gates to me for testing new systems; given me a better feel for what's important. I study 5 P.M. to dinner and three hours on Sunday."

Army Major Kevin G. "Joker" Scherrer, thirty-five. Rockville Center, New York. Married. U.S. Military Academy; master's from Stanford. Helicopter pilot. His parents—George J. Scherrer, a personnel manager, and Jo Anna Riegle Scherrer, a music teacher— were "well to do, relatively left-wing, participated in sit-ins. . . . But I was one of these kids who always wanted to fly." Taught theory of vertical and short takeoff and landing aircraft and fluid mechanics courses at West Point. A constant organizer of Class 100's activities, he was always helping out his classmates. A popular man.

Civilian engineer Jeffrey T. Semenza, twenty-seven. Scranton, Pennsylvania. Single. Bachelor's and master's degrees from Penn State. Joined Rotary Wing at Pax River in 1987; worked on ways to make it easier and safer to land on a ship by analyzing motion as the plane and the ship came together. Appreciated Pax River's letting engineers "get a whole lot of responsibility at a really young age." Considered TPS "the culmination of everything." Said the school would "fill out my credentials. In the flying, I'm learning something new every time I go out."

Lori Melling was more than an unusually striking and gifted woman who dared to be different. She was a revolutionist in the spirit of Captain Chambers, the man who forced airplanes onto the fleet. Melling wanted to force fully equal female pilots onto the fleet.

Looking at Melling in civilian clothes, no one would guess that she was a one-time tomboy with grease under her fingernails, or that she had earned two engineering degrees and then become a Navy jet pilot with the intention of taking her place alongside the men in a carrier fighter squadron. Passersby would more likely guess that Melling was a California fashion model, for she stood nearly six feet tall and had long, blonde hair. If they heard her speak, Melling's aw-shucks manner and Midwestern twang would have dispelled the notion that she was a standoffish model. She comes across as down-home and, if born male, would have been considered a regular guy.

"Lori has always wanted to make it on her own," her mother, Joan C. Meimburg Melling, told me. While Lori was growing up, her first love was cars. She fixed up old ones as a teenager, even overhauling and installing engines, knocking the dents out of the fenders, and spray painting the bodies. Her pride and joy during her years at Thornwood High School in South Holland, Illinois, was a red and black Firebird in which she had installed three different engines. "She always had dirt under her fingernails," Mrs. Melling recalled. Lori's father, Ralph H. Melling, an insurance agent, laughed about having to park the family's car in the driveway so that Lori could work on her wrecks in the garage.

"I pumped gas to feed my car," Lori recalled of her teenage years. Her master plan was to become an automobile designer for some big company like General Motors.

But as Mrs. Melling explained, "A boyfriend took Lori up in his plane, and that was it."

At TPS, Lori did everything she could during the working day to be just another test pilot under instruction. She wore an olive-drab flight suit and scuffed black flight boots, tucked her hair away in a bun, and gave as good as she got in the kidding that went on during the breaks between classes. One day Spike Long, just to needle Lori, ripped her name tag off the Velcro patch on her flight suit and threw it on the floor. "You're a dead man!" she snapped, then walked over to pick up the name tag and put it back on her flight suit. Then they both laughed. End of incident.

According to fellow aviators, Melling was thoroughly professional every time she went aloft. "A good stick. Adds a lot. Does her part." These were all things the supposedly male chauvinists of Naval Air told me about Lori. She had been a flight instructor in the T-2 Buckeye training plane, but she did want the chance to be all she could be as a Navy pilot and fought for it.

During the school year, she occasionally went to Washington, D.C., to try to convince lawmakers to repeal legislation that said women could not serve in combat. Congress lifted that ban but left it up to the Pentagon to decide how and when to give women full equality. Yet another Pentagon study commission was named to examine the question, frustrating Melling and her allies one more time.

As part of my effort to get to know the personal side of future test pilots, not just their flying, I asked Lori to explain why she was fighting for the right to fly on and off carriers, in war or peace, just like the men.

"Women's advance toward full equality in Naval Aviation has been a series of slow steps," Lori lamented as we talked over a tape recorder in an empty classroom at TPS. "We went from a few women flying, to women getting their wings in props and helicopters, then jet transitions, and then the full syllabus in the A-6s [bombers], A-7s [light-attack aircraft], and A-3s [electronic-warfare planes]."

Even if female naval aviators achieve full equality "tomorrow morning," she said, "it's going to take years for women to get through the RAGs [now called FRSs, or Fleet Replacement Squadrons, but the old term, replacement air groups, is ingrained into aviation lingo], into their squadrons, through workups [the exercises at sea during which the entire air wing, made up of many different types of aircraft, practices together and with the ship before going out on a long deployment], out on cruise, through department-head tours." Naval aviators must pass those milestones before they are considered for leadership positions running upward from commander of a squadron to commander of an air wing to skipper of an aircraft carrier.

Lori said that even if she realized her dream and got assigned to a carrier squadron, "it would be hard to compete" for advancement. "I don't have the experience of my male contemporaries. I have 1,600 hours [of piloting Navy aircraft]. That helps a little bit. When I'm screening [being considered] for command, I'll have a very short time at sea under my belt.

"If I do get out there" on an aircraft carrier to fly as a fully equal member of a squadron, "I think I could come back here as a test pilot with fleet experience and do a lot better job as a test pilot. That's what my goal is. I want to go to sea so I can come back here and be a better test pilot."

What if there is a war?

"I want to go. If there's a war, that's what we train for."

And if you get shot down?

"Bad luck!" she quipped, then laughed.

How about the danger of being raped if captured?

"Men get raped. And women get raped here in the States. That's ridiculous. There are all sorts of horrible, unspeakable tortures that men endure. It's not a pleasant thing."

What about the claim that women aboard carriers would be more trouble than they are worth because of sexual polarization and pregnancies?

"It's a leadership problem. It needs to be managed. If you put a bunch of young people on a ship you obviously have to set some rules. It's not the Love Boat, and here are some rules, and here are the consequences if you don't obey the rules. And then it's not a problem. We're all professionals."

How do you allay the fears of the wives or girlfriends at home that their husbands or boyfriends would carry on with the women at sea?

"You're not going to do that stuff in a squadron because it's going to ruin unit cohesiveness. It's going to screw things up. It's like messing in your own bed. It's a violation of Ranger Rick's rules of camping. I think it's overblown. It's like saying we better not have any port calls because husbands might cheat on their wives. It's a personal problem. If they [wives ashore] have problems with their marriage, it's not my fault. Most guys just want to go to work and do their job. That's what I think."

How would you define complete victory for women in the Naval Air community?

"I don't define winning as being CAG [the commander of an air wing on an aircraft carrier]. I just define it as having the opportunity all the way."

One afternoon I looked at the desk of this deceptively feminine looking woman who can do fifty-four pushups, and I saw stacked there books with these titles: *Statistics; Plane Trigonometry; Airplane Aerodynamics; Analytical Geometry; Airplane Performance; Aerodynamics for Naval Aviators; College Algebra; Calculus and Analytical Geometry; NATOPS Flight Manual, T-2B/T-2C, TA-4F;* and *Flying Qualities of Piloted Vehicles.* There was little sentiment displayed in her study cubicle. Lori Melling's pinup poster was a photograph of her A-7 attack plane.

Another revolutionist—without meaning to be—was Navy Lieutenant Robert L. "Beamer" Curbeam, Jr., the only black person in the class. After having covered as a military reporter the black-white racial problems that the Navy had experienced during the 1970s, which included the sabotaging of ships and constant confrontations, I marveled at the graceful way he conducted himself week in, week out at TPS. He had none of the chip-on-the-shoulder militancy that I had seen in other blacks isolated in an infantry unit, but a natural pride in himself and empathy for others. You forgot the color of Curbeam's skin as quickly as you sensed that he had forgotten the color of yours. His white wife, Julie, told me that Bob was the most tolerant man she had ever met, even of the racists in St. Mary's County who sometimes hurled insults at the couple.

I asked Beamer one day where his inspiration had come from. "My mother," he laughed. "She told all of us: 'You will do well! You will get your education!'"

Only after I met and interviewed Yvonne Ramona Evans Curbeam, Bob's mother, did I fully understand how this young black had soared so early in life, becoming an outstanding naval officer without picking up any hostility along the way. She has the erect bearing of a prideful lady who knows who she is and speaks with precision without sounding overbearing. When I talked with her at Beamer's home in 1991, she was teaching science at Dunbar High School in the Partnership Program, affiliated with Johns Hopkins University in Baltimore.

Mrs. Curbeam was born in Sparrows Point, Maryland, in 1938 in one of Bethlehem Steel's worker houses—surrounded by other worker houses occupied by black steel workers. She said all the blacks living on just three streets in the complex—I, J, and K—were proud people. Blacks and whites in the tight neighborhood got along, but integration of the schools and other public facilities was still decades away.

"My father worked in the mills, and my mom was a housewife," she told me. "I'm the twelfth child of thirteen children. During these times it was customary for the older children to help educate the younger children. So I was one of the chosen ones who had to go to school to get a formal education."

Yvonne Evans took two buses past three all-white high schools to reach the black Sollers High School in Dundalk, where she won awards in chemistry. She graduated from Sollers in 1956 and enrolled at Morgan State University in Baltimore. Her older brothers kept sending her the money they made working in the Bethlehem mills and in the post office. Their generosity enabled her to live on campus rather than commute.

In 1959 she met and married Robert L. Curbeam, Sr., who was building cables for Western Electric. Beamer was the third of four children born to the Curbeams. All have done well, with three of the four college graduates. So what magic advice did she give them?

"You need that formal education no matter what you do. And we will always be here for you no matter where you are or what you do.

"It was a little different with Robert. We told him that, but I'd say, 'You can go anywhere you want, but you're going to the Naval Academy.'"

To the Curbeams, the Naval Academy represented the pursuit of excellence by gifted young people. They thought their third son, Robert, was gifted and motivated and had stamina. Also, he did not want his parents to pay for his college education. The Academy seemed a good fit.

"Robert had my study habits," Mrs. Curbeam said, eyes glowing. Then with a laugh she added: "He got one B in high school." All the other grades were As.

"I told myself that if I'm going to push my children to do that, that, and that, I had to push myself. So I was pushing myself a lot" while they were growing up. She took evening courses from 1968 onward, leaving the house so often that a child would occasionally hide the keys to her car so that she would have to stay home. She earned her master of science degree in physics from the University of Maryland in 1974 and kept going to class, determined to earn a doctorate. She left home the summer of 1978 to take nuclear physics courses at Drexel University in Philadelphia; left home again for the summer of 1981 to study at Penn State in State College, Pennsylvania; and completed the class work near her Baltimore home by taking courses at Loyola College and Johns Hopkins University the summers of 1982 and 1983. Johns Hopkins awarded Mrs. Curbeam a doctorate in material physics in 1983.

For all of her educational credentials, Mrs. Curbeam seems even prouder of her ability to get into the hearts and minds of young black men and women and light fires of pride and determination. The Dunbar Partnership Program is an attempt to inspire disadvantaged children to take control of their lives during their high-school years and climb upward. Mrs. Curbeam shared with me a letter she received from one of her students, a seventeen-year-old daughter of a drug addict, to illustrate the relationship she and other teachers at Dunbar are trying to build with their students:

> There is one individual who has influenced me regarding leadership skills. Ms. Yvonne Curbeam, my chemistry teacher, has taken me under her wing and guided me through high school. She has also helped me make sense of the most important decisions of my life as well as prepared me to maturely make others by myself.
>
> Mrs. Curbeam has influenced me most because she is a strong minded, successful black woman who has been a role model for me. She has seen parts of me that I have yet to see. She balances her busy life as I do mine. She has qualities within that are important to me and that I some day aspire to have. She lives her life on the edge and never knows what is next, which to me is exciting and healthful because it keeps you in check with who you are. . . .
>
> Ms. "Curb" has assured me of my leadership abilities, confidence, dexterity, assertiveness and the right level of aggressiveness. . . . She has also believed in me at times when I didn't believe I could complete the task. She has been a mother away from home and corrected me when I stepped out of line. She has shown me the perfect example of how to be a successful black woman and a leader.

On the questionnaire I sent to all the Class 100 students, I asked why they had wanted to go to TPS. Beamer's mother would have approved of his answer: "Why not?"

One twilight several weeks into the course I walked up to a modern house in a subdivision called Cedar Cove adjacent to the southern edge of Pax River. The family of a young IBM executive could fit comfortably into the surroundings. But the occupants of this house were two of the members of Class 100, Lieutenants Ramon A. "Babaloo" Collazo and Darryl J. "Spike" Long. Babaloo was the only Hispanic in the class; Spike had already emerged as the class character. The two had flown in the highest-tech plane on a Navy carrier—the E-2C Hawkeye, which watches the skies for hundreds of miles around with its ungainly looking donut of a radar sitting on top of the plane. If high tech was what turned them on, why would they leave this most high tech of all Navy aircraft and detour to TPS—a detour that might take them out of the running for a coveted squadron command? Their answers would throw additional light on who went to TPS and why.

Once inside their house, I decided an IBM executive and his family could not live there after all. The downstairs living area gleamed not with new furniture but with the steel of weight-lifting machines. The aviators were trying to keep in shape despite their long hours doing geek work at the computer.

Spike Long, who at five feet eight inches tall looks the fullback he was at the University of Santa Clara, started off the answer to my question by saying that he had no quarrel with the Navy but wanted to do something different within it than keep piloting E-2s. Collazo, too, said he wanted a new challenge after years of watching scopes and dials in the back of the E-2. "We close up our windows, and we're in a dark tube," he said.

Both had tried to get assigned to the faster, more glamorous jets after flight training, but the Navy had had other ideas for them. They said the E-2 performed a vital role and could make or break an air wing, but with its slow flight and big donut on top it was far from glamorous.

"If they made a movie about the E-2, they'd have to call it 'Top Dome,'" joked Spike Long in reference to the movie *Top Gun* in which Tom Cruise plays a hotshot F-14 pilot in the sky and a motorcycle-riding Mr. Cool on the ground. "In 'Top Dome,' instead of having Tom Cruise on a motorcycle, you'd have a couple of geeks in a Ford Valiant cruising down some dirt road with 'Highway to the Fordhams' in the background."

"With a Macintosh laptop or something," chimed in Ray Collazo.

Over pizza and beer, the young aviators revealed that they and almost everyone else in Class 100—whether he or she admitted it or not—harbored the dream of going into space as an astronaut. "I think everybody here would like to do that," Collazo said. "I can't think of anybody who hasn't at least thought about it. Going into space would be just incredible. If I did that tomorrow, I could die a happy death. Well, I'd like to have a family.

"As far back as history has been recorded," Collazo continued, "people have been looking up at the stars and thinking, 'God, what is that? What's going on?' It has only been a few hundred years that we have understood what's going on up there. Being in orbit, seeing the earth as a globe. . . ."

Ray Collazo was out of words. He could only shake his head at the enormity of such an experience.

Why not climb Mount Everest?

"That's been done," Spike said dismissively. "Most people with a little bit of training can go up and scale a mountain."

"Because I'm in TPS," Collazo said, "I am closer than probably 99 percent of the population in getting up there in space" because the National Aeronautics and Space Administration picks mostly test pilots as its astronauts. "Whether I'm close enough or not, who knows?"

Like his housemate, Long said he applied to TPS to broaden his horizons. He said the school is "infinitely more challenging" than continuing to fly the E-2. At the least, he said, he flies different airplanes at TPS.

"As an E-2 pilot I'll never be a mission commander," Long continued. "I'll never have the responsibility that he [Collazo] has in the back of the airplane. I'm envious of that. Yeah, I'd rather be a pilot than an NFO [naval flight officer who flies in the airplane but does not pilot it]. That's no slam on an NFO here because I think our [E-2] NFOs are worth their weight in gold. The E-2's NFOs make or break your air wing. If you have a good set of NFOs who really know what they're doing, you're going to have a shit-hot air wing.

"The overall worst thing about being an E-2 pilot is that I have no input in the way the mission is going outside of what I can hear on the radios. My information is so limited that I don't have enough to make a good input. A lot of us E-2 pilots want to get involved. Some don't mind being a taxi driver, and that's fine. That may be enough for them right there because the airplane is not easy to fly at times. But I want more out of being in the Navy. You get to a certain point in the E-2 and the challenge goes away; it becomes drudgery."

E-2 pilots like himself who want a new challenge run into this Catch-22: Because the drudgery drives so many pilots out of E-2s, those who remain become so valuable that the Navy does not want to let them transfer to different airplanes. "We have a difficult time getting out of our community. The really good E-2 pilots I know get out [of the Navy] because they're not challenged.

"Another thing, you need 1,000 hours in tactical aircraft to be an astronaut. There's never been an E-2 pilot in the astronaut program because our airplane—even though we fly in a tactical regime where we're constantly working with fighters and constantly working around the boat and generally have a high stress load—it's not good enough for the astronaut program. Understandably so, because I think the work load in a single-seat fighter for the pilot is an infinitely higher work load than the work load of being half a pilot in the E-2 where the copilot does the radios.

"They could offer me more money to be a Navy pilot, but the money isn't important to me," Long explained. "I want to get out of the airplane excited, and I want to be there when my country needs me."

I knew that Long would have to spend another two years flying E-2s as a test pilot after finishing TPS. The E-2 was getting new engines. Long expected his test-piloting job after graduation would be to measure in great detail what effect the new engines were having on the old airframe. He would help write a new performance book for the E-2. I could not resist asking whether this did not amount to going from one tedious job to another.

"Hey!" Long replied. "It's better than going up to 18,000 feet and putting the auto-pilot on and waiting for the guy to tell you when to turn around. This was the best I could do to improve my challenge."

Class 100—How They Fly

Jerry Gallagher, the instructor pilot, was in the front seat and I was in the back seat of the T-2 Buckeye training jet whistling through white clouds and blue air on the way up to the patch of sky 23,000 feet above the Chesapeake Bay where we intended to spin the airplane—both right side up and upside down—and then do aerial somersaults. I was hoping my breakfast would stay put when I found myself hanging by my legs and watching the bay rush toward me as the upside-down airplane spun down through the clouds. All I knew about the somersaults was that the first one would be forward and the second one backward.

My purpose in going aloft with Gallagher this bright morning was to duplicate the spin training future test pilots receive. I wanted to do, see, and feel what they did so that I could describe their passage from regular pilot to test pilot. I had been thrown around the sky before in the F-14 Tomcat and other jets while deployed on the aircraft carrier USS *John F. Kennedy* in 1983–84. But we did not spin those planes. The F-14, for one thing, is too dangerous to spin. Its engines usually blow out like candles during a spin. The F-14 pilot, if he did manage to get the Tomcat out of a spin, would have to dive the plane steeply to force enough wind into the windmilling compressors of the engines to restart them. By that time he most likely would be out of the altitude needed to avoid crashing into the sea or land. Ejecting from the F-14 would be the better gamble.

The two-place T-2 Buckeye jet trainer is not like the Tomcat fighter. The T-2 is safe to spin if you know what you are doing. And Jerry Gallagher, forty-four, certainly knew what he was doing. He was as serious in his work as his comedian brother, Butch Gallagher, was funny in his. A former Navy jet pilot, Gerald L. Gallagher was now a civilian hired by the Navy to instruct future test pilots at TPS. Spinning was his specialty. "The reason we do spins," he told me before takeoff, "is that somebody has to go out and write the book about what happens when you fly these machines to the limits." Besides, he said of test pilots under instruction, "we want them to see as much aviation as they can." Knowing an airplane's limits and what to do when they are exceeded is part of test piloting and could save an aviator's life in aerial dogfighting, Gallagher said. "To a large extent, the outcome of a fight is [determined by] who can get closest to the limit."

What Jerry Gallagher and other test pilots learn in putting various aircraft through spins is distilled into written do's and don't's, why's and wherefore's. Their findings end up in thick instruction books called NATOPS, for Naval Air Training and Operating Procedures Standardization, written at Naval Air Systems Command in Crystal City, Virginia, an office complex on the edge of Washington, D.C.

"Would you like to fly this test?" Gallagher asked me as we started the step-by-step series of aerial exercises leading up to the spins. Instructors call these incremental tests "the buildup."

"OK," I replied, wondering if I would remember anything I had learned years ago when I had piloted light, private planes, which were not supposed to be spun.

"You've got the stick," Gallagher said through the radio line connecting us. "We'll leave the trim at about eight [notches] up." The trim is a system of tabs on the horizontal elevator on the tail, and it is used to alter the lift to hold an airplane in the desired up or down position against the oncoming flow of air.

"We've got the throttles at idle.

"Now just hold the wings level and make about a 1- or 2-knot deceleration by pulling back on the stick a little bit to change nose attitude."

I pulled back the stick ever so gently, too gently, to make the airplane go uphill and slow down.

"Hold the nose up," Gallagher directed. "Select a nose attitude that will give us a 1- or 2-knot decel [deceleration]. We're just looking to see if the airplane exhibits any adverse handling here."

If this were a new, unknown airplane and a problem exhibited itself at this nose-high position, the test pilot would note it either by writing on a knee pad or speaking into a tape recorder hooked into the radio line as mine was now. The whole idea of test piloting is to observe and record everything noteworthy about an airplane so that its unknowns become knowns.

I felt the pedals that work the rudder of the T-2 shaking under my feet.

"OK," Gallagher called back. "There's the pedal shaker to warn you that you're getting close." The pedal shaker is an electric motor in the cockpit that shakes the pedals when another device outside the aircraft signals it to do so. The signaler is a tube on the nose that feels at what angle the air is flowing over the wing. When this angle-of-attack tube senses that the plane is flying at too steep an angle to the airflow to maintain the lift needed for normal flight, it shakes the pedals to warn the pilot that his vehicle is about to go from flying machine to falling machine. I felt the pedals shake. The plane struggled up its hill of air like a car kept in high gear too long. I refused to give the plane the relief it was asking for by pushing the nose downhill.

"Apart from the pedal shaker, the airplane hasn't done anything else, has it?" Gallagher asked.

"No," I replied, not bothering to add the obvious—that the plane was either going to get more air under its wings within the next few seconds or become that free-falling machine.

"Keep it coming toward the stall. Keep the nose up a little bit more. There: a little buffet is coming through. You can kind of feel the airplane shake a little bit."

More than a little bit. I felt the plane shuddering. It was begging to be let off this hill.

"We should feel a little bit of pitch break from the stall," Gallagher warned. "Then ease the stick forward and we should recover immediately from it."

The hell with this, the plane said to itself, and pitched downward as if it had fallen into a hole in the air. I pushed the stick forward at last.

Oncoming air was pushing up on the wings again. The plane went from falling to flying. I could imagine the plane's saying, "Thank you" as it went happily downhill.

"I got it," Gallagher said as he took the flight controls from me. In the T-2 trainer, each seat has its own set of flight controls, unlike the F-14 fighter, in which the backseater has no way to fly the plane no matter what happens to the pilot up front.

"What we discovered on the Phase A stall was that it's pretty docile," Gallagher instructed as he started to dispose of this first step so that we could get on with the other ones leading up to spins. "There's no adverse airplane characteristics, and there's no adverse handling characteristics. It's just straightforward. We noticed we got some warning when the pedal shaker came on. And about 19 units [on the angle-of-attack indicator] we caught a little bit of airplane buffet."

If the T-2 training jet had behaved violently rather than docilely during the type of stall we had just completed, the Navy test pilot who had first put the plane through its paces would almost certainly in his developmental-testing report have termed this characteristic a "Part I deficiency" because it would have posed a danger to student pilots.

"Now what happens if we go into the stall at a little higher deceleration rate?" Gallagher asked rhetorically. "Let me show you what happens there. We're looking to see if there is anything that changes because we are doing the stall at a little higher decel rate. I'll park the nose up a little higher this time" to make the plane lose speed at a quicker rate. "Now notice we've got a big deceleration rate. We'll see if we can mark the same events that we had before. This is the speed we stalled at last time. OK. There's the pedal shaker. There's the buffet. And there's the stall. I think you can notice that things happen a lot faster with that high-decel rate, so you have less of a warning in terms of time. So if you get caught with your nose up, you don't get much warning."

If we were test pilots wringing out the T-2 for the first time, Gallagher and I would be obliged to warn in our written report that if a beginning pilot slowed down the trainer too quickly while its nose was up, he or she might stumble into a stall at such a low speed that the plane would be hard to control. It would be like pointing a sailboat so sharply into the wind that its forward motion slowed to the point that the rudder no longer steered the boat. Such an observation would have to be backed up with specific data. Gallagher was going to show me how test pilots gather the specifics.

"We'll do the slow decel and mark the stall. When I call, 'Mark!' just call your airspeed indication, OK?"

We flew up the hill again to make the airplane stall. I was looking at the instrument panel, not the horizon or the clouds outside the plane. I watched the needle on the airspeed indicator fall.

"Mark!" Gallagher ordered just as the plane went into its pitch break and stalled.

"One eighteen!" I replied.

"That's the slow-decel-rate stall speed," Gallagher explained. "Now I'll do it with a little higher decel rate, and it [the speed at the stalling point] should be much lower than that."

He slowed the plane more suddenly this time by pointing the nose up more steeply. The T-2's pedals shook; the plane's body shivered.

"Standby!" Jerry called just before the plane stopped flying and started falling. "Mark!"

"Ninety-nine," I replied as I saw the needle on 99 knots of airspeed.

"Yeah, so it looks like that first pitch break was at 99 instead of 118 [knots]. That's quite a significant change."

The lesson to be learned was that sudden slowdowns brought stalls at slow speeds, at which a plane becomes mushy, unresponsive. So be careful, Student Pilot, you may get into a stall before you know it and have a hell of a time getting out of it. Keep your speed up. Speed is life in an airplane. In a full-fledged test-pilot report, a graph of what happened to the plane at the various speeds, angles of attack, altitudes, and rates of deceleration would back up the warning. We would have gathered more points for the graph. The test pilot's words and graphs on stalls would be only a thin slice of his or her thick report on how the plane behaved in the air. Slow, steady, tedious, exacting flying and writing. The test pilot is more like a lab technician in a white coat than an aviator with a white scarf while testing an airplane. The pilot has to feel challenged when asked to fly to specified points in the sky for no other reason than to gather information for a report on how the airplane performs during a series of preplanned maneuvers. Yes, the truth is that test piloting is often boring, seldom exciting. It is glamorous only to those who do not do it. Jerry Gallagher was showing me the realities of the trade this bright morning over the Chesapeake Bay.

"As kind of a demonstration of what I mean by departure," Gallagher said after we had performed several more stalls at ever-shrinking rates of deceleration, "let's have a look at what happens when you try to control the airplane normally beyond the stall.

"I want you to fly this particular test. I want you to keep your feet on the floor. We're not going to make any rudder inputs at all. What I want you to do is hold the wings level and keep coming back toward the stall like you did before, except when you get to the stall, keep going past it" rather than recovering by lowering the nose so that the plane can fly rather than fall. "We'll end up with full aft stick. Try to keep the wings level by making aileron inputs. OK?"

"OK," I replied.

"You've got the airplane.

"Slow down."

I pulled back on the stick to cause deceleration. The nose went higher. All the old warning signs leaped to life. I kept the nose up. The plane staggered.

"Keep the wings level just with the aileron input," Gallagher directed.

I swung the stick left when the right wing dipped; right when the left wing dipped. I kept the wings level for a few seconds even after the plane had started its fall after stalling. The nose was still up, but I was having a harder and harder time keeping the wings level no matter how much I moved the stick to the left or to the right.

"Keep pulling back; keep pulling back," Gallagher instructed. "There we go. Now it's starting to go to the right, and left stick isn't helping. OK. I got it.

"That was an indication of a departure. That is, the airplane is going one way even though you're commanding it to go the other. So it's not under normal command anymore. So what we're showing here is that the airplane handles very nicely up to the stall, but once you get beyond the stall, then it starts to diverge. In this particular case it felt like it yawed off to the right. And after it yawed off to the right, it started to roll a little bit, and giving it left aileron didn't help at all. In fact, if anything, it made it worse."

The lesson here—one that would have been put in the book on the T-2 if these had been the plane's first tests—was that if you want to keep control of the plane after it stalls without pushing down the nose, the ailerons will not do it for you.

The other way to control a staggering airplane is by using the rudder. "Let's see if we can control that yaw divergence with the rudder pedals this time. We'll repeat the test. This time we're not going to use the ailerons. We'll just use the rudder pedals. So I want you to look out forward and keep the nose going straight. Ready?"

"Right."

"You got the airplane. Same kind of test except this time we'll use the rudder pedals. And you've got to be kind of rough with them. So go ahead and kick the pedals to keep the nose where you want it to be. Don't let it take off sideways."

The struggling, nose-high plane swung left. I kicked the right rudder. I was too late and too gentle. The nose slid left.

"Oops!" Gallagher called out. "OK. I got it.

"Now we noticed something that time. The nose started to wander a little bit. But you had plenty of control with the rudder to kick the nose around. The problem was that it tended to roll in response to that rudder and it got out of control, didn't it?"

"Right."

"So the airplane has a departure beyond the stall. In fact, it tends to depart even when you try to fight it with the controls because the normal control inputs are just not going to make it.

"Now, just let me show you that if you alter your control technique a little bit, you can control it."

He quickly decelerated the plane, let it stall, and then kicked the rudder pedals back and forth so hard that I could hear the thumping despite the radio noise pouring into my ears. But damned if Old Jerry did not keep the wings level even when the plane wanted to fall off to the side.

"See. I can keep the wings level at 30-units angle of attack, full stall. The problem is that if I would try to use the ailerons, I would have run into the same thing that you did. The airplane would slice off and depart. Notice I was kind of dancing on the pedals."

Someone as skilled as Jerry Gallagher could with the rudder keep the airplane up after a stall for what might be precious, lifesaving seconds if the plane stalled while dangerously low or if the pilot needed to stay out of an enemy's gun range for another instant. But the lesson for me—and for others trying to master a stalled jet—was this: Don't mess around with trying to keep the nose up after a stall. Push the stick forward right away to get the airplane flying again. But if you cannot do that, rely on the rudders, not the ailerons, to control the beast.

"Let me check the tip tanks," Gallagher called back. Tip tanks are those bomb-shaped fuel containers at the ends of the wings. Spinning with the tip tanks full and heavy puts too much strain on the airframe. "The tip tanks are dry. We can start our spins here. Grab the spin checklist here, and we'll make sure we've got everything ready. Make sure your map case is closed so we don't have things that will float around."

The map case was behind me on the right side of the airplane. I could not get its hinged top snapped shut. My shoulder harness and lap belts prevented me from twisting around so that I could see what I was doing. I felt stupid about delaying the spin. Test piloting is such a long list of little, but all important, things. I pushed the lever that loosened the grip of the jet pilot's straitjacket. This gave me enough twisting room to feel the lid and get it snapped shut. I told Gallagher I was ready.

"OK, check your harness."

"I've got it back into lock."

Gallagher read off other items on the spin checklist to make sure we were really ready to start swirling around the sky: "Visor tightened; pedals are adjusted; shoulder harness locked. Gear, flaps, and speed brakes are in; airspeed, battery, angle-of-attack, turn-needle gauges normal; yaw dampers off; anti-ice is on; smash lights are off."

We were indeed ready. Gallagher took the airplane at slow speed up another incline, just as he had done for the stall tests. He was going to force the T-2 into a spin by doing the wrong thing after the stall—just as a student pilot might do with this training airplane. Knowing how dangerous a training plane is to pilots who mishandle it is important information in deciding if an aircraft should be bought at all and, if it has been purchased, whether it should be modified to make it safer.

"OK. We're passing 16 units [on the angle-of-attack meter] at 135 [knots].

"There's 130. Mark! Pedal shaker at 127.

"Standby! We're at 120. There's the stall."

"Then there's the misapplication [of ailerons]." He pushed the stick to the right and stomped on the left rudder pedal, holding the controls at those cross purposes for what felt like several seconds but was really only one. With the plane starting a slow spin to the left, I saw the bay and land revolving below us. He returned the stick and rudder pedals to their neutral positions. The plane flew out of its brief spin, just as a heeling sailboat on the verge of tipping over would sail itself out of trouble if you let go of the sail and rudder.

We had spun only one and a half revolutions. But even in this first, brief spin I found it difficult to make my eyes flit from the horizon to the ground, to the needles on the instruments inside the cockpit. The varsity test pilot, however, has little difficulty doing all these things at once. I better understood why today's pilot is grateful for tape recorders and computers, which record what the plane is doing to back up his own recall and handwritten notes.

"You can see what happened on this one," Gallagher called back. "It took off in one direction to the left. And we went around one and a half turns."

I did not reply. My instructor up front must have thought the spins had left me deaf or sick.

"You may have to Valsalva here to pop your eardrums back out," he advised.

Antonio Valsalva was the eighteenth-century anatomist who discovered that people could relieve the pain generated by different air pressures inside and outside their ears by holding the nose and mouth and blowing hard against them. Doing the Valsalva makes you feel as if you are on the verge of rupturing your ears before they clear. I had always had trouble doing Valsalvas while wearing an oxygen mask, as I was during this flight. I settled for swallowing hard. My ears still felt stuffy but did not hurt.

"How you doing back there?" Gallagher asked while setting the plane up for another spin.

"Good so far." I was telling the truth. I did not feel nauseous from the first spin. But more were coming, including the upside-down one. I had never gotten airsick or seasick. But Terry DeLay, the always genial and helpful para-rigger, had handed me an oversized barf bag when he learned I was getting dressed for the spin mission. I feared he knew something I did not about the effect of spins on first timers.

"Good," Gallagher said and then told me what we had just learned from the first spin. "Even with neutral controls, it took about one and a half rolls for the airplane to finally get back into what you would consider normal flight." If we were writing a report, we would have noted where the controls were when the plane started to spin, how many seconds and turns it took the plane to recover itself, and how many feet the plane fell in its one and a half circles.

"OK, here we go again.

"One hundred thirty, 127 [knots], pedal shaker is on. Little bit of buffet. 120. Stall. Standby!"

The plane stopped flying again. Gallagher put the controls at cross purposes again, holding the stick to the right and rudder to the left for three seconds rather than the one-second "misapplication" of the first spin. He put the controls back to neutral after three seconds. The T-2 had started to spin to the left. Its nose was down at a 45-degree angle. I felt comfortable. It was a fun ride, not a scary one. I was beginning to enjoy spinning right side up. I still worried about how I would feel when we started spinning upside down. The plane righted itself after making three complete turns in the sky, an abbreviated spin.

"Smooooooth," I exulted to Jerry at the controls up front.

"That one was more docile than the other one, wasn't it?"

"Yeah! What did you do with the power? I didn't notice."

"I left it at idle for all of these tests.

"What we've noticed," Instructor Gallagher continued, "is that the airplane is a little sensitive to the timing of the controls beyond stall. The airplane is flopping around. It is probably related to what the airplane is flopping to when you make your control inputs.

"Let's see what happens if you put the controls on the same side this time. Left rudder and left stick. We're going to hold them in beyond three seconds to see what the airplane does. Usually we'll see an oscillatory kind of mode. We'll kind of be oscillating. Go around once. Kind of hesitate. Fade back in the other direction. Then we'll let it go for a couple of turns because we don't want to exceed 160 knots, which is our rudder limit.

"OK. Setting up. This will be full left rudder, full left and back stick.

"The shaker at 125. . . .

"There's the stall. . . .

"OK. The inputs are in. Full left. And full left. Notice the airplane kind of rolls left, yaws left, hesitates back to the right, and it snaps again. . . . We'll recover.

"OK. How you doing back there?"

"Good."

"OK. Notice on that one that the airplane tended to go into a spin kind of maneuver. Yawing. And then it would hesitate."

"Yeah. Why is that?"

"It's a combination of factors. The aerodynamic things going on are that you're commanding a left yaw with the rudder; but stick to the left actually gives you adverse yaw input to the right. So it's kind of fighting aerodynamically. In addition to that, you have some inertial coupling going on because the airplane is pitching while these yaw motions are going on." Inertial coupling comes from the airplane's accelerating motion, which generates several different forces at once. Inertial coupling occurs, for example, when a plane does an ever-quickening clockwise spin on one axis while its nose and tail bounce up and down faster and faster on another. The forces generated can combine or compete—producing spins, disrupting them, or even causing the plane to somersault. The inertial-coupling gymnastics were still ahead of me.

"Now, in this one we're going to take it into the normal spin. What we call the baseline, but we're going to use cross controls because that's going to generate the best yaw rate. Things we're looking at for this particular maneuver—once we get it into the stall we'll see it go through a couple of post-stall gyrations. And then pretty soon it will just kind of wrap itself up into what looks like a spin. And we'll notice that while we're en route to that, that the airplane is yawing and rolling to the left. And then once we get it into the spin we'll look at indications for the spin, which are pegged angle of attack at 30 [units], airspeed around 120 knots. And then the fully deflected turn needle right under the attitude gyro will show us the direction that we're spinning."

I got the rough idea of what we were going to do. But how the hell was Jerry going to keep track of everything?

"Once in a spin, do you look inside or outside the cockpit?" I asked.

"Primarily outside. But in order to tell that you're spinning, you have to verify your inside instruments: angle-of-attack, airspeed, and turn needle."

We went up the hill again to force the T-2 to stall.

"OK. There's the stall," Gallagher said.

"I'll put in full cross controls and back stick. Notice that we're rolling left. And from the turn needle we can tell we are yawing to the left. So it pretty much feels like a spin now, doesn't it?"

"Right."

"OK. After a couple of turns, it starts to steady out and continue the spin. You can see the angle of attack at 30 units. Turn needle is pegged to the left, and airspeed is about 120 knots. . . . OK. To recover, we'll put in full right rudder. Ease the stick forward. . . ."

Once again, I felt I was falling gently toward the ground. Yes, the bay and ground were still spinning. But the plane was not jagged or wild in its fall. I had faith Jerry could get us out of this before I felt anything violent in my rotating perch in back of the jet. The spinning stopped after Jerry pushed the nose down.

"Happily, it came out," he said once the plane resumed normal flight.

"Good-O!"

"And we bottom out by 17,000 [feet]," Gallagher said.

"Better than an amusement park."

"Say again."

"Better than the ride in the amusement park."

"OK. How are you feeling back there?"

"Good."

"See, it's not that bad. The airplane does a few gyrations. But from the backseat it's not too violent."

"I got a little dizzy toward the end there, but I expected that."

"Yeah," Jerry said knowingly.

"OK. The next thing we'll have a look at—what does that spin look like from upside down?"

"Why would a pilot get into an upside-down spin—aerial combat?" I asked.

"Some airplanes are real sensitive to inverted spinning: the A-4, for example," Jerry replied. "If you let the airplane's tail slide, it generally goes into an inverted spin all on its own. So it's nice to know how to get out of an inverted spin if you get in one. There's really no tactical use for it." Flying upside down, but not spinning, might be useful in a dogfight, he said, if you were trying to keep track of an enemy fighter underneath you.

Gallagher elaborated on how we were going to get ourselves into an inverted spin. He would roll the plane over on its back as we proceeded uphill toward a stall. He would continue going uphill after we were upside down to reduce airspeed until the plane stalled. Once we were upside down, he would be pushing rather than pulling the stick. The controls would have to be worked the opposite way from the right-side-up procedures. Once pushing on the stick had slowed the upside-down plane into the stall, the nose would drop. Then Gallagher would kick it into an upside-down spin.

"OK. I'm running my seat down. If you want to run yours down a little bit. Let me know when you're ready."

"I got it down about three-quarters," I informed Jerry. I later would fervently wish I had levered my seat down lower so that my head did not end up pressing hard against the plastic roof of the upside-down plane.

"We'll just do it from here.

"I'm going to raise the nose."

I felt the familiar run uphill we had done so many times before. We were still right side up.

"Now I'm going to slowly roll us over.

"Now we're kind of upside down. You'll probably feel yourself hanging in the strap a little bit," Jerry said casually.

A little bit! I felt like an upside-down carcass hanging from a meat hook. I was confused as I tried to figure out which foot pedal I would tramp and where I should put the stick to get the airplane off its back. The airplane was staggering again. Jerry was holding the nose high to make it stall upside down just as he had made it stall right side up. How could a test pilot possibly read the altimeter, alpha (angle-of-attack) meter, and airspeed indicator while hanging this way over the water by his legs? I asked myself.

"OK. Everything looks good," Jerry said calmly.

Looks good? I saw an upside-down world full of dust. Turning the T-2 jet on its back had allowed its pockets to empty out. My map case stayed closed. But the dust from every crevice seemed to be drifting down over me. The upside-down plane stopped flying and started falling.

"There's a stall inverted," Jerry informed me as though it did not make any difference whether we were right side up or upside down.

"I'm going to put in the control inputs. Notice that we're rolling to the right, but the turn needle says we're yawing to the left."

He could not prove it by me. From my upside-down, hanging position I could not focus my eyes on the instrument panel far less find the gauge he was talking about and read what it said. If Jerry had asked me to write down the altitude, I could not have fished out my pen. I might be able to say the number into a tape recorder. But everything in the cockpit seemed to have moved to a different place. I would have had to hunt for the altimeter. Happily, Gallagher did not call back, "Mark" during this strange-feeling upside-down spin.

"This is what it kind of looks like in an inverted spin," Jerry said. For the first time there was laughter in that professorial voice.

"Pretty wild, huh?"

It was that, all right. The clouds seemed to be on the verge of drifting up my nose as we fell through the sky in a steady, upside-down spin. The water and land below were turning faster this time. I could not keep track of how many circles we were making. I did not feel sick— just kind of otherworldly. The falling dust gave an ethereal quality to the spinning.

"OK. Now to recover. I'll let it go a little bit more. Opposite rudder. Neutral on the stick. . . ."

After what seemed like a long time to me but was probably only a few seconds, the plane stopped spinning, turned over, and flew right side up.

"Isn't that something?" Jerry asked.

It sure as hell was. I figured space flight must be like that. I began to understand why almost everyone in Class 100 wanted to go into space.

"How did you fare through that?" Gallagher asked.

"Good," I replied. "But I'm going to have to work that seat pan back a little bit." While I was upside down and hanging by my leg straps, the seat cushion with survival equipment inside—called the seat pan—had slid forward off the metal seat. I was trying to push it back in while sitting right side up. But doing this while tied down by harness and lap belts was proving difficult. The seat pan is attached to your harness, so if you eject, it goes with you and dangles below you after the parachute opens.

"Let me unload [the lift force on the aircraft] a little bit here. I'll make it a little bit lighter here. That helps."

"I'm going to unlock my harness so I can push myself up off the seat and slide the pan underneath me, OK?"

"OK."

I worked my hands gingerly to push the seat pan back in. I was conscious of the ejection handle right where I was working. The last thing I wanted to do right now was accidentally yank it and rocket myself out of the cockpit. I finally worked the seat pan back in place. There never seems to be any wiggle room in jet cockpits—at least I could not find any. I'm six feet tall and weigh 170 pounds.

"That was quite a show, Jerry," I said, recalling the fascinating look and feel of the upside-down spin. "I'm going to put my seat up again, OK?"

"OK.

"Now, when you go to air shows and see those guys doing that inverted spin, you'll know what's going on," Jerry said.

"Yeah. . . . They better not have any dust in the cockpit."

"How does it feel to be hanging in the straps?" Jerry asked with a snicker.

"You were right. I wasn't used to hanging by my legs. I said, 'Did I latch that fucker?'" meaning the wide lap belt worn expressly to hold you down during spins and upside-down flying.

"OK. Would you like to see that inertial-couple tumble, where you get the airplane to kind of somersault a little bit?"

An aerial somersault at 23,000 feet? I asked myself. What the hell. You're up here. May never get another chance. Go for it. Jerry knows what he's doing.

"Yeah," I replied. "Whatever you say. Let's try it. Just explain if I were a student why I'm doing this."

"OK. We've looked at the upright spin, and we've looked at the inverted spin. What normally follows is three more spins. Remember I said we're going to look at the elevator effects, the aileron effects? When we're done with them, we look at what can happen to the airplane if you get inertial coupling. Inertial coupling occurs if you get a rate of spin built up, like on a spinning gyroscope, and then make an input on another axis. The force will couple into yet another axis. You can actually make the airplane kind of somersault."

You cannot do this just by pushing the stick forward and backward to make the nose pitch up or down, Jerry explained. "If I just threw the stick forward, it would do a high-negative-G pushover, but it wouldn't somersault. On the other hand, if I can get it to inertial couple, then it might." As I got it, he had to marry up two or more forces to make the plane somersault.

Was the purpose of demonstrating inertial coupling to warn the pilot against piling more force on an airplane once it is spinning in the sky?

"It's just to show that you can generate motions in an airplane with the aerodynamic control as well as with inertial coupling. And so you have to be very careful. For example, with the F-14, they were looking at how much yaw rate they could tolerate before the airplane would spin. You have to look beyond how much yaw rate you can generate with the rudder pedal. You have to look as well at how much yaw rate you can generate through inertial coupling because you can go beyond normal limits.

"On this one, I'm going to pull the airplane until we're going kind of straight up, and then I'm going to get it rolling to the right. While it's rolling to the right, I'm going to kick on the rudder pedal a little bit, and the nose will start to go down. As it does, I'll feed forward stick, and the nose should go down even farther. So we should get what appears to be kind of a tumble. It'll do it. And it may be a little bit violent for maybe about two or three seconds, and then it will stop. But what we're looking at is that kind of nose-down kind of somersaulting. All right?"

"OK," I replied.

"It's liable to feel like the negative G you had in the inverted spin," Gallagher warned. Negative gravity force pulls the passenger toward the roof of the cockpit while positive gravity pushes a body down into the seat. "You'll be right side up. But you may feel thrown in the straps a little bit. So you might want to run your seat down a little bit. I'm going to run mine down for this, too. You need to hold onto your tape recorder real good for this one."

"OK."

"Don't let it loose," Jerry warned, for fear my tape recorder would go flying through the cockpit like a black brick.

"Here's how we'll start it. We'll get it going straight up so it will be kind of into the sun. OK, here we go.

"OK. Now I'll start it rolling to the right, yawing a little bit, and keep forward stick.

"See, you can see that kind of violent maneuver. It exceeds what you'd normally get in the aerodynamic world. You with me, George?"

I was with him, but I was trying to figure out what had just happened. I had felt us go into a forward somersault. Then I was somehow on my back doing a backward somersault. What the plane was doing at each point of these two successive somersaults looked like finger painting rather than a clear diagram in my mind. The blurry recall reminded me of being catapulted off a carrier deck in the F-14 fighter. By the time the impressions had been printed on my mind, I was way out in front of the boat and climbing into the sky. During the somersaults, I knew the plane was violently pitching. One second I felt I was about to be pitched through the plastic roof of the plane, the next second I was being pushed down into the seat, and then we were whistling through the sky straight and level as if nothing violent had ever happened. Jets do things so damn quickly.

Jerry was already thinking about something else—the weather, no less.

"Look at the thunderhead off to the right," he suggested, just as if we had somersaulted the airplane five years instead of five seconds ago. The test pilot cannot savor an unusual test like the somersaults right away, I decided, because he or she must move down the "to do" list and set up the airplane for the next point. Maybe that is why pilots talk so much on the ground about what they did in the air. Also, they can't use their hands to talk while they are flying the airplane. So hold the stories. Keep your mind on your work. Poets need not apply.

The hell with it. I survived the upside-down spins and somersaults. Take in the view. I studied the clouds that had been laughing at this intruder trying to fit into their world. They knew neither I nor any other person could stay up here long. The unsmiling instruments inside the plane would command us to go home to the ground before long. The beautiful, blackening thunderhead far off to the west reminded us who had the real power in this domain five miles above the earth.

"OK," Jerry called back, breaking my reverie. "Roll your seat back up if you haven't already done it. We're done with the upside-down stuff."

"No more suspense—from my legs," I joked.

Jerry went up the hill, provoked the stall, and went into what he called the "normal spin," although there was nothing normal about it to me even though I had experienced several spins already.

"Remember this when we get into normal spin," Jerry instructed:

"full cross control"—meaning left rudder and right stick, or right rudder and left stick. He had the controls crosswise at the moment. "You can see that it's building up the yaw rate. And this is about what the steady spin feels like. Now if I move the stick forward, watch what happens. Feel the spin accelerate?"

"Yeah, it's spinning faster," I replied.

"OK. I'll slow it back down.

"Now, I'll move the stick to the left a little bit, and see if you can detect anything happening to the aileron. . . .

"Not much. Now I'll just recover." He brought the stick back to the center, or neutral, position and then pulled it all the way back as he tramped the right pedal.

"That one got you wound up, didn't it?" Jerry asked knowingly.

"Yeah. Did that one get you dizzy, too?"

"What happens is that it gets your ears going round and round. Then when you stop abruptly, your ears are still going around. Particularly if you pull G [gravity force] at the bottom, you can really get yourself disoriented.

"Well, if you've got another spin in you, what I can do is demonstrate the data-taking routine for a normal evaluation flight. Normally, we would use a tape recorder or a voice link to the ground."

"Sure, we can do one more," I said.

"OK. Now the data we're going to want to get is the steady-state spin characteristics. And in particular, we're interested in the spin rate—that is, how long does it take to go around. We're interested in how much altitude we lose per turn. We're interested in how much altitude it takes to recover, and how many turns the airplane takes to recover.

"So here's my attack for that. We'll get the airplane into the steady spin to the left. When it gets steady, I'll pick up a geographic landmark and call a 'Mark' at that point. I'll call out the altimeter reading at that point, so we'll have the altitude and the time. Then I'll wait for three spin turns. At the end of the third turn, I'll call, 'Mark!' and give an altitude reading while I simultaneously put the recovery controls in. Then I'll call out when the turns stop. I'll say like a turn and a half, then I'll start to pull out, and at the bottom I'll mark the altitude. So we'll have the total altitude loss during recovery and the turns."

"Great!" I replied, looking forward to playing data-gathering test pilot but doubtful I would be able to get all the data read as we spun down through the sky.

"That must be a bitch, though, because I would want to look outside if I were in a spin rather than study instruments inside."

"You've got to kind of pay attention to what's going on," my instructor said in typical understatement. "I would expect three turns is going to take around ten seconds.

"OK. You ready? Here we go. There's the stall. Spin controls are going in. We'll wait until it gets steady state. We'll use that thunderhead as my mark.

"OK. Standby!

"Mark! Twenty-five two [25,200 feet] is the altitude.

"One turn!

"Two turns.

"Standby.

"Mark! Ten seconds. Twenty-three two [23,200 feet altitude].

"One turn and a quarter. Mark!

"And the pull-up. And at the bottom of the pull-up, eighteen one [18,100 feet].

"Data complete.

"So went in at twenty-five two; and after three turns we were at twenty-three two or so. So we lost about 2,000 feet in three turns, which is about 650 or 700 feet per turn about, in ten seconds. So it was about three seconds per turn, and the altitude loss and the recovery was in the order of 5,000 feet. It took a turn and a half for the yaw rotation to stop. OK?"

"Right," I replied. I understood what Jerry had done but marveled at how test pilots could gather all that data in about fifteen seconds while being spun around.

"Any questions?"

"Nope."

"That's pretty much it. The only thing we didn't look at was the control float of the spin. Generally, what you see there is that if you let go of the controls, the control surfaces will float whichever direction the wind is pushing them. And for an airplane with reversible kind of controls like the T-2 has, they all float into the pro-spin direction. So letting go of controls in a spin will sometimes recover and sometimes won't."

"OK. I'm ready for the barn. Thank you."

"You bet." And to the control tower, Jerry radioed: "Advisory, Tester Two One."

"Tester Two One, Advisory," answered a female voice in the tower.

"Complete in south spin [area]," Spinmaster Gallagher advised. "RTB [Return to base]."

Imagine yourself flying low at night over enemy encampments in a fragile helicopter lit up so brightly that any rifleman for miles around could carefully aim at you and try to knock you out of the sky whenever you came close enough.

This is what CWO4 Reginald C. Murrell did night after night in Vietnam in 1971. "We were basically a target," he told me in the monotone of a pilot who had been through too much to get emotional about any one thing.

Reggie flew a UH-1H Huey with a cluster of seven landing lights from C-130 transport planes rigged at the chopper's open, right door. The Huey's machine gunner crouched behind the lights as they shone on the bush below. When enemy soldiers could no longer resist firing at the helicopter beckoning to them like a beacon, other helicopters with no lights pounced out of the dark sky and blasted them.

"Never took a hit," Reggie said in the same monotone. But he could not help smiling as he said it. More of a smirk. His hunter/killer missions were only part of the flying he did in Vietnam. "I flew almost 1,300 hours in ten months. I was flying every day, seven days a week." How, I wondered as he told about his combat flying, could TPS be anything but boring to this forty-one-year-old who already had done everything a pilot can do in a helicopter, often at great risk?

When I met Reggie in 1991, he was teaching future test pilots how to evaluate a helicopter's performance. I discovered that passing on what he had learned since receiving his helicopter wings in 1970 stimulated his intellectual juices the way combat flying had stimulated his physical senses during the war. And Reggie Murrell, like the other instructors, wanted a thinking pilot in the cockpit, not a daredevil. He and the other veteran pilots had been to enough funerals of those who had pushed it.

"You don't want to look for that kind of guy," Reggie told me. "Nowadays, what we're looking for is somebody who can get the job done without an extra risk. We teach the buildup approach. You nibble at the unknown slowly so you don't get into trouble with something you can't handle."

This particular June day we were going to nibble at the danger of dropping from the sky in an OH-58 observation helicopter whose engine was not turning its rotor blades. Reggie was going to show me how a skillful pilot can land a helicopter from most places in the sky after the engine quits if he or she knows what to do and does it fast enough. "If a guy loses an engine and doesn't do something in a few seconds, he's going to die," the combat veteran said matter-of-factly.

As test pilots always do, especially instructor test pilots, Reggie detailed exactly what he was going to do with the OH-58 helicopter once we got in the air. He was going to drop out of the sky from various altitudes and at various speeds without engaging the engine to turn the overhead rotor blades. Although the engine would be kept at idle for safety's sake, it would be of no help in slowing our free-fall. How hard we landed, Reggie explained, would depend on how successful he was in exploiting the lift created when the passing wind turned the rotor blades, as with a windmill. This windmilling is autorotation, short for automatic rotation.

He would have two levers to make the engineless helicopter land softly like a pinwheeling maple seed rather than hard like an acorn. On his left in the OH-58 was a lever called the collective. Pushing the collective down or up makes the blades twist to change their angle as they bite into the air during their rotation in a counterclockwise direction. A push of the collective changes the bite, called pitch, of all the blades at the same time, that is, collectively. Hence the name.

The second lever, between the pilot's legs, called the cyclic or stick, raises or lowers the cutting edge of the blades one at a time rather than collectively. Imagine the helicopter is on a clock face with its nose at twelve o'clock and its tail at six o'clock. If Reggie pushes the stick to his left toward the nine–o'clock position, each whirling blade will rise up to bite the wind by the time it reaches three o'clock. The blade flattens after it passes nine o'clock, rising for another big bite into the wind when it returns to three o'clock. These big bites into the wind at three o'clock tilt the rotor blades to make them high when they are on the right side of the helicopter and low when they are on the left side. This slant toward the left moves the helicopter left. Pushing the stick to the right makes the blades bite hardest when they pass nine o'clock, slanting the blades left to right and pulling the helicopter toward the three–o'clock position—to the right. Pushing the stick forward to twelve o'clock pulls the helicopter's nose down and makes it go forward. Pulling the stick back to six o'clock pulls the nose up and makes it stop or even go backward. Foot pedals control the pitch in a small tail rotor whose thrust counteracts the twisting force, or torque, generated by the big rotor.

Even if the pilot in free-fall works the collective and stick correctly, he or she can still crash if the no-engine descent starts from certain positions in the sky called "dead-man zones" or "avoid areas." Each helicopter has a different dead-man zone that the pilot tries to fly out of as quickly as possible. Test pilots and engineers working for the helicopter builder chart the dead-man zones before delivering the helicopter to the military. The graph of these zones is called the High-Velocity Diagram. Military test pilots take the newly delivered helicopter aloft to determine if the dead-man zones are correctly charted. This requires simulating engine failures from different points in the sky to verify the High-Velocity Diagram. Reggie and other helicopter instructors teach future test pilots how to do this verification. We climbed into the OH-58 so he could show me how to do it too.

"There's our 500 feet and 60 knots," Reggie told me as we reached one of the jump-off positions for gathering data for the High-Velocity Diagram. He was sitting in the right seat of the OH-58 helicopter, and I was in the left. Command pilots sit in the right seat in helicopters and in the left seat in fixed-wing aircraft.

"Throttle chop on three. . . . Thousand one. Thousand two. Thousand three."

He twisted the motorcycle-style throttle atop the collective to reduce the engine to idle. The engine was no longer rotating the rotor blades overhead. The helicopter was losing the lift provided by those whirling wings. Reggie hesitated before he took any corrective action, simulating how a surprised pilot would react.

Wee-whoop! Wee-whoop! The stall warning was shouting at us. It was warning that the overhead wings were not turning fast enough to keep lifting the helicopter. The aircraft would stall out, just as the T-2 had when Jerry Gallagher flew it uphill before going into those spins. We had to get those overhead blades to windmill faster.

If you put your hand out the window of a moving car, you feel less resistance if you hold it horizontal against the oncoming wind rather than vertical. Reggie pushed the collective lever down so that the blades would be more horizontal to the wind passing through them. This decreased their resistance to the wind and allowed them to windmill faster. He wanted to get the blades whipping around faster and faster as we fell to recover the lost rotor speed. He used the stick to make us fall to the ground in a slant rather than straight down. The degree of slant would help determine how fast we would fall. He knew he could suddenly pull up on the collective just before we hit the ground to make all the blades bite into the wind at once. This would provide the lift needed to pull us back from a hard landing. But if he used the collective as a skyhook too soon, while we were too far above the ground, the blades would stop windmilling too soon. We might stop falling while we were still too high. The blades, twisted to face into the wind at a sharp angle, would quickly stop spinning with no engine to keep them turning. We then would fall the rest of the way to the ground like a rock, perhaps killing ourselves and certainly damaging the helicopter. Autorotating to earth requires skillful fiddling with the collective on the left and the stick in the center to end up with a soft, happy landing.

We had been falling for three full seconds from 500 feet. The flattened blades were spinning faster and faster. Reggie was watching the needle of the rotor-speed gauge on the instrument panel indicate revolutions per minute. It was moving out of the red danger zone toward the green. The stall siren stopped. "Turns are life," Reggie said.

"Rotor's in the green.

"We got our rotor speed back. So from here on out it's just a normal autorotation descent. Piece of cake. . . . About 100 feet we'll start our progressive deceleration"—going down fast at first and then slowing up in stages.

Our free-fall felt comfortable to me. We were falling to earth on a slant like that pinwheeling maple seed. Reggie's next move was to gradually increase the pitch on the windmilling rotor blades to provide more lift, slowing our descent progressively. I felt a bump and heard a scrape as the skids under the OH-58 hit the runway and skidded forward a few feet. Reggie had autorotated us to a soft landing on wind power alone.

Reggie took up the OH-58 again and again, starting our free-fall from steadily decreasing altitudes and at decreasing speeds. We were getting the points needed to chart a graph of how the helicopter behaved as we got nearer and nearer the dead-man zones.

"What we're doing is changing the conditions very slightly each time," Reggie explained. If our tests showed the danger zone was larger than the contractor claimed in the High-Velocity Diagram, "we would start seeing more difficulty in handling the maneuver before it got to the point where it was unsafe—if we do everything right. We'll say: 'We disagree with the diagramed conditions. It's not a safe entry condition. We need to redraw the boundary of the avoid area.'"

While testing the High-Velocity Diagram, "you're working on the boundary of a cliff. It's very critical that you be right on condition. Yes, it can be boring. It requires a lot of effort. If you're not precise, you could step off that cliff and hurt yourself and the aircraft." A test pilot should not miss the entry conditions, or point, by more than 1 knot in airspeed or more than 20 feet in altitude, Reggie continued. A pilot on most tactical missions, he said, is doing acceptably if he or she is within 5 knots of specified airspeed and 100 feet of the specified altitude.

Even though he knew from hundreds of proof-testing flights in the OH-58 that the contractor's High-Velocity Diagram was correct, Reggie, the veteran combat pilot, fervently believed every helicopter pilot—not just test pilots—should master autorotation because knowing how to do it could save his or her life. Military test pilots in proof testing an unknown helicopter's dead-man zones have in their hands the lives of the pilots who will follow them into that aircraft's cockpit.

Army CWO4 Reginald C. Murrell was obviously aware of this. He flew like the perfectionist he was—and perhaps had always been. Left fatherless at age five, he looked around at his opportunities and made the most of them. He wanted to go to the U.S. Naval Academy, "but you needed to know somebody, and I didn't know anybody." He joined the Air Force Reserve Officer's Training Corps at Clemson University in his native South Carolina in 1968 when the Vietnam War was raging. He wanted to fly for the military. "My eyes started going bad," he recalled, ruling out flying jets for either the Air Force or the Navy. He learned that his eyes were plenty good enough for the Army's warrant-officer flying program. And he could join right away rather than wait until he finished college. He went for it, graduating first in his flight-school class at Fort Rucker, Alabama, in December 1970.

"My first instructor was a character," he recalled. "He had only two fingers and a thumb on his collective hand. He'd reach all the way over and whack you with his other hand if you weren't doing well. Whenever I did an autorotation better than he did, he blamed it on him not having all his fingers."

When Reggie started flying Huey's in Vietnam in 1971, he found some of the warrants flying with him lived up to their legends. One of them, for example, got angry one night with a captain in the helicopter outfit. The warrant threw two smoke grenades into the captain's hooch and nailed the door shut. "He had been drinking heavily and probably would have died if somebody hadn't hauled him out of the room," Reggie recalled. The flying warrant who tossed in the smoke received an Article 15—a minor punishment—and kept flying. The warrants could be wild men, but Reggie never was. He was always the skillful, meticulous, and careful pilot. Maybe that is why he lived and so many other helicopter pilots died in Vietnam. Back on the ground, we talked some more about what he was trying to teach future test pilots in the flights like the one we had just completed.

"We don't want students who jump to conclusions. We want them to know the difference between letting someone know what is wrong with an aircraft as opposed to telling them what it is doing. You always want to tell somebody what it is doing because you can be very objective and very correct about that. You may or may not know why it's difficult to fly some maneuver because in the helicopter world there are so many things going on. Stability derivatives in fixed-wing aircraft are pretty straightforward. But in a helicopter, you can never really isolate one stability derivative. You usually have three or four of them working. The test pilot should be able to tell the engineer [on the ground] very accurately what's happening and then be inquisitive about what he can do to narrow down why we are having this problem. To determine the performance of an aircraft, there is a lot of very dull but precise flying. I think a lot of people getting into the business don't understand that that is what it is all about."

Leslie E. Scott, a retired Army warrant officer fourth class who also saw heavy combat while flying a Cobra helicopter in Vietnam, was the senior flight instructor of the Rotary-Wing Branch within TPS when I flew with Reggie in 1991. He defined the ideal test pilot:

"He's a positive kind of person with an affinity for details. He has good hand and eye coordination and almost an intuitive understanding of things mechanical. A test pilot needs to be relatively comfortable going from aircraft to aircraft. You have to have the ability to fly precisely and still analyze what's going on around you because on some tests you may have to hold the controls absolutely fixed and divorce yourself from the motion of the aircraft but still analyze the motion without getting excited because the pitch and attitude have gotten real big. 'We'll deal with that in a minute.' A lot of guys are not happy doing that."

Army Maj Eric L. Mitchell took me up to continue the instruction started by Reggie on how to test the autorotation capabilities of a helicopter. He planned to warm up by demonstrating a few autorotations over the field at Pax River and then move to the less-congested Webster Field southeast of the base.

"You've got it," Mitchell said as he took his hands off the stick and lifted his feet off the tail-rotor pedals. We were circling over Pax River, trying to reach the right point to start the free-fall maneuvering. Flying helicopters, I have to confess to my jet-pilot friends, has always been more exhilarating to me than flying fixed-wing aircraft. The helicopter stays low to the ground so that you still feel connected to the world below. You even feel smug looking down at the busy earthlings because you can see so much more of their world than they can see. And you are dressed in a comfortable flight suit, not straitjacketed by the belts, buckles, snaps, parachute, leg restraints, vest, face mask, and hoses of the jet pilot. The difference between flying a helicopter and flying a jet straight and level is the difference between sailing a small sailboat and steering a big powerboat. The helicopter, like the sailboat, requires doing several things at once to stay on course. You keep the jet on course just by working the stick. Helicopters are bouncier, trickier, and more fun to fly, I think. But Mitchell's calls showed I was not keeping the OH-58 on course.

"More right pedal until that ball comes in the middle," he instructed.

"Bring the nose up. . . .

"OK, I've got the controls. We're getting to the point where I've got to go into a hover. What we're going to look at now is the different flare types" to achieve soft landings while in the engine-off, autorotation mode. "We'll start with the one-step flare, with the nose about 10 degrees up." When a helicopter falls through the sky with no engine, the air flowing past the rotor spins it and builds up energy in the rotor. But this energy must be used carefully to assure a safe, no-power landing. The one-step technique calls for using up this rotor energy in one tilting-back maneuver, called a flare, while the helicopter is falling on a slant toward the ground. Tilting back the helicopter puts it more broadside to the oncoming air, decreasing forward speed. Pulling up the collective so the blades provide more lift slows both the forward speed and descent of the helicopter. The challenge is to time the flare so that the energy in the rotor is not used up while the helicopter is still dangerously high above the ground. A helicopter out of rotor energy falls like a rock and crashes. Getting the helicopter in the right "entry conditions"—proper forward speed and altitude—to start the flare is the key to making a soft, no-engine landing. Rationing the rotor energy during the fall to permit two flares, one after the other, on the way down is called the two-step. Using up the energy a little bit at a time in a series of flares is called the "progressive flare."

The toughest part of this is hitting your entry conditions, Mitchell said. "I say I want to be 60 knots at 100 feet" before starting the flare. "You got to work real hard at that. Otherwise, it's not a good data point because you weren't at the conditions specified for your test. The other hard thing for students is feeling comfortable in autorotation so that they can start being kind of a third party and being observant of what's going on. The actual flying is not that tough. . . .

"You see that my speed is down a little bit" from the desired 60 knots. "So I'm going to put my nose down a little bit to try to get my speed back before reaching 100 [feet above the ground].

"There's 100! Coming into a one-step, 10 degrees nose up. Now we'll pull initial [raise up on the collective] and level the aircraft" on the ground-effect cushion. "You can see I had no control over my ground speed [before the pull-up]. It was just going to run on to the ground at 30 knots."

We slowed up but did not land. Mitchell re-engaged the engine just before touchdown so that we could move on to the next event of demonstrating a two-stage flare of the helicopter—raising up its nose so that the bulk of the helicopter would press against the oncoming air and help slow our no-engine fall.

"I would like to use my flare to slow my initial rate of descent so I don't have to do it all with collective," Mitchell explained.

We went into autorotation again. Mitchell pulled up for the first step of his flare as we neared the ground, using both the body and the blades of the helicopter to brake our descent. The helicopter slowed its drop but was still shooting forward too fast to land on the long skids. It is dangerous to land on skids at high speed because their front ends may dig in and flip the helicopter over onto its back. Mitchell pulled up on the collective a second time to provide more lift to slow our forward speed and descent, the second step of the flare. This virtually stopped our forward motion. We would have been able to plop safely the rest of the way to the ground if the engine had really been dead.

We set up next for the "progressive flare," in which the pilot keeps pulling or pushing the collective to make the nose move up or down to adjust descent and ground speed. The pilot does not reach one point in the sky and then hold the nose in the constant 10-degrees-up position as in the one-step and two-step flares but rather feels the way in to the soft landing.

The progressive flare is the one TPS teaches and the one Reggie had shown me. The progressive flare is more difficult to master than the one- and two-step flares, but its flexibility increases the odds for making a safe landing in an engine-out autorotation.

"This is going to be a full touchdown," Mitchell said as we neared the point for disengaging the engine from the rotor.

"Entering. . . . Throttles to idle. Rotor is staying in the green. I'm in trim. I've got 60 knots; 58 and starting" the progressive flare. The stall warning shouted at us again. Mitchell used the combination of hiking up the nose and changing the pitch on the blades as we dropped in autorotation from 100 feet. We landed gently with very little forward speed. We just settled on the grass and skidded a few feet.

"I'll give you an A on that one," I quipped as we sat safely on the ground at dead stop.

"Successful landing," he replied. "We get to go do another one."

We flew to Webster Field to practice gathering data on helicopter performance.

"Our scenario is that the contractor has said 60 knots [descent speed] and 100 feet is the optimum flare," Mitchell began when we were over the field. "So what we're going to do is try to verify this by varying those parameters around the optimum and see how it changes the autorotating landing characteristics. We want to look at how airspeed and flare altitude are going to affect it to see if we can maybe come up with a better technique or a better pair of numbers here to do the autorotation at, or confirm what the contractor has given us here is indeed the truth. That generally is the business we're in. We're checking the contractor to make sure what he's telling us is the truth."

When it comes to graphing the dead-man zone on the High-Velocity Diagram, Army test pilot Mitchell said, "The marketeer wants a real small one so he can sell his airplane. The lawyer wants a real big one so that the company isn't liable. If you're in this red area, supposedly you can't shoot a safe, successful autorotation. Pilot's fault" if the airplane crashes when the engine quits because "you're in the avoid area."

Mitchell flew a series of autorotations while I called out the relevant data. If this had been an actual test flight, an automatic taping system that recorded every move the helicopter made would back up my handwritten data so that the test pilot and engineers could exhaustively analyze the helicopter's performance after the tests had been completed.

Mitchell ran our OH-58 tests in the same incremental, fastidious way Gallagher and Murrell had done them. "One parameter, one increment" is the way to test, Mitchell said. Change only one condition during each test, see what happens to the aircraft; move on to the next condition, and see the effect of that one. Test pilots of the high-tech 1990s work like highly educated technicians in a laboratory whether they are in the cockpit or at an office desk. Happily for the pilots, their aerial laboratory has no walls.

LCDR Mark G. Feuerstein, thirty-two, another driven man who delivered so many newspapers while still in high school that he had $10,000 in the bank by the time he graduated, took me up in the T-2

Buckeye jet to give me an insight into the ways a test pilot determines the basic flying qualities of a fixed-wing airplane.

"Incredibly boring," instructor pilot Feuerstein said in describing the routine test pilots follow in determining whether a newly developed plane handles well enough in the air for the military to buy.

One such FQ, for flying-qualities test, we were to conduct would show how much arm strength it took to pull the twin-engine T-2 out of a dive. We would subject the plane to more and more gravitational force, called Gs, by pulling it out of a dive steeper and steeper each test. Then we would graph the results.

To understand how we were going to generate Gs, imagine circling your car clockwise at 20 miles per hour around an empty parking lot. A wide circle at 20 miles per hour would not push you against the side door. A very tight circle at that same speed, however, would push you hard against the door. The tighter circle would increase the G force. Feuerstein said he was going to do the same kind of thing with the T-2. But the ever-tighter turning would be vertical, from up to down, instead of horizontal. The tighter the arc he flew in pulling out of the dive, the more Gs he would put on us and the airplane.

How the stick feels and acts is crucial to a pilot, especially during aerial combat. In a dogfight, fighter pilots like to feel through the stick what their airplane is doing as they wrench it around the sky. They do not want the computerized controls to keep the plane trimmed to the point where they lose the feel of what is happening. Bomber pilots also want to feel in control of the airplane when they have a hand on the stick but do not object to the computer's adjusting the trim while they worry about getting the bombs on target.

"At 1 G, we've got breakout and friction of maybe 2 pounds" on the stick, Feuerstein said. This would be the first point on the graph showing how much strength was required to pull the T-2 out of a dive at 1 G—the natural pull of gravity. Then we would try 2 Gs, twice the pull of gravity; 3 Gs; and 4 Gs. If it took a lot of strength to pull the T-2 out of a dive at 3 Gs, flying the T-2 would be exhausting. If it took almost no strength, the pilot could get lulled into complacency and overstress the airplane, even go into such a violent stall that the wings would be ripped off.

"We're going to get trimmed up at 300 knots at 15,000 feet," Feuerstein said.

"Then we're going to get off the condition—by off the condition I mean off that airspeed and altitude—and be slower and higher. We're going to dive down into the point [of 15,000 feet] accelerating. As we get close to our target airspeed [of 300 knots], I'm going to start pulling back on the stick so that as the nose goes through the horizon on this sweeping arc with my airspeed at 300 knots, plus or minus 5, I've got a constant pull on the stick. My force gauge is going to be in between my hand and the stick. So then I can look and say, 'OK, it was 15 pounds at 2 Gs at 302 knots.' Then I can plot this point.

"Then we'll go back and start again at slow airspeed, and we'll come down steeper, and we'll wait until we get closer to that 300-knot airspeed because the energy is going to bleed quickly. I'm going to pull through that 300 knots again, this time targeting 3 Gs, and write down the same data."

Feuerstein ended the briefing with the customary what-if instructions for emergencies. I always listened but never thought anything bad was going to happen. I looked forward to every flight, never worried about anything except doing something stupid myself, like pushing the stick the wrong way or getting sick.

"For takeoff today we've got a fairly low ceiling," Feuerstein said. "So if we have a fire or an engine failure right after takeoff, we're going to clean up the airplane [meaning raise the landing gear and take other steps to reduce drag to make it easier to stay airborne on one of the T-2's two engines] and establish an IFR [instrument flight rules] climb because we're going to be IFR pretty quick. As always but more so today our first objective is to fly the airplane. When we're in stabilized climb and moving up off the ground, I'll bring the engine that is causing us problems back to idle. If there is a fire indicated, I'm just going to shut it off because you don't need it. I will ask for a GCA [ground-controlled approach] downwind. If there's secondary indications indicated with the fire, we're going to turn so we're out over the water, and when we're feet wet, we're going to jump out. If there are no secondary indications and it's a plain-vanilla engine failure, we're going to turn for a GCA downwind—hopefully get a foreshortened approach—and then come into a flare landing.

"If we're out of control passing 7,000 feet [on the way down to the ground], we have to eject.

"If we're out of control and it's a surprise to us, I'm going to neutralize the stick, bring the throttles to idle, check the trim to nose up, check that my harness is locked, and take a look at what we've got.

"If we're really in a spin, I'll apply anti-spin controls—opposite rudder and neutral stick.

"If we're not in a spin and we're in a spiral, I'll do much the same thing, only instead of using full rudder, I'm going to put in just a little bit of rudder. That's how you stop the spiral, which is more of a rolling motion vice a yawing motion.

"Again, 7,000 feet is the magic altitude. If we have to get out, I will call, 'Eject! Eject! Eject!' If for some reason we're not talking to each other, I'll rap hard on the canopy with my left hand three times.

"Bird strike. If we run into birds, the first things to check if I'm not awake [because a bird coming through the canopy could knock him unconscious] or incapacitated are airspeed and altitude. Make sure both are OK or improving. If it's not improving and you can't make it improve and you decide we have to get out, pull the handle back before you eject us." Pulling the eject handle back before pulling it up ejects both occupants of the T-2.

"If you don't pull the handle back," thereby leaving Feuerstein alone in the airplane after I had ejected, "just send flowers," Feuerstein quipped.

We took off without the engine's failing or catching fire. We zipped through the thick white clouds without hitting any birds, entering the unbounded world of clear air at 20,000 feet. As usual, I found myself studying the beautiful surroundings outside the cockpit rather than the instruments inside it. The solid mass of clouds below us looked like a floor to heaven's cathedral. I wrenched my eyes away from that scene and focused them on the instruments.

Suddenly, we were diving at 300 knots, just as Feuerstein had briefed on the ground. He pulled the plane up in ever-tightening arcs to increase the gravity forces while keeping the plane's speed constant. Again, this was exactly as advertised. During one of these flying-quality maneuvers, I held the force gauge—an instrument about the size of a two-cell flashlight—between the stick and the palm of my hand. I tried to read the pounds of force on the gauge as we reached the target G force displayed on a meter on the far right side of the cockpit. Trying to read both instruments at once at the correct altitude made me feel like a tailor trying to measure a man for a suit while he was running in place. No one thing is hard in test piloting. What is difficult is trying to do a number of things at once while the plane bounces around the sky. Get above the point; dive into it; pull up without exceeding 300 knots; remember everything that happens as you go; write it all down; set up for the next test. The fun of this test-flying is not what you do but how well you do it. The same kind of psychic income keeps the fisherman casting his dry fly hour after hour even when no trout rise to it. He makes his "point" when he drops the fly exactly where he intended. For purist test pilots and fly fishermen—masterful technique fulfills.

The flying-qualities mission—like the thousands of such tests conducted on the same tired T-2 before we took it up—confirmed that the trainer handled well enough to entrust to beginner pilots. Its stick forces were neither too light nor too stiff. Too light might result in a pilot's pushing a plane out of control accidentally. Its other flying qualities were satisfactory. There were no "Part I" deficiencies—the worst kind.

The ideal test pilot, Feuerstein told me after we had gotten back on the ground, "has a methodical, ordered way of doing things." I said a number of the hotshot pilots in Class 100 were worried that all their studying and tedious flying were turning them into geeks. Feuerstein laughed knowingly, adding, "My wife thinks the casting director of *Revenge of the Nerds* screwed up because he didn't pick me."

I flew in several other planes to get the cockpit view of test-pilot training. My flights were conducted on what the Navy calls a "not-to-interfere basis," meaning I would go fly when none of the students was waiting to do so and when instructors, who must fly frequently to keep their edge, were available.

Part of test-pilot instruction is how to evaluate the flying qualities of a fixed-wing aircraft when one of its two engines conks out. TPS uses an Army U-21, a King Air in its civilian life, to teach this. The U-21 is a propeller-driven airplane. It makes a good flying laboratory because the results of an engine failure are dramatic without being dangerous. The old, low-tech planes have a lot to teach the new, high-tech test pilots. TPS keeps an assortment of the old planes in the hangar, just as a library keeps classic books on its shelf.

"Now see if you can keep this thing on course," Instructor Mitchell told me after he had feathered the left engine of the U-21. "My foot is tired." I took over the stick, which was easy to handle, and the rudder pedals, which were not. It took a constant, strong push on the right rudder pedal to keep the right engine from pushing the airplane to the left. Other one-engine tests, including takeoff and landing, showed the U-21 lived up to the contractor's advertising about being capable of flight after losing an engine. The test pilots in evaluating the U-21 years ago had done the tests Mitchell was flying with me in 1991. Again, the flying was systematic and often tedious. But a slow propeller plane like the U-21 speaks more plainly to the test pilot than a jet. The U-21 shouts what it is doing or will do if you keep messing with the power and the controls this way, like when the right engine tried to muscle the airplane after the left engine stopped pulling. The jets just whisper their warnings and then quickly carry out their threats.

"Your airplane," Karl T. Hutchinson, sitting in the left seat of the flying laboratory his firm had made out of the Learjet 24 executive aircraft, told Army Capt Roger A. Arnzen, the Class 100 test pilot under instruction.

"I got it," Arnzen responded, taking over the controls of the twin jet. I was sitting in the jump seat directly behind Arnzen.

"What we're going to look at first is directional stability," Hutchinson, a former Air Force F-16 pilot, said over the intercommunication system connecting us all together. "This is going to be the tendency of the airplane to want to point back into the wind when you disturb it in sideslip. . . . Give me about 3 degrees of sideslip on the gauge. . . ."

As soon as Arnzen had achieved 2 degrees of sideslip, Hutchinson told him to lift his feet off the rudder pedals. The Learjet did not swing back on course on its own.

"Here's an airplane that you can give 1, 2 degrees of sideslip, raise your feet off the rudder pedals, and it stays there. This is neutral stability. The airplane is very easy to displace. . . . We want positive directional stability. We want an airplane that wants to point into the wind. We want an airplane that wants to fly pointy end forward. Let me give you a stable airplane."

With that, Hutchinson pushed a series of buttons on the console between the left and right seats. The behavior of the airplane changed.

It swung back on course on its own when Arnzen took his feet off the rudder pedals. The CALSPAN Corporation of Buffalo, New York, had elaborately wired the Learjet so that it would change its behavior every time Hutchinson called out of the computer the personality he wanted the Learjet to assume from that moment. The Learjet could go into sixty-four different flying modes with a simple push of buttons and more with additional programming. Arnzen struggled with twenty-five different flying modes during the two-hour instruction flight.

Many military leaders believe high-tech simulators will play an ever-expanding role in teaching people to design, evaluate, and fly the aircraft of the future. While ground simulators are cheaper and safer, Hutchinson said flying ones may carve out a larger role for themselves in the future. One possibility, he said, is to use the same flying simulator to teach pilots to fly two or more different airplanes. This would save training and maintenance costs, he added.

The cost of computerizing different flight characteristics into an aircraft the size of the Learjet 24 would be between $500,000 and $700,000, Hutchinson estimated.

We were gliding along in the high-tech F/A-18 when the instructor sitting behind me explained with his question why I was having so much trouble believing I was flying at 400 knots in the Navy's most modern warplane.

"See how quiet it is?" marveled Marine Capt Alan G. McKillip from the backseat.

The F/A-18 flew so quietly that it was more like sitting in the fish-globe front seat of a peaceful glider than a combination fighter and bomber designed to kill. The F/A-18's engines are hung so far behind the pilot that little of their noise penetrates the cockpit.

The smoothness of the flight controls enhanced the sense of quiet. The computers do almost all the work of keeping the plane steady. I felt no bumps or vibration as I held the stick in the neutral position. This plane—nicknamed the Electric Jet because of all its modern electronics—was flying itself.

But the really dramatic difference between the new generation F/A-18 and its predecessors is the information it presents to the pilot, much of it on the windscreen. Imagine the readings you see on the instruments of your car's dashboard—miles per hour, temperature, oil pressure, and everything else—suddenly showing up as numbers in between the two layers of glass of your windshield. The F/A-18 displays information that way, all kinds of information. Numbers, arrows, warnings, dials, and bars all appear magically in the plastic of the windscreen. This feature is called a heads-up display, or HUD, and it lets you read about your own flight as you fly along.

McKillip dove the F/A-18 on an island in the Chesapeake. The plane's HUD showed me arrows, numbers, and squiggles, more than I could keep track of during the dive. The plane seemed to be saying to me, "Pay attention, Stupid. I'm telling you what's going on."

We then went into mock aerial combat against Marine LtCol Robert A. Price, who was piloting a T-2 training jet. Randy Hepp, a civilian photographer for Pax River who specializes in photographing aircraft performance and once had to bail out of a TA-4 while photographing the separation of F/A-18 bomb racks, was flying with Price. Once again the F/A-18's radar and HUD came alive with numbers and arrows. I found the amount of information dizzying.

Although the data the F/A-18 was generating overwhelmed me, I had no trouble maneuvering the airplane itself. It was similar to the sudden ease of parking a car with power steering after wrestling for years with mechanical steering. The F/A-18 was sweetly responsive. Its computers compensated for my clumsiness with the controls. I concluded early on in the flight that for the pilot, the F/A-18's biggest challenge is not in flying the plane but absorbing all the information it presents.

Back on the ground, flight instructor McKillip and adversary pilot Price agreed with my conclusion as we reconstructed the flight that seemed to take only minutes rather than its actual hour.

"There is so much neat stuff in the airplane that you forget to fly it," said McKillip, a former A-6 pilot. "You start looking at all the systems and everything else. The aircraft trims by itself. There is no noise. Sometimes you ask yourself as you fly along, 'Why is this aircraft suddenly feeling rough when I'm only doing 250 knots?' Then you find you're actually doing 500 knots. The airplane flies beautiful. The big thing is aviate, navigate, and communicate. But you've always got to fly the airplane first."

"The hardest part in flying the F-18," said Price, "is assimilating all the information that is being presented to you by the aircraft. Once you assimilate that, you're there. The aircraft is very user friendly and easy to fly. It will do so much for you. You just have to manage that system."

Several of the leaders of the directorates at Pax River who employ TPS graduates complained to me that the school spends too much time on teaching students how to evaluate the performance of an aircraft and not enough on its systems, which are the keys to successful missions. The most successful combat pilot, goes this argument, is not the one who can fly the best but the one who can exploit the aircraft's high-tech systems the most. High tech is forcing pilots to become managers of the systems in their office—the cockpit—but TPS is not restructuring its curriculum to address this change, according to the school's critics.

Bernsen and Price, director and deputy director of TPS in 1991, agreed that the mix of instruction will have to be changed eventually but said the hard questions are how fast this should be done and what instruction should be eliminated. "I see performance testing being reduced over the years but still being there," said Price. TPS has launched elaborate studies on how it should change its mix of instruction in the future.

However, the coming changes will be slow, not sudden. Test pilots, no matter how smart computers become, still will have to go to class to learn the why of aircraft behavior, to understand the theoretical as well as do the hands-on actual I had just experienced in the sky over Pax River. Going to class every day is, and always will be, part of learning how to be a test pilot. I decided to sit through enough of TPS classes to see what this high-tech ground school was really like.

Class 100—Honing and Boning

"I can teach calculus to a fence post—or a marine," quipped JJ McCue, the liveliest teacher at Test Pilot School.

Day after day I watched him write long formulas on the blackboard with both hands, stamp his feet, thump the board with an eraser, and twist his body like an airplane bucking the wind to hold the attention of the thirty-four members of Class 100.

"You've got to simplify," he told us over and over during the eleven-month course as his chalk galloped across the blackboard to solve calculus problems, "then all this shit goes away."

Or before showing us the numbers to explain how much a wing quivered under stress, he would intrigue us with the promise of an explanation he could put on the blackboard as hard numbers: "I can give you a warm and fuzzy for this one."

One morning he asked us, "Do we know why F-4s [Phantom fighter-bombers] have flat spins? Yes."

Then picking up two pieces of chalk, one for each hand, he warned, "Like the girls in Naples said when the carrier came in, 'There's five thousand of them and one thousand of us. This is going to be painful.'"

But a few minutes later he had all the numbers, arrows, and circles up there on the board to explain mathematically why the F-4 goes into a flat spin.

When JJ sensed we were falling asleep with our eyes open despite his best efforts at the blackboard, he would turn away from it and needle the students as people, not aviators and engineers.

"Who are you flying with this afternoon?" he asked Nancy Fechtig one morning.

"Otto," she replied, using the nickname of F/A-18 pilot Wes Nielsen.

"You're going to fly with an old guy like him?"

"Look who's talking!" Otto retorted to the older JJ.

"George," JJ pleaded, seeing me smiling from my seat at the back of the classroom, "help me."

"I can't," I replied. "I'm Methuselah back here."

"No," JJ smiled, "that's him," pointing to thirty-seven-year-old Jack Kirk, the oldest aviator in the class.

Inevitably, though, the class work was often tedious, boring, and seemingly unending in the four one-hour class periods starting at 8 A.M. I felt as if I were revisiting my ancient past. As a naval-aviation cadet in the V-5 program, I had taken engineering courses at Georgia Tech, and I remembered the long class lectures, heavy homework, and three-hour labs. This time I was not doing the homework or going steadily to the classes. I was studying how the future test pilots were being taught, not trying to become one. But even as an in-and-outer, I saw and felt important differences between TPS and my instruction at Georgia Tech that went way beyond the substitution of calculators and computers for the slide rules used in the 1960s.

One big difference was that TPS's teachers had college-educated adults sitting in front of them. These students wanted to know how all those equations they had learned during their undergraduate courses in calculus and aerodynamics could help them in their future work as test pilots and engineers.

The biggest difference of all, I think, was the sense of mission that fired up most of the teachers and flight instructors at TPS. None of the teachers was saving his energy to write academic tomes, nor riding the job because he already had tenure. There was focus to their instruction.

"Remember the game plan," JJ said after he had explained how lasers work. "If you want to understand how to test a laser, you better understand what's going on. You've all used systems. Now you want to learn how to test them. There's a huge difference."

Besides giving lectures, TPS teachers give homework assignments in such texts as *Naval Flight Test Pilot School Flight Test Manual; Fixed Wing Stability and Control, Theory and Flight Test Techniques.* It covers the hard part of testing—the evaluation of flying qualities as distinguished from performance.

"Most people don't realize that evaluating flying qualities and evaluating performance are two different things," Syd Sherby, founder of TPS, told me from Washington State in one of our many telephone conversations.

Finding out how fast a plane can fly and climb and how far it can go on a tank of gas has always been relatively easy, Sherby said. Instruments record those hard facts of performance. But assessing flying qualities means making judgment calls and expressing the feel of the airplane. How much strength should it take to push the stick forward, backward, or sideways? How fast should the plane execute a roll? Are the flying qualities dangerous or safe? Acceptable or unacceptable?

To learn how to gather the data for evaluating flying qualities, TPS still teaches its students to follow specific procedures, just as Sherby taught his first class in 1945. Those procedures have been refined, but the principle remains the same: Find out how the plane handles in the air, and express your findings as precisely as you can.

For example, if the pilot pushes the stick to the left, he or she expects the plane to bank to the left almost immediately. To have to wait too long for the bank would be like waiting too long for your car to turn left after you've turned the steering wheel in that direction. But how much pause should the test pilot tolerate? The TPS manual on flying qualities gives this guidance:

> The results of flying qualities investigations have revealed that the roll mode time constant [how long it takes the plane to bank left or right after the stick has been pushed left or right] should be no greater than one second for high maneuverability airplanes in flight phases or tasks which require precision tracking or precise flight path control.
>
> For all airplanes in all phases of mission accomplishment, a roll mode time constant greater than 1.4 seconds generally results in objectionably sluggish roll response and requires a change in piloting technique. Determination of the roll mode time constant from in-flight tests

requires special sensitive automatic recording devices (oscillograph, magnetic tape, telemetry, etc.) and a special data analysis procedure to be presented later. . . .

So the test pilot under training at TPS goes aloft to find out how long it takes the plane to go into a roll. He or she varies the conditions slightly and tries again, and again, each time recording the results. Once back on the ground, the pilot graphs the data. This is typical lab work at TPS. The pilot usually works with an engineer who flies along on the testing missions. The pilot's findings are "qualitative," how the airplane felt, how soon it responded to his or her touch, what it did when subjected to the various conditions, and how forgiving it was of a pilot's mistakes. The engineer takes the pilot's hands-on findings and, through calculations, extends them by figuring out how the airplane would roll at speeds slower and faster than the pilot flew. The engineer's findings are "quantitative"—they show every inch on the yardstick, not just the pilot's "points" every six inches.

At TPS pilots and engineers work together on small teams to evaluate an aircraft. They learn how to speak each other's language—qualitative and quantitative. The idea is to enable them to communicate, to appreciate each other, to learn how several people can write one report, and then to brief superiors on their findings.

In one team effort, pilots Boomer Hamilton, Spike Long, and Fish Mason and civilian engineer Andy Maack were told to find out if the Douglas TA-4J Skyhawk had the range and endurance to be an effective daytime bomber. They followed the detailed procedures and applied the formulas discussed in class and cited in the TPS performance manual. They spent ten hours collectively in the two-place jet and did their calculations about its range in their study cubicles at TPS and on their computers at home. They argued back and forth about what to say and how to say it in their evaluation report, as would be the case in real life. Their report concluded that "the extremely limited combat radius of the TA-4J airplane will force the battle group commander to position the carrier within the enemy's effective area of operation. . . ." The team received an A on their report.

"What we're trying to do here," said Robert B. "Doc" Richards, head of academics at TPS, "is make them understand—physical, hands-on understand—what you're trying to teach them. That's where I think the colleges miss it to a great extent. Everything we're teaching is taught in college. What the colleges have missed is the hands-on application—really understanding the physical application. Here it is right on a piece of hardware.

"The guy has heard differential equations before in college, but here is why we're going to use them. This is what it looks like in a time plot. Our real mission is to show them the engineering applications."

Then, with wistfulness, Doc allowed as how he missed the old days when there was more of the actual and less of the theoretical in evaluating aircraft. "Doing inverted flight in an open-canopy T-6 Texan [Navy SNJ], where I got a lot of my training, you can slide the canopy back," recalled Richards, a former Air Force pilot. "The wind is blowing in your ears. You've got sight cells in the gas tanks so you can see how much fuel you've got. You pump a few strokes of gas into the carburetor, and you can fly that airplane upside down for thirty or forty seconds before the oil all drains out. Things like that are the guts of aviation, which you don't get these days. You're not really flying the F-18; you're flying the computer."

He said this lack of direct, hands-on feel of the aircraft requires today's test pilot to be "more adaptable, more knowledgeable about the systems" that do much of the flying, most of the detecting and firing of missiles.

"Back in the earlier days, all you really had to know was how to fly the airplane. Turn on the ADF [automatic direction finder] or something like that. The big evolution is that the seat-of-the-pants pilot is kind of gone now. You don't fly the airplane by the seat of the pants anymore—by the feel, by the noise. It's masked by the automatic flight controls. Pilots are migrating from being pilots to being systems managers.

"Maybe because I'm an old bastard, I like the old way better. It was more flying, if you think flying is pulling on the stick and feeling the Gs and feeling the buffet on the surfaces. All that real aerodynamics.

"On the other hand, flying today is more sophisticated. You've got to be smarter—less motor skills, maybe, and more technical skills. Today's aviator does so much in systems management that he's not much of an aviator anymore. Lots of people—and I'm one of them—are concerned about losing the seat-of-the-pants aviator."

To make up for this loss of the direct connection between man and machine—the blocking off of real feel, or what he calls "flying the computer"—Richards said he and his fellow teachers must make sure they make the man and machine connect. They see this as their big challenge as they stand day after day before classes of future test pilots and their engineering partners.

Bob Miller is a gentle, soothing kind of teacher who prepares so meticulously for class that the students feel guilty if they do not hold up their own end by doing the homework and listening to what he says. Because he is a modest man, I had to pry his credentials out of him. He went through TPS himself with Class 49 in 1968, earned his master's degree from Princeton University in aerospace and mechanical sciences, and flew gliders for fun.

As the teacher who worked most closely with the helicopter pilots, Miller said his main mission was to teach them how to think, talk, and write like engineers so that they will be understood when they express themselves on the good and bad of an aircraft. To be successful in the world of evaluation, he said, the test pilot has to be able to say, "'I need this' in engineering terms."

Miller started out as an engineer at the Carrier Suitability Branch of the Strike Directorate, and in his twenty-six years at Pax River, test-flying, he said, had undergone a quiet revolution.

"When I first came here it was more of white scarf, kick the tires, light the fires. That was the dominant attitude. It has gotten more and more professional. A test pilot now is more like a business person.

"Rules and regulations and the bureaucracy have regulated out the old kind of individualistic flying, like flat-hatting. Early on it took that kind of guy to take on the risk of being a test pilot. Then you had accidents. Then you had more rules to prevent them from happening. You ended up with lots of regulations.

"The same kind of guy who was willing to be a test pilot doesn't make it through the training command today. This makes the accident rates come down, but all the regulation changes the whole personality of the organization."

Marine LtCol Robert A. Price was the deputy director of TPS while I was auditing class. He succeeded Bernsen as director on 10 January 1992. A big (six feet four inches), rangy, affable man, he threw a 90 plus mile per hour fastball at age eighteen and was drafted by the Baltimore Orioles. He opted for a college education, joining the Marine Corps before the draft grabbed him for the Vietnam War. "I'll always wonder whether I would have made it in the big leagues," he told me one day.

After graduating from Trinity University in San Antonio and flying helicopters in Vietnam, he was accepted for TPS. He graduated with Class 86 in 1984 and became the chief test pilot for the Rotary Wing Directorate at Pax River after graduation.

As good as the TPS teachers are, Price said, a would-be test pilot is still in for lots of boring hours, honing and boning his or her skills at TPS and at the subsequent test-pilot assignment. The number-one quality of a successful test pilot is the patience to fly each and every long, boring test flight with enthusiasm.

"Of course, you also have to have pretty good hands to hold that point. You have to understand the theory behind that test and the methods. And you have got to have a love of flying."

Almost everything the students at TPS do—homework, lab work, and flying—requires them to write about it afterward. Their most important writing is for their reports evaluating an aircraft they have tested. As working test pilots, their future reports could theoretically make or break a billion-dollar aircraft project and decide what planes go to the fleet. I say theoretically because history shows test pilots' reports are often ignored. More on this later.

Although TPS puts great stress upon teaching its test pilots and engineers to write airplane-evaluation reports, I found this the weakest part of the curriculum. As I read through the TPS manuals on report writing, they seemed to set forth a theory and then promptly contradict it. For example, the Navy's *Report Writing Handbook* states the following: "As the Naval Air Systems Command's primary field activity for development, test and evaluation of aircraft weapon systems, the Naval Air Test Center must communicate the results of technical evaluations in a clear, concise and timely manner" and "in non-technical language." But the accompanying textbook, entitled *Report Writing Instruction*, cites as a model this description of the ejection system in an experimental plane:

> Lack of a sequenced command ejection capability will require each crew member to initiate his own ejection which could result in fatal delays during critical in-flight emergency situations and would preclude safe ejection of an unconcious [*sic*] or incapacitated crewman.

That is the way test pilots are being taught to write—never use one word when you can use five. Do not say it bluntly and clearly, like this:

One crew member cannot eject the other from this airplane. This omission is unacceptable because it could cost an incapacitated crew member his or her life.

On one student's report, an instructor wrote, "Great!" next to this sentence on the F/A-18's attack radar:

TDC [throttle designator controller] oversensitivity and the associated absence of adequate tactical feedback to indicate TDC activation status resulted in eight miscued target designations during the course of a 1.6 hour flight.

I think, but am not sure, that this would be the plain-English translation of that sentence:

The throttle designator controller is too sensitive. It also fails to show whether it is in the active mode. These flaws caused eight errors in designating targets during 1.6 hours of flight.

I doubt if any Secretary of Defense, Secretary of the Navy, senator, or representative—unless he or she had been a test pilot—could understand the original version or act upon these descriptions.

On the positive side of the report-writing training at TPS, instructors do demand that the students be specific in their criticisms, as this example from a report on the A-6 bomber's cockpit illustrates.

A student wrote, "The obscured location of the direct view indicator is a Part I deficiency and must be corrected prior to delivery to operational squadrons."

Steven Enewold, the chief flight instructor, scolded, "I don't think you explained why I will die or can't do the mission." Those are among the criteria used to determine if a problem is categorized as a Part I deficiency.

Test pilots are taught to grade a plane's flaws from most serious to least serious.

A Part I deficiency is considered so serious that it must be corrected before the aircraft goes to the fleet. By definition, the aircraft would have one or more of these faults: is not airworthy, is unable to accomplish its mission, prevents the crew from being fully effective, or poses a "real likelihood" of injuring the crew or damaging the aircraft.

A Part II deficiency does not prevent the aircraft from accomplishing its mission but does keep the aircraft from realizing its potential.

A Part III deficiency "is minor or slightly unpleasant and appears too impractical or uneconomical to correct in this model but should be avoided in future designs."

The Navy tries to make writing an evaluation report as systematic as painting one of those outlined pictures with numbers designating where to put what color. As TPS teaches its students, a test pilot evaluating an aircraft must organize the all-important "Results and Discussion" section of his or her report around these six topics: (1) conditions of the test; (2) data collected; (3) analysis of the data and observations, both positive and negative; (4) what the information collected says about the ability of the aircraft to perform its intended mission; (5) conclusions; (6) recommendations. This is what TPS calls the six-part paragraph.

I can understand why Navy leaders want uniformity in the way the test pilots' findings are presented. But nowhere is the test pilot allowed to speak loud and clear, in plain English, whether he or she thinks the airplane is worth buying or sending to the fleet. It seems to me that the test pilot should be allocated a space outside the rigid outline to write what he or she really thinks of the aircraft for its intended mission. If the test pilot's opinion is not worth considering, whose is? I submit that any system of evaluation that mutes or muzzles the evaluator defeats its purpose.

As a summing-up exercise to the instructional flying, report writing, and briefings, future test pilots toward the end of the eleven-month school year are sent out on their own to assess an airplane, usually one he or she has never flown before. This equivalent of a thesis for the test pilots under instruction is called a DT 2, for developmental testing phase two.

The students wait with much anticipation for their assignments, hoping to get an airplane in a foreign country to brighten the drudgery of DT 2 testing and report writing with a touch of adventure. Of all the students in Class 100, LT Charles "Scott" Anderson, a P-3 antisubmarine-aircraft pilot, drew the most glamorous assignment. He was told to fly by commercial airliner to Adelaide, Australia, to test a heroic World War II aircraft, an Australian Air Force C-47 that had participated in the allied invasion of Normandy in 1944. Anderson was born in 1961!

Anderson and LCDR Mark G. Feuerstein, a TPS flight instructor, stayed in a hotel in Adelaide for ten days and were fervently embraced by the Aussies in between Anderson's test flights in the C-47. Anderson did not have to contend with high technology in his testing and writing because the C-47 is an old-fashioned, stick-and-rudder aircraft. His report employed the same methodology, however, that he would have used to evaluate an unknown, modern aircraft. Because his findings are free of the clutter of high-tech terms, they provide a clear insight into how a test pilot's reports are researched and written. Here are excerpts from Anderson's key "Results and Discussion" section of his report on the venerable C-47:

"Field of view from the left seat [of the cockpit] is depicted on a rectilinear total vision plot," a diagram of the blind spot on the right side of the plane when it is sitting on the runway. Anderson asked an associate to walk around in the area on the right side of the C-47. Anderson signaled the associate to a spot when he got to the edge of the pilot's vision. That spot was marked on the ground. The associate kept marking the edge of the blind spots on the ground until Anderson had enough points for a graph. He measured the blind area with a tape measure, then graphed it to show the location and size of the pilot's blind spot as he sat in the cockpit and taxied the plane. Primitive, slow, and painstaking work—but accurate.

> During taxi, the closest point on the taxiway centerline that could be seen was approximately 100 feet ahead of the airplane nose, making centerline control during straight taxi difficult to judge. Turns to the right were nearly blind for the pilot, causing extreme discomfort in line and hangar areas. During ground operations at small, unprepared fields the restricted forward field of view will prevent the pilot from adequately scanning the airplane path, greatly increasing potential for obstacle impact and airplane damage. The restricted forward field of view during taildown ground operations is a Part I deficiency which must be corrected as soon as possible. . . .
>
> [The handle for locking the tail wheel of the C-47] was evaluated for location and ease of use during ground operation. . . . To reach the control handle, the pilot had to unlock his harness, lean forward and right approximately 18 inches, completely losing his forward field of view. During taxi in line and hangar areas, the pilot will be "heads down" while operating the tail-wheel control handle, making him unaware of crucial directions from his lineman, which greatly increases potential for obstacle impact resulting in airplane damage and person-

nel injury. The location of the tailwheel control handle beyond the functional reach of the pilot is a Part I deficiency which must be corrected as soon as possible.

The propeller control levers were mistaken for the throttle levers several times during flight [because they were so close together and looked so much alike]. The unconventional arrangement of the power control quadrant is a Part I deficiency which must be corrected as soon as possible.

The escape hatches in the cockpit were too dangerous to test while the aircraft was sitting safely on the ground. They would be even more hazardous after a crash landing or during a fire. "The inadequate emergency egress system is a Part I deficiency which must be corrected as soon as possible. . . ."

Crosswinds of 15 knots caused the C-47 to act like a weather vane once it was on the ground, making the plane difficult and dangerous to taxi. The pilot's limited vision and the plane's

strong weathercocking tendency while taxiing will combine to make taxiing in winds greater than 15 knots at small airfields hazardous, severely restricting mission operations. The hazardous ground handling characteristics during taxi in high winds is a Part I deficiency which must be corrected as soon as possible. . . .

During low altitude cruise flight in light turbulence, maintaining heading within plus or minus five degrees was difficult, requiring accurately timed rudder inputs every two to three seconds to suppress the Dutch roll. Suppression of the yawing motion was unrealistic over an extended period due to pilot fatigue. During long transit periods, the easily excited Dutch roll yawing motion will cause extreme discomfort for passengers. The easily excited, practically unsupressable [*sic*] Dutch roll . . . is a Part II deficiency which should be corrected as soon as practicable. Dutch roll characteristics in configuration CR [cruise] failed to meet the requirements of the specification [in the military's contract with Douglas Aircraft Co., builder of the C-47].

The fuel gauge was so inaccurate that the pilot could have 20 gallons less or 60 gallons more in the plane's tanks than the amount shown on the gauge,

causing conservative mission planning, thereby limiting mission range and endurance. The inaccurate fuel quantity indication system is a Part II deficiency which should be corrected as soon as practicable. . . .

The airplane was very sensitive to gusts. . . . During approaches to landings, the gust oversensitivity will greatly increase pilot workload to maintain heading and glide slope control. The gust oversensitivity is a Part II deficiency which should be corrected as soon as practicable. . . .

The insufficient climb performance will restrict the pilot from low level maneuvering in mountainous terrain, forcing him to transit at higher altitudes, causing increased chance of detection and degrading mission effectiveness. The insufficient climb performance is a Part II deficiency which should be corrected as soon as practicable.

In his "Conclusions" section, Anderson wrote: "Within the scope of this test, the C-47B airplane displays limited potential for the combat airlift mission. It will be satisfactory upon correction of the Part I Deficiencies." His report documented twelve Part I deficiencies, twenty Part II deficiencies, and seven Part III deficiencies.

The C-47 went to war with none of those deficiencies corrected and became the most celebrated transport plane of the propeller age. The plane's heroic record does not mean that Anderson was wrong or too picky. Test pilots are supposed to be demanding. Anderson's predecessors who tested the C-47 and planes like it in the 1930s and early 1940s were less critical because neither they nor anyone else knew how many things could be done to make a bulky plane like the C-47 fly better. Designing and building flyable airplanes is still an art less than one hundred years old. The planes and their testers keep changing.

First Navy Test Pilot

Lieutenant Theodore Gordon "Spuds" Ellyson was not only the Navy's first uniformed pilot but, by necessity, its first test pilot. Every flight in the early days of Naval Aviation was not only an adventure but an experiment. Here, Spuds Ellyson—so nicknamed because of his love for potatoes—is at the controls of the Navy's first aircraft, the Curtiss A-1 biplane, in 1911 at Hammondsport, New York. Ellyson survived several crashes while piloting early Navy planes, only to die in one while flying as a passenger. (Smithsonian Institution)

Boat Rocker

Captain Washington Irving Chambers did more than any other officer in the early 1900s to add aircraft to the fleet. Battleship admirals in Chambers's day dismissed planes as little more than bothersome kites that had no place in naval warfare. Undeterred, Chambers schemed with airplane builder Glenn H. Curtiss and others to give the Navy eyes that could see over the horizon. Chambers, the first Navy director of aviation, was banished to a closet office and was retired early by the Navy establishment. (U.S. Naval Institute)

ABSOLUTELY FIREPROOF.   W.S. DUNNING, MANAGER.

· THE ANTLERS ·

Colorado Springs, Colo.

April 12, 1911.

Secretary of the Navy,

Navy Department,

Washington, D. C.

Dear Sir:

I have the honor to report that Lieut. Ellison is now competent to care for and operate Curtis aeroplanes and instruct others in the operation of these machines. Mr. Ellison is a hard worker and has acquired considerable knowledge of the art of aviation. He has been especially successful in operating the machine and is easily capable of qualifying for a pilot's license. It is a pleasure for me to recommend Mr. Ellison as a man who will make a success in aviation.

Yours truly,

G.H. Curtiss

Spuds Gets an "Up"

There was nobody in the Navy to teach its first aviator to fly, so aircraft builder Glenn H. Curtiss did the job. Curtiss taught Theodore Gordon "Spuds" Ellyson how to fly in 1911 in the wilds of North Island, San Diego. Curtiss made Ellyson and other student pilots run the plane back and forth over the ground for days before allowing them to jump it into the air for hops of a few hundred feet. Ellyson used the same method when he became the Navy's first flight instructor. (Chambers Collection)

Master and Apprentice

Glenn H. Curtiss is at the wheel of the A-1 biplane he designed, built, and sold to the Navy. Note the wheels, which enabled the A-1 to operate from land as well as from water. The plane's water, land, and air capabilities inspired the name Triad. This photograph was taken in July 1911, when Curtiss and Ellyson were flying the A-1's Navy acceptance trials at Lake Keuka in Hammondsport, New York. Hammondsport, Curtiss's hometown, became known as the cradle of Naval Aviation. (Ellyson Family Collection)

Get Up!

Breaking the grip of the water on the floats of the Navy's first seaplanes proved to be a challenge. Pioneer designer, builder, and flyer Glenn H. Curtiss experimented with all kinds of shapes at his flying camps at North Island and Hammondsport. Seaplanes at first were thought to be the future of Naval Aviation. The A-1, trying to take off here in 1911 from Lake Keuka, had its engine and propeller behind the pilot. Leaning into shoulder bars worked the ailerons. The wheel controlled the rudder and elevators. (Ellyson Family Collection)

Spuds's Taxi

Captain Washington Irving Chambers, the Navy's first director of aviation, clutches a makeshift life preserver as Spuds Ellyson prepares to fly him from Hammondsport to Penn Yan at the far end of Lake Keuka in 1911. The July night was so hot and windless that Spuds could not generate enough lift to get the A-1 off the lake. So Naval Aviator Number One taxied his boss all the way to Penn Yan, where Chambers caught the train back to Washington, D.C. Chambers was elated by the novel taxi ride. (Ellyson Family Collection)

History Makers

Spuds Ellyson at the wheel of the A-1 is teaching his first student, Lieutenant Jack Towers, how to fly, on the lakeside training field at Hammondsport in 1911. The two rivals shared many adventures and scored many firsts in aviation. Ellyson, Naval Aviator Number One, and Towers, Naval Aviator Number Three, moved the Navy's flying encampment from Hammondsport to Greenbury Point, Annapolis, Maryland, in August 1911. In October 1911 the two aviators took off in the A-1 from Annapolis for an endurance test. (Ellyson Family Collection)

First Navy Trainer

This is the four-cylinder Lizzy trainer the Navy's first student pilots drove across grass fields to master the controls before attempting to get airborne. In crashes, they often suffered injuries from being thrown against the elevator on the plane's nose. Lieutenant Jack Towers, typifying the experimental flight-testing of the early 1900s, removed the front elevator to see how it affected the plane's flying qualities. The plane flew just as well without it. The front elevator was abandoned. (Ellyson Family Collection)

Familiar Sight

People living near Lake Keuka in Hammondsport, New York, became accustomed to seeing biplanes orbit over the lake in the early 1900s, as the A-1 is doing here. Boat owners stayed alert for sudden crashes and were usually the first to come to the rescue of aviators clinging to plane wreckage in the lake. The lake stayed cold all summer. Early aviators had no sophisticated life preservers nor anti-cold "poopy" suits. Lieutenant Jack Towers swam in the lake religiously to build up resistance to its coldness. (Ellyson Family Collection)

REGULATIONS
For Operation of
AIRCRAFT

━━━ Commencing January 1920 ━━━

1. Don't take the machine into the air unless you are satisfied it will fly.
2. Never leave the ground with the motor leaking.
3. Don't turn sharply when taxiing. Instead of turning sharp, have someone lift the tail around.
4. In taking off, look at the ground and the air.
5. Never get out of a machine with the motor running until the pilot relieving you can reach the engine controls.
6. Pilot's should carry hankies in a handy position to wipe off goggles.
7. Riding on the steps, wings, or tail of a machine is prohibited.
8. In case the engine fails on takeoff, land straight ahead regardless of obstacles.
9. No machine must taxi faster than a man can walk.
10. Never run motor so that blast will blow on other machines.
11. Learn to gauge altitude, especially on landing.
12. If you see another machine near you, get out of the way.
13. No two cadets should ever ride together in the same machine.
14. Do not trust altitude instruments.
15. Before you begin a landing glide, see that no machines are under you.
16. Hedge-hopping will not be tolerated.
17. No spins on back or tail slides will be indulged in as they unnecessarily strain the machines.
18. If flying against the wind and you wish to fly with the wind, don't make a sharp turn near the ground. You may crash.
19. Motors have been known to stop during a long glide. If pilot wishes to use motor for landing, he should open throttle.
20. Don't attempt to force machine onto ground with more than flying speed. The result is bouncing and ricocheting.
21. Pilots will not wear spurs while flying.
22. Do not use aeronautical gasoline in cars or motorcycles.
23. You must not take off or land closer than 50 feet to the hanger.
24. Never take a machine into the air until you are familiar with its controls and instruments.
25. If an emergency occurs while flying, land as soon as possible.

Simpler Times

Today's military flying regulations, in contrast to this one-page set of rules promulgated by the U.S. War Office in 1920, fill books as thick as telephone directories.

Me and
G. H. Curtiss

Special Relationship

Spuds Ellyson, at the wheel of the the A-1, was in awe of the man wearing the life vest, Glenn Hammond Curtiss. He discovered that this wiry man with an eighth-grade education could do almost anything with his head and hands. Curtiss would sketch out modifications for an aircraft on the walls of his shop in Hammondsport and then help mechanics turn them into wood or metal. One day a janitor caused consternation by whitewashing over the sketches—covering up Curtiss's only working drawings. (Ellyson Family Collection)

North Island in 1911

This camp run by Glenn H. Curtiss was the first flying school for the Navy's first aviators. Curtiss realized he could not sell his planes to the Navy unless some of its officers knew how to fly them. So he offered free flying lessons to an officer of the Navy's choosing. The Navy on 23 December 1910 cut Spuds Ellyson's orders to report here. Curtiss launched from North Island many of his spectacular flights designed to show skeptical admirals the potential of aircraft for naval warfare. (Ellyson Family Collection)

Ouch!

X marks the spot where the head of Spuds Ellyson smashed into the ground of North Island on 14 March 1912 after his crash in the Curtiss A-2, the Navy's second plane. Ellyson had been running the biplane across the ground to determine if the winds were too tricky for student flight training. The plane jumped off the ground, shot 25 feet into the air, slammed back down, turned upside down. Ellyson recovered and resumed his flying career but suffered permanent injury to his neck. (Ellyson Family Collection)

Free Instruction in the Operation of the
CURTISS FLYING BOAT
Will be given
To Those Taking a Regular Course of
Training at the

CURTISS SCHOOL OF AVIATION, SAN DIEGO, CAL.

First Hydroaeroplane Races at Hammondsport, N. Y.

David McCulloh in his "Flying Boat" leads; he is accompanied by Mr. Curtiss,
Lincoln Beachey is second, accompanied by Lansing Callan, while Francis Wildman,
instructor at Hammondsport School, is third with the standard hydroaeroplane.

Among the men who have learned aviation at Curtiss Schools are: Lieut. T. G. Ellyson, now in charge of the aeroplanes of the U. S. Navy, Lieut. J. H. Towers, who just established a new World's Hydroaeroplane Record of 6 hours, 10 minutes, 38 seconds, H. Robinson, who recently introduced the Hydroaeroplane in Europe and is now instructor in a Curtiss School, C. C. Witmer, now in St. Petersburg demonstrating Hydroaeroplanes to the Russian Navy and Army, Lieut. J. W. McClaskey, instructor in a Curtiss School, Lincoln Beachey, "The World's Greatest Aviator," S. C. Lewis, now instructor in the Morane School in France, J. Lansing Callan, now an instructor in a Curtiss School, Francis Wildman, now instructor in a Curtiss School, Beckwith Havens, now a demonstrator, W. B.

Atwater, now demonstrating to the Japanese Government, besides a score of men who own their own machines and fly in contests and exhibitions and a dozen others have taken positions with either manufacturers or exhibition concerns.

OUR San Diego, Cal., Aviation Training Grounds, situated on North Island, in San Diego Harbor, are the finest in America, if not in the world. North Island is leased by us exclusively for Aviation purposes, and comprises one thousand acres of flat, level sand, unobstructed by rock, tree, or building, thus offering every advantage as a flying course. The island is entirely private, yet within a few minutes of San Diego, one of the most progressive and attractive cities on the Pacific Coast.

THE FIRST CLASS BEGAN INSTRUCTION DECEMBER 1st.
ANOTHER CLASS WILL START JANUARY 1st, 1913.
A $100.00 DEPOSIT WILL RESERVE A PLACE FOR YOU IN THIS CLASS. MAIL OR WIRE IT TO-DAY.
OUR BOOKLET "*TRAINING*" MAILED UPON REQUEST.

THE CURTISS AEROPLANE CO., HAMMONDSPORT, N. Y.

Early Brochuremanship

This 1913 poster illustrates how the Navy's first aircraft contractor, Glenn H. Curtiss, tried to develop a market for his products by teaching people how to fly them. (Library of Congress)

Commander Ellyson

Theodore Gordon "Spuds" Ellyson in 1921 when he was executive officer of the Naval Air Station at Hampton Roads, Virginia. He left flying in 1913 to serve with the surface fleet. He won the Navy Cross during World War I for developing tactics for subchasers. He returned to aviation in 1921. In 1928, while executive officer of the USS *Lexington*, the Navy's second aircraft carrier, he was killed when the Navy plane carrying him as a passenger crashed into the Chesapeake Bay. Ellyson was flying to Annapolis to be with his hospitalized daughter, and his death came on his forty-third birthday. (U.S. Navy)

Unheralded Architect

Edward W. Rounds, shown here when he was a commander coordinating aircraft testing at Patuxent River in the 1940s, had as a young man successfully pressed Navy leaders to systemize the evaluation of aircraft. His farseeing memoranda led to coordinating the expertise of engineers on the ground with test pilots in the air. Complained Rounds, a former test pilot, in 1926: "One of the greatest handicaps is the lack of reliable data concerning the performance of Naval airplanes." (U.S. Navy)

Boom Times at Pax

More than seven thousand workers were housed in temporary, tar paper–covered barracks like these at Pax River during the construction of the base during World War II. Life was often wild inside these barracks, with high-stakes card and dice games among the diversions for the isolated workers. One night at the gate a guard caught a man trying to smuggle in a prostitute hidden in a rolled-up rug. Winds turned the base into a dust bowl in the summer, while rains in the spring and winter created a sea of mud. (U.S. Navy)

Pax Comes to Life

Commander William T. Rassieur, the first commander of the Naval Air Station at Patuxent River, presides over the commissioning of the base on 1 April 1943. Seated directly behind him is Rear Admiral John S. McCain, Chief of the Bureau of Aeronautics. He warned against allowing the new facility to be used for anything except testing, for fear of diluting its purpose. McCain's warning was heeded for almost fifty years. But in 1992 some Navy development functions were added to the test center at Pax River. (U.S. Navy)

SECNAV Knox Sees for Himself

World War II Navy Secretary Frank Knox proved to be a strong supporter of the
Naval Air Test Center at Patuxent River. Flanked here by Captain William T.
Rassieur (foreground) and Commander Thomas Booth, Knox agreed that the stun-
ning advances being made in aviation during World War II required the Navy to
improve its capabilities for evaluating them. Transforming daring but underedu-
cated combat pilots from the fleet into meticulous test pilots was one of the biggest
challenges the Navy faced in the 1940s. (U.S. Navy)

First Schoolmaster

In 1990 Sydney S. Sherby studied the portrait of himself made in 1944, when he was ordered to teach test pilots and engineers at Pax River what made aircraft behave the way they did. He had no textbooks, no faculty, no laboratory. With big assists from experts at the National Advisory Committee for Aeronautics at Langley, Virginia, he wrote a textbook, rounded up a faculty, and joined them in teaching test pilots and engineers how to evaluate an aircraft. What evolved was the U.S. Naval Test Pilot School. (U.S. Navy)

Future Student

Lieutenant Donald Boecker (right) at this joyous moment in 1965 had no idea he would not only go to the Test Pilot School that Sherby had founded but would end up running the whole Naval Air Test Center. He and Lieutenant Donald Eaton (left) had just been rescued from Laos after ejecting from their burning A-6 Intruder bomber. Skipper Leonard Alexander "Swoose" Snead (center) of Attack Squadron 75 joined in welcoming the heroes back to their aircraft carrier, the USS *Independence.* Swoose Snead urged Boecker to become a test pilot. (Ralph Clark)

A-6 Bomber

This is the type of plane Boecker and Eaton flew off the USS *Independence* on 14 July 1965 to bomb the Ho Chi Minh Trail in Laos. Their bombs exploded prematurely under the right wing, shooting fragments into fuel tanks and hydraulic lines. The aviators ejected, landing in hostile territory, and were pursued day and night by enemy soldiers until Air America helicopter pilot Sam Jordan swooped into the jungle and carried them to safety. The ordeal gave Boecker an appreciation of the need for test work. (U.S. Navy)

USS Independence

This venerable carrier was the launching pad for Boecker and Eaton when they flew off to Laos on the fateful mission that almost cost them their lives. The ship's band saluted their safe return, while sailor after sailor shook the hands of the aviators, saying, "Glad you made it back." (U.S. Navy)

Boecker the Admiral

The teenager from Naperville, Illinois, who kept winning ribbons at local fairs for his airplane models had risen to the rank of rear admiral by the time Class 100 reported to Pax River in 1991 to begin Test Pilot School. Boecker welcomed the students aboard, telling them they would become friends for life through sharing the rigors of TPS. As commander of the Naval Air Test Center, Boecker was the Navy's top liaison officer with St. Mary's County. He adopted the area as his permanent home. (U.S. Navy)

Modern Schoolmaster

Commander Thomas J. Bernsen, director of TPS in 1991, represented the new breed of highly educated, disciplined test pilots. He majored in mathematics in college, was a meticulous helicopter pilot, and strove to create an atmosphere of mentoring at TPS, in contrast to the sink-or-swim approach of some of his predecessors. He was unforgiving of recklessness in the cockpit, however, telling the students that he had already been to too many funerals of fellow aviators. Nobody at TPS was killed on Bernsen's watch. (Author)

Chief Test Pilot

"We are here to teach you how to test, not to give you some neat-o things to play with," Commander Steven "Smiley" Enewold told the students of Class 100 when they reported to TPS. Enewold, Chief Test Pilot for the school in 1991, stressed that "test pilots are not born; they are trained. We're here to train you how to be test pilots. When you graduate from here, you've got a learner's permit to be a test pilot. If you don't quit, you'll make it." (Author)

Mr. Intense

Army Captain Arthur T. Ball, sitting at a computer in his work space at TPS, typified the intensity of the students. Wives often complained that they tired of looking at the backs of their husbands' heads as they sat at computers at home, doing schoolwork. The U.S. Naval Test Pilot School trains Army and Marine aviators as well as Navy fliers. Army graduates leave Pax River, while most Navy and Marine test pilots stay there to practice their trade. (Author)

Family Man

Lieutenant Commander Steven R. Eastburg, holding his son, Gregory, has the deep engineering background that the founders of TPS found lacking in the first aviators sent to Pax River to evaluate aircraft. He strives to be on the forward edge of technology and is intensely interested in the potential of unmanned aircraft. Like most of the new breed of test pilots, he goes home to his family in the suburbs after work, not to the officers' club. But airplanes still break. Steve almost lost his life while testing one in 1992. (Author)

Engineer

Katy Fleming, a flight engineer at Pax River, discovered that working and flying with future test pilots in Class 100 provided insights she never would have gotten at her former desk job. TPS puts engineers and aviators on the same team to evaluate aircraft. This forced association is designed to show the rival specialists what they can do for one another. Engineers and pilots plan test flights before takeoff and analyze the results together afterward. (Author)

Wild Blue Yonder

Captain Mark "Fish" Mason was the only Air Force pilot in Class 100 but said TPS picnics like this one kept him from feeling like an alien. Daughter Grace is on his shoulders. The Navy and Air Force exchange students for their respective test-pilot schools. The downsizing of the American military may bring a merger of the Navy school at Pax River and the Air Force one at Edwards Air Force Base, California. (Author)

Hard at It

Civilian engineer Jeffrey T. Semenza was among the students who often worked at their TPS desks on weekends to finish reports. School Director Bernsen said some students in the past brought sleeping bags into their study cubicles so that they could stay overnight there. "That's not the answer," he told TPS students. He urged them to set aside time during the school year for personal fun and to keep their sense of humor. Jeff did. (Author)

Beaming Beamer

Lieutenant Robert L. "Beamer" Curbeam proudly shows off his daughter, Eva. Beamer, the only black in Class 100, was an exceptionally talented radar intercept officer who was awarded the class prize for writing the best reports. A graduate of the U.S. Naval Academy, Beamer credited his mother, a teacher who grew up in a poor section of Baltimore, for inspiring him to excel. "You will do well! You will get your education," she kept telling him. (Author).

"You'll Be Sorry"

Class 99 threw a "You'll Be Sorry" party for Class 100 at the Pax River Officers' Club. Class 100 celebrants from left to right: Air Force Captain Mark "Fish" Mason, Navy Lieutenant Charles "Scott" Anderson, Italian Air Force Captain Sergio Comitini, Navy Lieutenant Darryl J. "Spike" Long, and Navy Lieutenant Robert D. "Bullet" Allen. (Author)

Spinmaster Gallagher

Jerry Gallagher, former naval aviator, specializes in teaching future test pilots how to evaluate an aircraft's performance during spins. Here he explains aircraft behavior by using a model of the T-2 Buckeye trainer. The T-2 is the plane used for spin trials at TPS. Gallagher puts the T-2 in an upside-down spin during the instruction flights. (Author)

Learning by Doing

Author (right) with flight instructor Mark G. Feuerstein just before going aloft in the T-2 to receive the same kind of instruction future test pilots receive in the air at TPS. This flight was to evaluate the flying qualities of the aircraft through such exacting tests as measuring with a hand-held gauge the pressure it takes to move the stick under varying conditions. (U.S. Navy)

Learning by Analyzing

Marine Captain Alan G. McKillip (foreground) brainstorms with two TPS students, Lieutenant Ramon A. "Babaloo" Collazo and Lieutenant Nancy D. "Nofun" Fechtig, in a study cubicle at TPS. Every flight is analyzed exhaustively after it is completed. Aircraft performance is shown with graphs as well as texts in the steady stream of reports TPS pilots and engineers write all during the school year. (Author)

JJ Lays It On

"I can teach calculus to a fence post—or a marine," John J. McCue, Jr., aerodynamics instructor at TPS, contended. He spiced his lectures on calculus and aerodynamics with jabs and jokes and frequently pounded the blackboard to hold everyone's attention. Many of the students conceded by the end of the school year that JJ could indeed teach calculus to a fence post, or a marine. (Author)

Too Much Geeking!

Lieutenant Darryl J. "Spike" Long registers overload as he is confronted with the demand to write yet another report at TPS. Spike applied for TPS to break the monotony of flying the E-2 Hawkeye command-and-control aircraft. One of his biggest thrills came when he flew the F/A-18 fighter-attack jet at TPS. His high-jinks enlivened the school year. (Author)

Andy Knows

Civilian engineer Andrew C. Maack exemplified the help-one-another spirit Bernsen and other TPS leaders tried to generate. Before coming to TPS, Andy had won an award for his work on putting a plastic wing on the A-6 bomber and was credited with figuring out why an A-6 from the Strike Directorate had crashed. Andy happily shared his aeronautical expertise with his classmates on the ground and became a popular backseater with the pilots in the air. (Author)

The Old Master

Robert B. "Doc" Richards, chief academic instructor at TPS, believes the way to make course work come alive for pilots and engineers is to relate it directly to what they will be doing in evaluating aircraft. A pilot from the stick-and-throttle era, Doc Richards acknowledges that the day of computerized controls and systems has arrived and that TPS courses have to deal with these new realities. But how much to change TPS is an ongoing debate. (Author)

Rotor Heads' Headwork

Marine helicopter pilot Stephen C. McCulley (foreground) teams up with Navy helicopter pilot Jeffery D. Hood to get yet another report into the computer. Test pilots and engineers work in teams at TPS to simulate the group approach they will take in actual evaluation projects. Helicopter and fixed-wing pilots take different courses at TPS. (Author)

"How's This Sound?"

Lieutenant Christopher L. "Spanky" Frasse (foreground) and Lieutenant Charles S. "Scott" Anderson, fixed-wing pilots, try to describe the good and bad points of an aircraft they have tested. Test pilots under instruction are trained to assess but not judge aircraft in their reports. This requires them to pull punches and word their evaluation reports guardedly rather than stating forthright opinions. (Author)

The Graduates

Front row (left to right)—Porter, Collazo, Fleming. Second row—Maack, Mannella, Eastburg, Frasse, Anderson. Third row—Hamilton, Arnzen, Mari, Hood, Kirk, Semenza, Mason, Hilditch. Fourth row—Ball, Linnell, Nielsen, Dungan, Long, Curbeam, McCulley, Erdos, Comitini. Back row—Scherrer, Rusher, Melling, Knaust, Fechtig, Allen, Fitzgerald, Portnoy. (Randy Hepp)

The Half-Graduate

Captain Robert Parkinson, acting commander of the Naval Air Test Center on Class 100's graduation night on 13 December 1991, hands the author a certificate for "partial" completion of the engineering test-pilot course. TPS Director Bernsen, promoted to captain during the school year, shares the laughter. (U.S. Navy)

Point Woman

Lieutenant Lori J. "Wrench" Melling, sitting in the T-45A Goshawk trainer, went out on the point while in TPS in 1991 to fight for equal opportunity for female jet pilots like herself. She contended there is no reason female pilots should not be given billets in carrier squadrons and go into combat along with men. Congress agreed in 1991, but President Bush appointed a commission to study the question. (Randy Hepp)

Test Pilots' Wives

Cathy Eastburg (left) with son, Gregory, and Sandi Brennan, with daughter, Megan, know that their aviator husbands have chosen dangerous work. They have to learn how to wall off anxiety, pursue careers, and raise children. Whenever a plane is missing, they pray their husbands are not aboard. But in April 1992 they lived the special agony of being informed that it was their husbands, Steve Eastburg (left) and Sean Brennan. The wives waited, prayed, and then celebrated when they learned their husbands had survived. (Author)

S-3 Viking

This is the type of plane that shook apart in midair while Lieutenant Commander Steve Eastburg of TPS Class 100 and Lieutenant Sean Brennan of Class 99 were testing it over the Chesapeake Bay on 29 April 1992. Steve, sitting in the right seat, ejected himself and pilot Sean at the last possible split second. Eastburg survived the ejection with minor injuries, while Sean landed in the water unconscious and suffered burns over most of his body. They were both rescued. (U.S. Navy)

Mishap Victims

Captain Steven A. "Axle" Hazelrigg
(with cap), chief test pilot of the Strike
Aircraft Test Directorate at Pax River,
and Lieutenant William C. "Catfish"
Davis took an A-6 aloft on 15 August
1990 to test how the bomber handled
a newly designed bomb. Without
warning, the flight controls broke. The
bomber hurtled to earth. Hazelrigg,
perhaps unable to eject because of the
negative Gs, rode the plane down to
his death. Davis ejected, suffering
major injuries. The A-6 lacks a command ejection system, so Davis could
not eject Hazelrigg. (Courtesy of
Michael's of Whidbey Island; U.S.
Navy)

Superstar

Keith E. Crawford proved to be a superstar at TPS, winning both the outstanding-student and report-writing awards when he graduated with Class 73 in 1978. Moving on to the Strike Directorate, Crawford developed a spring to make the F/A-18 more responsive during exhibition flying by the Blue Angels. Commander Crawford was killed on 22 October 1986 while flight-testing the spring over the Chesapeake Bay, prompting a far-reaching investigation of safety practices. (U.S. Navy, by PH2 Jerry Ferguson)

Tragic Aftermath

The crash that killed Keith Crawford led to Captain Lewis W. Dunton III's losing his job as director of Strike. Although not a formal Navy punishment, Dunton felt humiliated by the transfer and concluded he had no choice but to resign from the service he loved. The Navy had been the core of his life. He became depressed and committed suicide in 1987, leaving his wife, Marjorie, and two sons, Lewis W. Dunton IV (left) and James Cable Dunton. (U.S. Navy)

Captain George C. Duncan, standing here in front of an F-4 Phantom, brushed against death time after time during his Navy flying career. He somehow managed to come out alive every time, living to enjoy his retirement. He shot down thirteen and a half Japanese planes during World War II, almost becoming a triple ace, and survived two crashes while serving as a test pilot. The pictures that follow, which show his Grumman F9F-5 Panther slamming into the ramp of the aircraft carrier USS *Midway* in 1951, dramatize how miraculous was his survival. (U.S. Navy)

Ramp Strike

"I hit a burble," Duncan recalled of his approach to the *Midway* in this F9F-5. "I remember pulling back on the stick. I saw the flames and closed my eyes. That's the last thing I remember until I felt them sewing up my head in sick bay." (U.S. Navy)

Fire!

A jet like Duncan's F9F-5 is a flying fuel bomb. When a plane is ripped open, its fuel usually ignites. The fact that the flames were coming from tanks behind Duncan as the front half of his plane hurtled down the deck saved him from being incinerated. (U.S. Navy)

The Straps Hold!

The impact and the tumbling down the deck breaks the canopy loose and rips the helmet off Duncan's head. But his safety harness keeps him inside the somersaulting cockpit. The main part of the flames mercifully stay behind him as fuel spills out on the carrier deck. (U.S. Navy)

Stopped at Last

Duncan and the front end of the plane finally stop tumbling and come to a stop in the middle of the flight deck. Rescue teams race to extract him from the cockpit before the galloping flames catch up to it. (U.S. Navy)

Flames Catch Up

Flames eat up the fuel leading to Duncan's cockpit and come close to engulfing him as rescue workers struggle to extract the unconscious aviator. They freed him from his harness, but not before the fire had burned off his ears—exposed by the loss of his helmet—and burned his forearms. He suffered no other major injuries and was back flying six months later. (U.S. Navy)

Paddles

Lieutenant Commander Barry "Puppy" Love, serving as landing signal officer on the USS *John F. Kennedy* on 4 December 1991, awaits the arrival of the T-45A Goshawk. The Navy trainer was slated to make its first carrier landing that morning but was held up by stormy weather. Love stood ready to give corrective commands if the T-45A pilot strayed out of the landing groove while approaching the carrier. (Author)

First Trap

Commander David "DJ" Venlet makes history by landing the T-45A trainer on an aircraft carrier for the first time. Venlet landed the afternoon of 4 December 1991 on the *Kennedy* while the carrier was orbiting in the Atlantic off Florida. "Paddles" Love did not have to give DJ any corrective calls. (U.S. Navy)

T-45A Navy Team

This foursome shepherded the T-45A single-engine intermediate and advanced trainer through its evaluation at Pax River in 1991. The plane exhibited one problem after another, but the team kept working to solve them. Left to right: Commander David "DJ" Venlet, project chief; civilian manager Joseph Wascavage; Marine Captain Craig "Bowser" Bowers (standing on inlet), and Navy Lieutenant Wade "Torch" Knudson. (Author)

Problem Child in Flight

The T-45A was supposed to be a simple modification of the British Hawk but turned into an expensive rework of that plane. By mid-1992 the plane had fallen behind schedule, was way over cost, and kept developing problems in flight, including engine stalls that apparently only a new engine could cure. Uniformed Navy leaders blamed former Navy Secretary John F. Lehman, Jr., for forcing the T-45A on them, but he said he left the choice to them. (U.S. Navy)

Rebel with a Cause

Captain George J. Webb, Jr., former chief test pilot at Strike, complained that test pilots keep writing reports, "but I don't know who the hell ever reads them." He said he warned in 1983 about the problems the Navy would encounter in trying to make the British Hawk suitable for student pilots to land on aircraft carriers. He recommended that policy makers pay more attention to test-pilot findings so that problems are addressed before a plane enters production. (British Aerospace)

1992 Skipper

Marine Lieutenant Colonel Robert A. Price had the helm of TPS in 1992 when everything about Naval Aviation was being debated, including the training of test pilots. How many test pilots should be trained for the changed world of the twenty-first century? What should they study? Price, as director of the school Sherby started in 1945, was confronted with the transcendent question: "Where do we go from here?" (Randy Hepp)

TPS Today and Tomorrow

The building for the future U.S. Naval Test Pilot School was nearing completion on the hill in front of the existing facility in 1992. Optimists said there would always be a need for the school at Pax River and its graduates, no matter how small the Navy became. Pessimists said the downsizing of the American military clouded the future of the school. (Randy Hepp)

Class 100—
Graduation and
Beyond

The night that the Tapooies and engineers in Class 100 thought would never come did at last arrive on 13 December 1991—graduation. No more class lectures; no more trying to hit points in the sky, missing them, trying again; no more report writing; no more long evenings at the computer at home; no more sitting in the stuffy cubicles at TPS on Sunday mornings.

So it was with relief that thirty-three of the thirty-four students who reported as Class 100 to Pax River on 14 January 1991 dressed up for the graduation night of formal dinner, hopefully short speeches, the handing out of diplomas, and then some serious drinking interrupted by only enough dancing to keep wives and girlfriends from going home mad. It was with pride that wives, one husband, parents, sisters, brothers, and friends of the graduates got ready for the big evening.

The missing thirty-fourth student had studied hard but, in the judgment of his flight instructors, could not adapt quickly enough to flying different kinds of aircraft. He was invited out of test-pilot training and sent to a job requiring less flexibility. This happens. Some members of Class 100 never forgave School Director Bernsen for washing out the student. I thought that was unfair to Bernsen. He had thought long and hard before acting and worked like hell to get the student a good next job.

As I wrestled into my tux, I reflected on how the upcoming evening would symbolize Class 100's passing from the known world into the unknown one. The thirty-three men and women who were graduating had all been born when the Cold War was at its coldest. They had entered their teens as the Vietnam War raged. They had grown up hearing and believing that they had to contain, and perhaps kill, the godless commies in Europe and Vietnam.

Then, with jolting suddenness, the American government had ordered a political all stop. As these children of the Cold War went through TPS in 1991, the American government was telling them something radically new: The Russians aren't coming after all. In fact, they are dead in the water. We Americans should help rescue them, not sink them. And the Vietnamese commies really aren't so bad either. They are helping us find our war dead. Perhaps it is time to normalize relations.

What the hell was happening here? What are warriors supposed to think? What war are they supposed to prepare for? What are they supposed to do with the rest of their lives? Will they have jobs in the American military in the year 2000? Will there even be an American military in the year 2000?

Such ironic twists, all in one year, I thought to myself as I headed toward the Cedar Point Officers' Club where the graduation was to be held. I doubted if any of the students in Class 100 had such heavy thoughts this winter night. Why should they?

The scene inside the club confirmed my expectations. Students, parents, relatives, and friends were standing close together, toasting one another with glasses of champagne in the circular front room overlooking the Patuxent River. The scrubbed faces of the young people shone; medals danced on dress-uniform jackets; mothers stood proudly by their sons; fathers acted as if they understood and belonged to this test-pilot fraternity. I thought I was seeing double when I spotted Chris "Spanky" Frasse. He and his brother, standing together, looked just alike.

I threaded my way through the celebrants to reach the side of the room where Margaret Acheson Hilditch, the wife of Royal Air Force Squadron Leader Laurence Hilditch, was playing the piano and Christine Scheidl Erdos, the wife of Canadian Air Force Captain Robert T. Erdos, the flute. When I reached them, I noticed a woman, sitting in a chair near the wall, who was weeping quietly but constantly.

"Want to meet the Hungarians?" Rob Erdos asked me with a smile. It turned out that the crying woman was his mother, Magda Weisz Erdos. The man standing at her side and looking off into the distance was his father, Joseph Erdos.

"Mrs. Erdos," I asked after we had been introduced. "Is there anything I can get for you?"

"No," she replied, smiling through her tears. "There are just too many emotions for me to handle tonight."

Pulling back the long left sleeve of her blouse, Mrs. Erdos held up her bared arm to show me the ugly tattoo the Nazis had put there when she was a terrified teenager sent to a hell she could not understand nor escape.

"I was in Auschwitz," she said.

Her story tumbled out as I, frozen with fascination, sat solemnly beside her in the midst of all the frivolity. Magda Weisz grew up in the tiny village of Satu Mare in southern Hungary and was herded into a Jewish ghetto with the rest of her family in 1942 when the Nazis occupied the country. The Nazis tried to keep food and medicine from reaching the ghetto in an attempt to starve to death the penned-up Jewish families.

One winter afternoon, when the Weisz and other Jewish families were sick and weak, the Nazis without warning pushed them into railroad boxcars bound for Auschwitz. The Nazis would not give fifteen-year-old Magda; her sixteen-year-old sister, Lily; or their parents, Rose and Arnold Weisz, time to dress warmly for the long trip. Magda remembers being clad in only a thin, cotton dress—no coat.

After a horrid trip in which many of the villagers died from exposure and suffocation, Magda said her family and other Jews found themselves standing before the cruelly smiling Josef Mengele at the Auschwitz railroad siding. Mengele, who became known as the "Angel of Death," looked over the Weisz family and ordered the older and stronger-looking Lily into the line of future slave laborers and the sickly Magda and her parents into the line leading to the gas chambers.

From some instinct Magda would never divine, her mother sensed what was happening and pushed her into the line with Lily when Mengele was not looking. The sisters were marched off. They never saw their parents or any other relatives again. "I've always felt guilty that I didn't pull my mother along with me," Magda told me that graduation night during a surge in her weeping. "I still have terrible nightmares."

Magda and Lily walked day after day from the prison camp to an aircraft factory three miles away. The sisters saw scores of fellow prisoners fall out of line and die at the side of the road. The Nazis just left them there and pushed the column of slave laborers onward. She remembers always being hungry and, in the winter, always cold.

In May 1945 Allied forces liberated the Auschwitz concentration camp. Magda said her health was broken. She had no relatives except Lily, and she wanted to forget the nightmare of her old life and start a new one. In 1949, feeling stronger from the treatments in refugee health centers, she sailed for Halifax, Nova Scotia. She journeyed on to Toronto where she met fellow Hungarian refugee, Joseph Erdos. Friendly police in the Budapest police station had hidden him from the Nazis all during the war in exchange for the youth's chores, which included repairing bicycles. Magda and Joseph Erdos married in 1950 in Toronto and on 26 February 1963 had a son they named Robert.

Mrs. Erdos brightened as she told me about how strong her boy's convictions were at an early age. "He quit the Boy Scouts because he thought they were too militaristic," she said with a smile.

"But he wanted to fly ever since he was eight," interjected Joseph Erdos.

Only at that moment did I fully understand why Rob Erdos had been so tolerant of my presence in Class 100. He obviously had absorbed the philosophy of live and let live. He might even have respected a free press, despite the obnoxiousness of many of us in it.

The enormity of Mrs. Erdos's experience hit me. Here she was, a survivor of Auschwitz and a thousand associated horrors, sitting in the middle of an American Navy base, waiting to see this handsome captain in the Canadian Air Force, her son, receive his diploma from the U.S. Naval Test Pilot School. I would have been weeping, too.

All through the graduation address by Sergei Sikorsky and the presentation of diplomas, I thought about the emotional distance Mrs. Erdos had traveled to reach Pax River. The human spirit can indeed be indomitable.

I felt warmed by another mother's pride—that of Yvonne Curbeam —as she heard the name of her son called to receive the award for writing the best developmental-testing thesis. It was really no surprise to either of us knowing Bob Curbeam and his work, but warming all the same.

Royal Air Force Squadron Leader Hilditch received the Outstanding Student award; Army Maj Kevin G. Scherrer won the "Sid Sherby Award" for the student most helpful to his classmates.

I knew Spike Long would do something different when he was called up to the head table to receive his diploma. He did not disappoint. He wore huge tiger paws on his feet and kicked them high in the air for all of us to see once his diploma was in hand.

To my surprise and delight, CAPT Robert Parkinson, acting commander of the Naval Air Test Center, called my name. I went to the podium to receive my TPS diploma from Director Bernsen. It read:

> Be it known to all persons that George Wilson is an honorary graduate of the U. S. Naval Test Pilot School having satisfactorily completed a portion of the academic and flight requirements of the Engineering Test Pilot course conducted during the period of 14 January 1991 to 13 December 1991 as a member of the 100th class.

Generous, classy, I thought as Bernsen handed me the certificate. One of my flight instructors, Eric Mitchell, yelled over his congratulations when I got back to my table. "I decided to quit while I was behind," I replied.

Dinner over, speeches concluded, diplomas and awards presented, the evening returned to its celebratory mood.

Christine and Rob Erdos were among those making the most of these last moments as members of Class 100. They danced as his parents looked on exultantly. Mrs. Erdos's eyes were dry now.

I repaired to the bar. It was crowded with happy people. CAPT and Mrs. Carl Anderson, parents of Scott, looked right at home in the club. It was no wonder. They had spent some of their happiest hours in Navy clubs all over the world during the retired captain's career.

Spike Long was getting as good as he gave from his ebullient mother, Alyce F. Hansen. Like the Andersons, she was at home with the Navy, especially at Pax River. Her first husband, Connie Olsen, had gone through TPS in 1960 with Class 27.

Lori Melling, looking lovely with her business-hours hairdo combed out into something feminine, was sitting at the edge of the dance floor with a Pax River aviator taller than her own five feet eleven inches. She would soon accept a marriage proposal from a hometown boy who had joined the Air Force. But none of us knew that on graduation night, least of all her Navy escort.

Bob "Bullet" Allen, in between squiring his lovely TWA pilot and wife, Cindy, and swapping flying stories with CAPT C. V. Campbell, his skipper when they flew F-14s together with the VF-41 Black Aces, apologized for the hostility some of the members of Class 100 had displayed to me and the book project.

"I hope you didn't let them drive you away," Bullet said with concern. He had been open, frank, and helpful from my first day at TPS.

Morty Linnell, the F-14 backseater who had bitched so vigorously about all the geeking at TPS, seemed to be enjoying himself this night. He looked like the model officer in his formal uniform. On the questionnaire I had asked all the members of Class 100 to fill out, Morty listed his "top 10 reasons for coming to TPS" and dared me to print them all. Here they are:

> (1) To hang out with Army guys. (2) To learn to hover. (3) To get good at killing roaches. (4) To help the handicapped—Air Force. (5) To become a Copymeister. (6) To meet blondes. (7) To totally fuck up my life. (8) To screw southern Maryland inbreds. (9) For the patch. (10) To end world hunger.

Before leaving the celebrants at the club, I asked Christine Erdos to look back at TPS to add a wife's perspective to the experience. She obliged, sending along this remembrance from the Erdos' new home in Cold Lake, Alberta, Canada, where Rob was evaluating Royal Canadian Air Force helicopters as only one of six test pilots in the whole air force:

> When Rob first came home in September, 1990, and told me he had a chance to be selected for Test Pilot School in Maryland, a thousand questions leapt through my mind.
> "Where? No, really—where? How long would we have to stay there? When would we have to leave? Where would we go next?"
> At the time Rob was talking about uprooting us we were living in Comox, on Vancouver Island, off the coast of British Columbia. I was in no hurry to leave the artistic community burgeoning in the rugged wilderness that I had grown to love. My interior design business had recently become successful. After two break-even years, I grossed almost $40,000 in ten months of work and had additional contracts for the coming year.
> We learned that TPS was a stepping stone for astronaut wanna-be's, an unheard of possibility for a Canadian, but the promise of flying over twenty different types of aircraft in the course of the year-long

program was an irresistible draw for my husband who had quite frankly explained to me the day we met that flying would always be his first love. (Later, in the "You'll Be Sorry" party the senior class at TPS threw for us, they explained that a TPUI would fly over twenty aircraft only if [he or she] flew over the TPS hangar.) Rob said TPS would provide an unparalleled chance to study flight and flying machines, and become more specialized in his chosen profession. How could I say no?

We arrived at National Airport in Alexandria, VA., on the 27th of December and got thoroughly lost amid the network of intersecting routes as we searched for the way south. Images of quaint, Southern style homes with low, wide verandas and creaking porch swings filled my mind as we drove along, passing signs saying Zekiah's Swamp, Dr. Mudd's House, Oakland, Hollywood and California.

Mile after mile of strip malls and fast food outlets lacked the quaintness I had imagined. Two days of extensive and fruitless searching with a kindly real estate couple reinforced the impression of poverty and neglect. I was devastated by the local tabloid's page after page of violent crimes, break-ins and robberies. Where were we?

By good fortune, we found a house in Wildewood nestled in the trees and only twenty minutes from TPS—an hour when the guards at the gate stopped everyone, everyday during the war.

Every class has its own personality. Some are known for partying; some are studious. Class 100 was competitive. Not only were the students classic over-achievers, but there seemed to be an ongoing contest among the wives as well.

Our first coffee was hosted by the course senior's wife, Ann Kirk, a tall stunningly beautiful woman, who was more than a little dismayed at finding herself the so-called leader of our little group by reason of her husband's rank and position. The position was little more than spokesperson for the group. To get us started, as she had been instructed to do, she encouraged us to get together and find common interests and activities to keep us sane.

The disparateness of our individual situations made it difficult to form a cohesive, supporting network. Many wives resented being uprooted from previous posts where the climate was warmer, the people friendlier and where they had friends or jobs. Some had children; others did not. Some wives were employed; most were not. On the whole, we were well educated in a number of fields.

Three of us were what the Navy classed as "aliens." Our respective countries—Canada, Italy and Great Britain—were paying for the course our husbands were taking. We three wives were in the country as guests and tourists. Elvira Comitini, Margaret Hilditch and myself enjoyed weekly excursions to museums and galleries in Washington, D.C., and to shopping malls. Our mutual friendship held us together all year.

We met George Wilson who was researching a book on the 100th class to go through TPS. Conversations with George, as we got to know him, allowed us a big picture perspective that just was not possible to view from being a student at TPS. He was one of the few who was actually interested in the countries of the aliens.

The initial pep rally effect of the TPS welcome wore off quickly as the reality became apparent. The hard work was there, of course, but so was a lack of serviceable aircraft. Complaints circulated among the students of disappointments and confusion. Various perks that were scheduled to maintain morale fizzled one by one. Visiting aircraft brought in for familiarization flights were reserved for staff instead. Course breaks, designed to give much needed time off, were occasionally loaded with assignments from theory classes while senior staff reminded everyone to relax!

As the pressures mounted for the husbands at the school, so did they among the wives. Several relationships showed the strain of the time-intensive workload imposed by the course.

Grumblings and complaints surfaced from some wives about unfairness in scheduling the three streams of the course: fixed, rotary and systems.

Ann was blamed for not making sure her husband controlled attendance at the weekly happy hour at the BOQ where some weary students gathered to slough off the week's pressures.

A complaint came from one woman that her husband was being compromised by having to do a group project with a female student. When I mentioned that Rob and I socialized with George Wilson, and enjoyed conversations with him, I was accused by that same wife of endangering her husband's career.

Competitiveness of an incredibly petty variety—vying for who suffered the most—infected our get-togethers. By the time summer break fell upon us the last week in June, dissension reigned.

Name calling at our evening coffees, and gossiping phone calls amongst our wives, reinforced my negative feelings towards that type of group. Once most people were aware that I was on speaking terms with the writer/journalist, no such calls were directed my way, fortunately. It was the first time that I had been involved in anything as a military wife, after having spent some time as an officer in our own military.

The coffee evenings continued, with reduced attendance, and despite the schism, the wives produced an artful musical production for the "You'll Be Sorry" party our class held for the junior class in August. But by the time graduation time rolled around, and it was time for our own farewell luncheon from the junior class, the intensity of the course climaxed. At this point, the final project of the DT 2 was just being tackled by our ragged, bleary-eyed husbands, and the final few weeks of the course loomed ahead.

The students of each class are responsible for the production and payment of their own graduation ceremonies, to which the staff are invited as guests. The dissenting wives felt that they had no say in the matter of the grad night details and attacked Ann at our final wives' luncheon for allowing her husband to deprive them of their rights. Our own farewell was colored by this event, which remained the final effect of our year's association as a group.

At graduation, problems and frustrations with school policy and administration were no longer in the forefront of our thoughts. As Rob and I packed to leave, we realized we had both profited from the association with TPS. Rob had developed an understanding of his craft that was hitherto unknown to him and had acquired an impressive addition to his curriculum vitae. I had found treasures like St. Mary's College with its high caliber teaching staff. I took sculpture and poetry there. Another treasure I discovered was the Lazy Moon second-hand bookshop on Solomons Island. And I had the opportunity to pursue my flute playing and other interests.

After shipping our belongings from Maryland back to the frozen wastelands of Alberta we were to call our next home, Rob and I embarked on a month long trip to Europe. In the wilds of the southern Spanish mountains I discovered that our graduation night celebrations had left their indelible mark: I was incapacitated by the nausea of morning sickness.

After reconnecting with the Erdos after graduation, I called other Class 100 graduates in the spring of 1992 to get updated on their activities.

I learned that Kevin Scherrer, Tom Fitzgerald, JD Hood, and Glen Knaust were among the graduates working at the Rotary Wing Test Directorate located behind the TPS hangars. Scherrer was coordinating the tests on the Army's MH-60K Blackhawk and MAC-47 helicopters. Fitz was flight-testing new software for the SH-60F helicopter, while JD was experimenting with a new cyclic stick for the SH-60. The stick was designed to break off when a pilot's head slammed down on it during a crash landing. The unbreakable stick had injured several aviators in crash landings when their seats had bent forward, allowing their faces to hit the cyclic. Knaust told me he was using what he had learned in TPS to test the H-2G Seasprite and LAMPS Mark I helicopters. He was also working on a master's degree in aviation science through correspondence courses with the University of Tennessee. Always achieving, these guys, I thought to myself.

I tracked down Roger Arnzen in his motel room in Yuma, Arizona, where he was staying while testing the Stinger missile on the Army's test range at Yuma flats. The good news, Arnzen told me over the telephone line, was that he had been promoted to major. The bad news was that he did not know how long he would be stuck out in Yuma away from his wife, Barbara Terry. She was in Dothan, Alabama, outside Fort Rucker, where the Arnzens were stationed.

Given what has happened to you since graduating from TPS, would you change anything about the school?

"Yeah," Arnzen replied. "I wish they had taught me how to test weapons. We learned a lot about how to evaluate aircraft performance and flying qualities, but not much about how to evaluate weapons."

The Army helicopter pilot reasoned that with a shrinking defense budget, all the military services would be putting new weapons on the aircraft they already had. They would not be building new helicopters and planes. Therefore, Arnzen said, TPS should reflect this new reality by teaching students more about testing weapons and systems, even if it meant cutting back on the aircraft-performance and flying-qualities portions of the curriculum.

Marc Mannella dramatized the systems-training gap. He said that he was testing laser and electro-optical systems slated to update the old Huey helicopter for the Marine Corps. To learn more about systems, he went back to TPS to audit some of the classes taught by George W. Masters, Jr., senior academic instructor in the wizardry of modern systems.

Conversations with other Class 100 graduates brought similar recommendations. The general conviction was that test pilots in the post–Cold War 1990s would be evaluating new gadgetry to go on existing helicopters and airplanes, not new aircraft themselves.

Bob Curbeam chortled when I told him what his fellow graduates had been saying. He said this had been his argument all through TPS. "We pretty much know nowadays if an airplane is going to have good performance and flying qualities," he said. "So TPS could cut down on those courses and broaden the systems curriculum."

Curbeam was at the Strike Aircraft Directorate, testing the systems designed to release bombs from a modified F-14 Tomcat fighter, nicknamed the Bombcat.

Morty Linnell, like Curbeam, was back in his rear seat of the F-14 and glad of it but was doing his testing at the other end of the country at the Naval Air Warfare Center Weapons Division at Point Mugu, California.

Otto Nielsen, F/A-18 pilot, said TPS had "really prepared me well" for his job at Strike. He was testing a new laser system designed to give more visual guidance to a pilot trying to land on a carrier deck.

Steve Eastburg sounded the happiest with his work. He had been named deputy program manager of the Unmanned Air Vehicle program at Pax, a field that was far more exciting to him than returning to his old job of testing the new software for the S-3B antisubmarine aircraft. While many of the other graduates thought they were stuck with testing new systems on old aircraft for two or three years, Eastburg felt he was out on the new frontier of aviation, and he loved this work. He did not know at graduation that the S-3 airplane he knew so well would soon break up in the sky with him inside.

Lori Melling had also lucked out. She had been assigned to test the only new plane at Pax River, the T-45 trainer. But the possibility of her realizing her dream of becoming an F/A-18 pilot in a carrier fighter squadron was fading. The Bush administration had named yet another commission to study if and when women should be allowed to take such combat jobs in the American military. By 1993 Melling most likely would be a lieutenant commander, probably too senior to be chosen to start the lengthy training needed to fill a fighter-pilot billet on a carrier. Not to worry, Melling told me. In 1993 she would apply to become an astronaut.

In the spring of 1992 civilian engineer Andy Maack was working to turn that old bus of an airplane, the EA-6B electronic jammer, into a fighting machine. I had frequently hitchhiked rides in the four-place EA-6B while deployed with the USS *Kennedy* in 1983–84. I never figured the bulky aircraft would be turned into a warrior. But Andy was working to make it so. He was helping arm the EA-6B with the

Harpoon missile and working on the problems that made the plane prone to spin and to have a nasty stall.

So what good had TPS done him, inasmuch as he was back to doing the same kind of work at Pax River that he had done before going through the school?

"I understand better what their qualitative flying is all about," Andy replied. "It's a different way of looking at goodness and badness" in an airplane.

Bullet Allen felt restless doing a teeth-gritting job at the Strike Directorate at Pax—reviewing the flight-test plans for the bomber version of the F-14 fighter from a safety standpoint.

Scott Anderson, who had flown one of the oldest planes in the world, the C-47, for his final exam, was testing the new doomsday E-6 strategic-communications aircraft. It would theoretically provide communications for national leaders during nuclear war.

Spike Long, who had applied to TPS to break the monotony of flying circles in the sky with the E-2C Hawkeye command-and-control plane, found his adventure after graduation. He was flight-testing the suitability of the C-2 aircraft, the Navy's truck for taking cargo and people from land to aircraft carriers, to fly spooky missions for the SEALs, the Navy's special-forces outfit.

"Leaving TPS was like the Air Force Academy," Fish Mason told me in our long coast-to-coast telephone conversation. "I said to myself, 'I never want to see this place again.' I didn't even buy a TPS T-shirt. Well, I just sent for a T-shirt. I'm starting to remember good things about the place. I learned from the Navy that there are other ways of doing things. We in the Air Force have paper wars when we want something we can't get. Navy guys just ask why can't you do this thing for me. They have made me a little more challenging."

I asked him if he had felt isolated as the only Air Force officer in Class 100. "No," he replied, "I felt very welcome." In the spring of 1992 Fish had not started in on heavy-duty test piloting but expected to do so early in 1993 at Edwards Air Force Base, California.

The most prevalent complaint among the graduates was the lack of flying time in their new jobs as working test pilots. "There are just not enough flying hours to go around," said one of the aviators. "I'm thinking of volunteering to go back to the fleet as soon as I can. There's just not enough for me to do here" at Pax River.

With the Cold War over, with the Navy building few new aircraft, and with the defense budget steadily shrinking in the 1990s, how was the Navy going to keep Class 100 and other TPS graduates productively employed? I put this question early in 1992 to VADM Richard M. Dunleavy, Assistant Chief of Naval Operations for Air Warfare.

"We're constantly upgrading the aircraft," which often "changes the flying characteristics of the aircraft," he replied. "Not substantially; just subtly. You need a guy with that kind of training to really evaluate from an operational perspective" how the modifications change the aircraft. "You'll always need a good cadre" of test pilots and engineers.

Given the cost of training test pilots and the growing complexity of the systems they have to master, would it not make sense to keep the graduates of TPS in their testing billets longer than the standard two years following graduation?

Dunleavy said he liked the present system because "I get the kid back in the fleet" after his or her eleven months at TPS and two years in a testing directorate. "And I get a group going through Test Pilot School who have just come from the fleet. Salt. I'm terrified of isolation. If you get away from something too long, you forget it. About the only things you don't forget are riding a bike and sex."

In the sixteen months I had been following Class 100, not one of their number had been hurt in an aircraft crash, despite hundreds of hours of flying the edge. I did not mention this. Nor did anyone else. Talking about such good luck is unacceptable within the aviation fraternity. It is worse than saying out loud that a pitcher has to put away only three more batters to have a no-hitter.

However, everyone in the aviation fraternity knows that accidents are bound to happen. "You're only as good as your next flight," TPS Director Bernsen often warned.

Pax River's command histories document how lucky and how unlucky aviators can be. Sometimes they make their own luck. Other times they crash and die without them or anyone else knowing why. Here are a few of both kinds of accidents as written in the emotionless prose of the command histories:

On 17 March 1947 while engaged in a test flight of an XBTC southwest of the station, Lt. L. T. O'Neill, attached to Flight Test, experienced an engine failure and had to make a crash landing in an open field near St. Mary's City. Due to faulty locking device, the hood slammed shut on landing, and Lt. O'Neill, his left arm broken, found himself imprisoned in a burning plane.

The quick actions of a sailor on leave, Frank Mkurawski, MOMM3, and his civilian brother-in-law, Michael Kohut, in kicking open the hood and dragging Lt. O'Neill free undoubtedly saved his life. . . .

Lt. E. R. Hanks [of the Service Test Division] crash landed an FH-1 type aircraft on 14 January 1948. Lt. Hanks was returning from a high altitude test flight when low ceilings caused him to shift to single engine flight to conserve fuel.

Immediately after shifting to port engine operation, RPM [revolutions per minute] began dropping on the engine.

After checking the position of the selector valve, Lt. Hanks attempted to restart the right engine.

Several attempted starts proved futile, and an emergency landing procedure was carried out.

The field selected, the largest in the immediate area, presented additional hazards in the form of two hills 75 feet high.

Lt. Hanks mushed the plane into the first hill and slid to the top where the aircraft again took to the air and landed against the second hill, skidded to the top and began a series of small circles, coming to rest atop the hill.

Lt. Hanks was uninjured although marks on his buffet helmet indicate that serious head injuries would have been sustained had he not been wearing a suitable protective type helmet.

Cause of the forced landing was found to be a broken torque tube.

[On 25 May 1948 Cdr. J. J. Hyland, assistant director of Flight Test, was flying an XF2H-1 Banshee in a fly-by over the base at 500 knots when he] struck a bird squarely with the vertical fin which was sheared off clean at the level of the horizontal stabilizer. The rudder was lost entirely.

Cdr. Hyland climbed his airplane to altitude, where, in testing its handling qualities for landing, control was lost.

Intensive efforts to recover from the ensuing spin were unsuccessful, and he was forced to bail out at low altitude.

Although badly bruised when he struck the airplane, he recovered and landed without further injury in Chesapeake Bay, from which he was quickly rescued. The plane itself was lost in deep water. Cdr. Hyland's skill and judgment were of the highest caliber.

[On 25 June 1948] Lt. Cdr. T. W. Ramsey [of Service Test] crashed in the Chesapeake Bay while flying an FJ-1 aircraft [and died]. His aircraft dived down from altitude in a steep dive and struck the water one mile east of the station. The cause of the accident is undetermined.

A Test Pilot School UH-1B helicopter crashed 22 January 1971 near Broomes Island, MD., killing the pilot, Army Maj. Milton R. Roberts. Navy Lt. Bruce L. Valley, co-pilot, was rescued by Mr. L. R. White who was in a fishing boat. Both students were members of Class 58.

[On 6 March 1971] a Test Pilot School glider (X-26A) crashed aboard the station while on a routine flight. Lt. Cdr. Thomas W. Hickman, attached to the Test and Evaluation Coordinator, was killed in the crash. Cdr. R. J. Sample, director of Test Pilot School, was instructor in the glider and escaped injury.

An F-8K aircraft crashed 22 June [1971] during a routine training flight, killing the pilot, Marine Capt. S. J. Erickson, a member of Class 59. . . .

Aviators love to talk about the narrow escapes or funny accidents in which nobody gets hurt. They hate to talk about fatal accidents. The official Navy term for accidents where pilots crash and burn and die is also minimizing. The term is "mishaps."

But test piloting is dangerous work. Men and women die doing it. If everyone knew for sure what a new or modified aircraft was going to do in the air, you would not need test pilots. Just let any old pilot take 'er up.

Aviators also like to believe that machines never make mistakes, only the men flying them. This is a comforting deception, probably a necessary one. Otherwise, aviators might always be listening and feeling for breakdowns, and they would be afraid of pushing their airplanes to their limits. Holding back makes for inaccurate tests and lost dogfights.

Aviators hate to hold funerals; they hate to dress for funerals; they hate to go to funerals. I asked Skipper John "Market" Burch of the

VF-31 fighter squadron on the *Kennedy* when I was aboard what his strongest emotion was when his squadron lost two F-14s in three days in November 1983, and two of his men died. "Anger," he replied. Burch's anger was directed at the mistakes the pilots had made in flying their machines into the Mediterranean, not against the pilots themselves as human beings and shipmates. Aviators can disconnect a wrong push of the stick from the person who did it. It is cursing your teammate for swinging at a bad pitch but still loving him or her as a person.

"We wouldn't have funerals if it weren't for the families," Burch told me. "We do it for their families."

I came to understand and appreciate this compartmentalization between flying and living and flying and dying. It was not being heartless and uncaring. It was being honest and professional. Dying was part of flying. But dying was not supposed to stop the flying. Push the wreckage overboard, whether physical or emotional. Launch the next flight. That is the code of Naval Air.

However, the families of the Class 100 pilots and other aviators get none of the highs of flying. They get the lows of wondering, worrying, and, if the chaplain comes to the door, coping with sudden loss. This is the part of the story not described by the minimizing term "mishaps" nor given a human face in the command histories. A book about test pilots, to be honest, should give the human dimension of mishaps, especially with regard to the families. Cathy Eastburg would be the first of the Class 100 wives to experience the special agony of mishaps.

Mishaps

LCDR Steve Eastburg of TPS Class 100 and LT Sean Brennan of Class 99, both thirty-three years old, were preparing to take the S-3 Viking antisubmarine aircraft up over the Chesapeake Bay to fly a "vomit comet" mission. The idea was to do the aerial equivalent of reverse engineering. First, they would fly the S-3 through a series of precise maneuvers while an elaborate network of instruments monitored and recorded what happened to the plane. Next, engineers and technicians on the ground would study the information gained and use it to fine tune the simulator. The payoff would be a more-realistic simulator for pilots trying to master the S-3 under various flying conditions, including adverse ones.

The flight plan had been studiously developed before Eastburg and Brennan were assigned to execute it. They discussed what they were going to do, step by step, with other aviators and engineers before climbing into the S-3 designated Waterbug 736. Nothing looked particularly risky. Engineers at the Chesapeake Test Range at Pax River would be watching for trouble the whole time they were airborne.

Eastburg, a naval flight officer, would be in the right seat of the S-3, working the radios, studying several of the key instruments in the cockpit, and taking down data. Brennan, the pilot, would be flying from the left seat and taking the plane from one point in the sky to another to complete a long list of maneuvers.

The rough part of their ride—the part that inspired the name "vomit comet"—would come when Brennan pitched the S-3 up and down, rolled it from wingtip to wingtip, and swerved it from left to right in a series of skids called yaws. The first set of these stomach-jolting maneuvers would be done at an altitude of 10,000 feet at a speed of 305 knots. The second set would be down in the rougher air at 5,000 feet at an even faster speed, 365 knots.

The S-3 is a twin-engine jet with thick wings and a tail so tall that it has to be folded over from the top to fit in carrier hangar bays. Pilots regard it as a solid aircraft that flies smoothly. Eastburg and Brennan felt safe in it. They had no fears the airplane would break during the maneuvers that lay ahead of them this sunny afternoon of 29 April 1992.

After a quick lunch and an extensive preflight briefing, the aviators took off without incident and steadied the S-3 at 10,000 feet in clear air over the Chesapeake a few miles east of Pax River. Brennan worked the throttles and trim until he had the plane straight and level at 305 knots. Eastburg watched the gauges and answered such standard radio calls from the ground as "Waterbug 736, you're five miles from the boundary." Sean Brennan pushed the stick forward and backward in ever-decreasing intervals. The plane pitched up and down like a bucking bronco. He swung the stick left and right in the same quickening sequence. The plane rolled like a canoe being smacked on its sides by higher and higher waves. Sean went into rudder sweeps to generate the yawing, pushing the left rudder pedal, then the right, then the left, then the right. The motion causes queasiness in the guts for even veteran pilots.

All that done, with lunch swirling uneasily in their stomachs, Steve and Sean descended to 5,000 feet. Sean put the plane through the same set of punishing maneuvers at 365 knots. The ride became rougher at this faster speed in the thicker air. He was in the middle of the same sickening rudder sweeps when Steve heard the noise of catastrophe coming from somewhere in the aft fuselage.

Craaack!

Steve had never heard such a chilling sound in an airplane. It sounded like a tree snapping in half during a windstorm. They knew the plane had broken, but not where. Telemetry would show that the top of the giant tail had broken off—meaning that Sean could no longer make the plane move left or right with the rudder pedals. At about the same instant one of the elevators needed to make the plane go up or down snapped off. The plane went out of control. It rolled, pitched, and yawed violently. Each new gravitational force pushed or pulled the aviators in a different direction as they sat in their seats, their shoulder and lap harness straining to hold them down. Steve glanced over at Sean and saw he was still fighting the airplane. His body was so twisted by the pile up of gravitational forces that Steve doubted he could reach the ejection handle even though it was now obvious that they had to leave the wrecked plane or die. Steve managed to get his hand around the ejection handle under his seat as Sean started the "Eject, eject, eject" command.

It was less than two seconds between when they were confronted with the emergency and when Steve pulled the ejection handle. They would learn later that waiting another split second would have killed them both. The rockets under the seats of Steve and Sean ignited, blasting them through the plastic roof of the cockpit just before it became a death trap. The S-3 skidded around until it was hurtling through the air tail first, and the right wing broke off at its root in the fuselage, pouring fuel into the onrushing air. The atomized fuel exploded into a fireball, probably from the engine exhaust.

Steve and Sean did not know what was happening to the airplane at the time. Only later would telemetry tell the story: so much force slapped into the sides of the rudder that it could not take it and snapped.

Everybody on the ground who was plugged into Pax River would learn what happened almost as soon as it happened. They knew the plane had broken up near Bloodsworth Island but not what had happened to the crew. Friends called friends and asked. I received one of those calls but would only learn much later what happened to Steve and Sean once they left their flying fireball.

For Steve there were sounds of Whap! Whomp! and then nothing but an eerie silence. For Sean, memory was mercifully blocked out by the ejection Steve initiated.

The whap was probably the noise of banging out of the cockpit at 3:18 P.M.; the whomp, the opening of the parachute; and the silence, the slow fall through the sky toward the surface of the bay.

"Am I still alive?" Steve asked himself as he experienced a sense of otherworldliness in his drift down through the sky. He saw plane wreckage floating through the sky with him. They were flotsam together. He struggled for a sense of reality. He looked all about him for assurance that he was still part of earthly existence.

Above his head, he saw the white blossom of his parachute canopy.

Below dangled his feet, shod in his flight boots.

Beside him, off in the distance, was a limp body hanging from another parachute.

And far below, on the surface of the water, were white boats.

He put it together.

They had ejected from the airplane. They were alive and of this life. He gave Sean a thumbs-up. No response.

His next thought was of his wife, Cathy. He told himself: "Boy! I've got to call her! She's going to be worried."

Navy survival training then asserted itself. IROK—the lifesaving acronym for his predicament. *I* for inflate your life preserver. He did by pulling the beads at his waist outward. *R* for raft. He pulled the handle alongside the metal cushion stuck to his rump, the seat pan, so that the raft and other survival gear could fall freely ahead of him, stopped by a tether whose yank inflated the raft. *O* for optional equipment. He checked those things: face visor, gloves, front snaps on his life preserver, oxygen mask. *K* for Koch fittings, which he must remember to unsnap when his boots touched the water, but not before. The Koch fittings kept him hooked into his parachute. Aviators worship their parachute while it is holding them in the air but curse it when they are in the water. Too many aviators have drowned when their still-attached parachutes filled up with water and pulled them under.

IROK completed, Steve was composed enough during this fall toward earth to fish the emergency radio out of the tight pocket of his survival vest and start talking over it.

"Mayday! Mayday! Mayday!" Steve radioed. "This is one of the S-3 crew members. Just had mishap one mile east of Bloodsworth Island. I'm OK. Condition of other aircrew unknown."

He then remembered that the automatic emergency radio beacon in the seat pan that was floating down with him would drown out his calls if he stayed on the 243.0-megahertz frequency. He dialed 282.8 megahertz and repeated his Mayday calls.

He wondered if any of the boats and ships he saw below had heard his calls or could see him in the sky above them. He need not have worried about being seen. Cpl. Thomas Shores and Officer Victor Kulyncz of Maryland's Department of Natural Resources had been horrified by the sight of a fireball in the sky above, followed by two parachutes dropping out of it. They had radioed the Maryland State Police in Salisbury to send out a rescue helicopter.

Steve saw the water rushing up at him. "Man, I don't want to get wet!" Executing his survival training, Steve unsnapped his Koch fittings connecting him to the parachute as soon as his boots hit the water. The parachute floated away from him, just as the survival instructors had promised. He climbed into the raft, which had hit the water ahead of him already inflated. He was safe if somebody saw him before he froze to death. He was shivering. Shock had drawn his blood into his vitals, leaving his body feeling cold.

Steve saw the Boston Whaler crewed by Shores and Kulyncz bearing down on him. While waiting for it, he looked around for Sean but could not see him for the two-foot waves. It was sunny and fairly warm, but the water—at 52.3 degrees Fahrenheit—had further chilled him. He discovered he was bleeding from gashes in his right knee, nose, and chin.

The men in the Whaler were like those crews in the landing barges that braved artillery fire from shore as they rushed toward Normandy beach during World War II. Shores and Kulyncz did not let the plane wreckage falling from the sky slow them up. They were soon alongside Steve's raft. With help from Shores and Kulyncz, he climbed over the port side of the boat and then asked the question that had moved to the top of his mind. "Did you see the other man?"

Shores and Kulyncz assured him they had. The Whaler raced off to rescue Sean and was soon beside him. Steve was not prepared for the sight.

Sean's face had been burned black when he shot through the plume from the rocket that had propelled Steve out of the cockpit just ahead of him. He had no eyebrows; the hair protruding from his helmet was frizzled; the front of his flight suit had been burned off, leaving much of him bare. He was lying unconscious in the water with his head tilted back. The life preserver, which had inflated automatically when it sensed salt water, was holding Sean up. But it was not snapped across the front. If Sean's head had fallen forward rather than backward after he was in the water, the pilot almost certainly would have drowned. Even if his head had stayed tilted back and no boat had reached him quickly, Sean—who had not been conscious to unsnap the Koch fittings attaching him to the parachute—would have been pulled under the water once the canopy filled up. Steve saw the parachute was already filling.

A Navy rescue H-3 helicopter arrived overhead and dropped a swimmer into the water. Steve signaled the helicopter to back away because its rotor wash was kicking up hurtful spray and complicating Sean's rescue. Steve saw that Sean, besides his ugly burns, had smashed his right shoulder as it caught on something in the cockpit while he was being rocketed out. Steve figured Sean would not survive being hauled out of the water on a helicopter hoist. The helicopter backed away from the Whaler. The helicopter swimmer was retrieved.

Steve, Shores, and Kulyncz unsnapped Sean from his parachute and life raft—no easy task while leaning out of the boat—and gingerly pulled the burned pilot out of the bay. They laid him as gently as they could on the flat spot in the bow of the Whaler.

Steve knelt over Sean, studied his breathing, and held him in his arms as the boat bounced eastward toward Deal Island. Steve was ready to administer CPR (cardiopulmonary resuscitation) if Sean's breathing staggered.

"You're going to be OK; you're going to be OK," Steve kept telling Sean. "We'll be there in just a few minutes."

Steve thought he heard Sean mumble, "Steve, are you OK?" in a brief break out of his unconscious state.

The two-foot waves were bouncing the speeding Whaler up and down. Steve worried what this was doing to Sean's smashed-up shoulder. He asked Shores and Kulyncz to slow the Whaler. They did. Steve asked for their coats to pile on the shivering Sean. They quickly handed them over. It took a seemingly endless eight minutes to reach Deal Island.

Steve saw islanders crowded on the Deal pier to gawk at the arriving aviators. He protested, "Vultures!" to himself. He would have been less angry if he had known an ambulance, a Maryland State Police Dauphine rescue helicopter, a Coast Guard helicopter, and the Navy H-3 chopper from Pax River were all on the ground behind the crowd.

Maryland Trooper First Class James C. "J. C." Collins, Jr., a flight paramedic with ten years' experience, pushed his way to the dock. He saw old friends from the Princess Anne Volunteer Fire Company who had rushed to Deal by ambulance. Lorenzo Cropper, ambulance captain; Jim Foote, duty medic; and Steve Willin, a cardio-rescue technician, deferred to J. C. and asked him what he needed.

"I need a KED Board and a stiff collar." A KED board has flexible sides so that it can be slid under an unconscious person easily but is stiff along its centerline in case the patient's back is broken. Collins also asked for and got from the ambulance crew the devices he might need to slide down Sean's throat to keep his breathing passages open. The medic, who had tended to many burn victims, was most worried that the pilot's singed breathing passages would swell to the point they would close. This would suffocate him. Sean was foaming at the corners of his mouth, a sign of "nose singing." He had evidently burned his breathing passages when inhaling the ejection-rocket fumes. Collins also worried about Sean's severe burns, which had robbed him of vital insulation, and which may already have been infected with germs from the bay water. Collins knew infection often killed burn victims too.

With help from several others, Collins got Sean out of the Whaler and onto the KED Board. Once they had Sean on the dock, they laid him in the Maryland police helicopter's stretcher. Collins inserted an intravenous tube into Sean's left arm and prepared to carry him to his elaborately equipped helicopter—virtually a flying intensive-care unit.

A Navy crewman from the Pax River helicopter said he was under orders to get Sean Brennan into the Navy helicopter. "Are you geared up for this?" Collins asked dubiously. Seeing the squeeze the sailor was in, Collins said he would tell the officer in the helicopter that the Maryland State Police should care for the critically injured pilot, not the Navy.

Collins, a former marine, ran up to the Navy chopper, saw that it had little if any of the survival equipment Sean would need to stay alive, and told RADM Barton D. Strong, the top officer at Pax River: "Captain, my name is Trooper Collins. I have your pilot. He's got first-, second-, and third-degree burns over 50 percent of his body. He's got to go to the East Coast Regional Burn Center. This man has got to get there."

Strong agreed.

Collins took the Navy crewman along with him in the police helicopter with Sean. The Dauphine's rotors had been turning the whole half hour they had been on the ground.

"Where we going, Buddy?" Joe McNair, the civilian pilot of the police helicopter, asked Collins.

"Straight to FSK," shorthand for the Francis Scott Key Medical Center in Baltimore. The Baltimore Regional Burn Center is part of FSK.

"No problem," replied McNair as he swung off the road where he had landed and headed north for Baltimore.

All this while, Steve Eastburg was watching over Sean Brennan like a soldier whose foxhole companion had been shot. Steve's bleeding had stopped to the point that the ambulance crew did not right away realize he was the second man in the plane and might be hurt. Ambulance Captain Cropper, fearing Steve might be more seriously injured than he looked, insisted he lie down on a stretcher board to keep his head immobilized. Cropper and his crew lifted Steve into the ambulance, intending to take him to Peninsula Regional Medical Center in Salisbury. Steve strenuously argued that it made more sense for him to fly in the Navy rescue helicopter to the hospital at Pax River, that he was not hurt. Duty medic Foote radioed headquarters for instructions and was warned that he should not turn Steve over to a lesser-skilled medic. The ambulance crew and Steve reached a compromise under which Willin of the Princess Anne fire company would fly with Steve in the Navy chopper back to Patuxent.

"You know," Willin confided to Steve after the Navy helicopter had lifted off Deal Island at 4 P.M. and began thwack-thwacking its way across the bay, "this is only the second time I've flown."

"You ought to be the one on this board," Steve quipped.

The first thing about his rescue that Sean remembered after ejecting from the S-3 "was the drone of a helicopter. But I didn't know I was flying in it. I must have asked where I was because I heard the medic say, 'You've been in an aircraft accident.'

"I kept coming in and out of consciousness. I realized I had to have had a plane crash. I kept asking these questions: 'Where's Steve? Is he all right? What happened to the plane? Did I kill anybody? Did it land on a house?'

"I remember the medic answering: 'He's OK. You didn't kill anybody. The plane landed in the water.'"

Collins said of Sean's conversation on their way from Deal Island to Baltimore in the police helicopter: "It was his training talking. When he got to asking about what happened to the airplane, I told him, 'Pal, don't worry about it. Your airplane is gone. They make them every fucking day.'

"I asked him how he was feeling." Collins recalled. "He said, 'I feel I've got a case of really bad sunburn all over.'"

Collins monitored Sean's blood pressure with mounting concern. The pilot's heart was having a hard time pushing blood through the vessels constricted by shock. The systolic blood-pressure reading had risen to 172, up from the normal 120. Collins gave Sean 5 grams of morphine to relax him. The systolic pressure plunged to 90. The medic put him on a respirator.

"Hey!" Collins yelled at Sean to keep him from passing out. "Don't you do that to me again." The systolic pressure rose and steadied at the desired 120.

The medic also worried about the pilot's heavy loss of fluids. He tossed tubing to the Navy crewman and asked him to prepare another intravenous tube. "Hey, Doc!" the crewman replied. "I'm not a medical person." Collins removed Sean's boot to find an unburned place to insert the tube. He found a full vein on the pilot's left ankle and started feeding in more fluids there.

The police helicopter landed on the pad beside the hospital. A six-person crew, alerted by radio, was waiting and whisked Sean inside. A former Army nurse, with a reputation for talking tough, saw that Sean was a Navy flier and asked, "What's he doing here? Isn't this guy military? He should go to Bethesda."

Collins, with little attempt to control his anger, lashed out: "Ma'am! You take a person who needs definitive care to a definitive facility!"

"Calm down," the nurse relented. "Go wash your hands."

Dr. William P. Fabbri, who was overseeing the team, winked approvingly at Collins and raced on with the job of saving Sean Brennan.

With Eastburg safely inside the hospital at Pax River and Brennan at Francis Scott Key in Baltimore, Navy leaders turned their attention to the delicate obligation of informing the wives of the aviators about the "mishap."

The Navy way is to send at least one officer, often with the chaplain, to the door of the aviator's home and inform the wife face to face. Aviators' wives dread an unexpected ring of the doorbell and feel stricken when they see an officer standing at their door.

Cathy Eastburg, Steve's wife, is a nurse. They met in the College Avenue Baptist Church in San Diego in 1985 and married in 1987. This late afternoon of 29 April 1992 she was chatting happily with Gayle and Gregory Crabtree, old Navy friends from California, in the living room when her doorbell rang. Gregory Crabtree answered the door while Cathy rose and held her two-and-a-half-year-old son, Greg, in her arms. CDR Julian Hart, a friend from Force Warfare, was standing in the kitchen just beyond the back door by the time she reached him.

"I had a big smile on my face," Cathy recalled. "I figured Steve had asked Julian over for dinner. But then I saw how solemn he looked."

"We lost an airplane," Hart began. "Steve's OK."

Images of Steve's broken body flooded Cathy's mind.

"Do you want to make a phone call?" Hart asked gently. Chief Bob Croker, also from Force, who had been waiting outside, joined Hart in the kitchen.

Cathy had seen all kinds of horrors as a nurse. But this was different. This was her husband, Greg's father. Her knees began to buckle. She told herself that if this was a minor thing there would not be two Navy men come to the house. Why not just a phone call from the hospital? Her fears escalated.

"You know," resumed Hart, "we just wanted to give you a ride to the hospital. Do you want to call somebody?"

Cathy called her mother and told her what little she knew. That Steve's airplane had crashed; that he had ejected; that he was in the hospital; that she was going to see him; that the Crabtrees were visiting and would look after Greg.

During the drive to the hospital Hart and Croker were politely evasive about what had happened to Steve's airplane. She had been a Navy wife long enough to know the system: Don't tell the family anything until we're sure. But it was still maddening.

An old hand at end-running hospital bureaucracies, Nurse Cathy Eastburg strode right into the emergency room, found Steve's bed, and leaned over him.

"Hi, Babe!" he greeted. "I'm doing just fine."

Cathy mechanically responded with something bland while her eyes and mind concentrated on their medical survey of Steve's body. "I knew it was a miracle he was alive." The gashes that Drs. Timothy Hannon and Gregory Johnson were sewing up while she stood beside Steve's bed did not bother her. It was the likelihood that he had broken his spine, or neck, or arms, or legs or suffered internal injuries. None of this had occurred from what she could see and what the doctors told her. "I was very thankful to God that He had spared Steve."

The official part of the Navy family started coming into the hospital to show Steve they cared: Rear Admiral Strong; CAPT Robert Parkinson, director of the flight test center; and CAPT Jim Keen, director of the Force Warfare Aircraft Test Directorate.

At 8:30 P.M., after what felt like hundreds of X rays had confirmed Steve was still whole all the way through, the doctors released him from the hospital. A Navy driver on duty drove Steve and Cathy to their home in a blue Navy van. Steve put his arm around Cathy and tried to sort out the events of his traumatic day. He tasted the salt of the bay and wondered how so much could have happened to him in so little time.

At 9:30 that same night, after taking a hot shower that finally warmed him, Steve Eastburg was sitting on the floor of Greg's upstairs bedroom, reading him stories from Dr. Seuss and Sesame Street.

"It was incomprehensible to me, surrealistic," Steve said later. "Here I was, five hours after almost losing my life, reading stories to my son. I had gone from something incredibly violent to a world of peacefulness with my little son and his innocent mind. I thank God every morning for sparing me."

Sandi Brennan, Sean's wife, was even more surprised than Kathy when she opened the door of her home in California, Maryland, and found an unexpected visitor, LT Dean Sawyer of Force, standing outside. Sandi had just come home from her job as an executive assistant to a defense contractor in Lexington Park and had relieved the sitter taking care of Megan, the Brennans' eighteen-month-old daughter. She did not know Sean was flying that day and was totally unprepared for the conversation that followed.

"Sandi," said Dean Sawyer, "we lost an airplane."

"Oh my God! Who was it?"

"It was Sean's airplane."

Sandi felt sick. Her mind spun. But she still managed to keep standing at the door, asking more questions.

"He's burned, and he's in Baltimore. And that's all I know. We've got a ride for you to Baltimore. Melinda and I are going to take Megan home with us."

Sandi packed a bag, made a few telephone calls, grabbed a picture of Megan to show Sean, and was inside the waiting room outside the Francis Scott Key emergency room by 8 P.M.

Sandi recollected that Sean had said his biggest fear was being burned in an aircraft accident. "I didn't know what to expect. I had never seen anybody burned."

She waited and waited. Dr. Fabbri was still working on Sean and came out of the emergency room long enough to describe the flier's condition. "He was just wonderful," Sandi said of Fabbri. "He didn't paint a rosy picture, but I could tell he was doing everything he could for Sean."

Captain Parkinson and Captain Keen, having already visited Steve Eastburg, joined Sandi and Julian Hart at Francis Scott Key. The three waited into the night. At 10:30 P.M. the emergency-room door opened, and a stretcher with a man bandaged until he looked like a mummy with tubes plugged in whipped by on a gurney.

"That wasn't Sean, was it?" she asked the captains. "Oh my God, that couldn't be him. I don't believe it."

It was. A nurse came to her shortly afterward and asked if she would like to see him before his eyes swelled shut. She brought Megan's picture to show him. She was shocked, sickened to the point of feeling faint when she looked at Sean.

"It blew me away. I was so choked up, I could say only a few words. I had to run out of the room."

The thirty-three-year-old aviator who had looked so strong when she last saw him had lost his eyebrows; tubes and wires crisscrossed his body; an oxygen mask was clamped over his nose; what skin that showed was greased over and black; his head looked like "a giant Brillo pad" of singed hair; there was a big gash above his right eye; he was shaking and trying to talk.

Parkinson and Keen stayed in the room. Sean kept asking them how Steve was. Parkinson put Megan's picture on the bulletin board in front of Steve's bed and said, "We want you to be able to sit up and look at her."

"That's my goal," Sean replied weakly.

Dr. Andrew Munster, head of the hospital's burn center, kept Sandi apprised of Sean's progress. His first week was extremely painful, consisting mainly of taking baths during which his burned skin was scraped off so that new skin could grow and infection could be deterred.

Sandi stayed in a motel near the hospital the first night. After that, she drove from her home to the hospital and back every day for five days. The second week she stayed in Baltimore. Navy friends mobilized. Sue Ehlers, wife of LT Mark Ehlers, called to say she was flying in from California to help out.

"You don't have to do that," Sandi said over the phone, "That's too much money."

"I know you'd be there for us. I've already got my reservations."

After two weeks at Francis Scott Key, during which his burns healed miraculously without grafting, he went to the Naval Medical Center in Bethesda, Maryland, for treatment of his shoulder and other bodily injuries. Then it was home and daily therapy at the Pax River hospital to get in shape to go back to testing airplanes.

I asked both wives after their husbands had healed whether they wished their husbands would give up test piloting. Their answers typified those of fliers' wives the world over.

"There's nothing you can do to prevent anything like this," Cathy Eastburg said. "It's part of life. Something like this could happen on the road.

"The best response is to see what you can learn from it. Life is extremely fragile no matter how invincible you think you are. Test pilots think they're invincible. They're not. There are a lot of things we can't control. We have to be trusting in Christ for our salvation.

"When I first heard about the accident, I asked myself, 'Am I going to be a widow at thirty-one?' I had faith God would provide. Greg understood. He said, 'Daddy had a boo boo.'

"What happened definitely makes me appreciate what's important. The little things don't bother me anymore. Steve is doing what he wants to do. I want him to be happy in what he's doing. This has made us appreciate each other more."

Sandi Brennan, who met Sean while she was in high school and he was living summers in her hometown of Harvey, North Dakota, while he worked on the railroad, said she and other test pilots' wives realize the work can be dangerous.

"At least he's doing what he wants to do. I worry more about him driving along Route 235. I look at this accident as a fluke. I can't worry about him going back to flying or I'll drive myself crazy. When there's an accident, I feel for that person, but you cannot help thinking, 'Thank God it wasn't my husband.'"

After the accident there was a lot of second guessing within the test-pilot community at Pax River. Questions included: Why had not the engineers at Force Warfare discovered the dangers inherent in such high-speed rudder sweeps before they wrote the flight plan for Eastburg and Brennan to carry out? Why did not the engineers and technicians watching the telemetry while the flight was in progress see the problems before disaster struck and call off the tests? Eastburg and Brennan did not join in on this second guessing, which comes in the wake of such accidents. I found myself wondering whether the accident showed the need for a better computerized data base of what had happened to the S-3 before on similar tests.

Lori Ann Peplinski Davis, thirty, a lovely woman with the high cheek bones of a fashion model, was pregnant on 15 August 1990 with her first child. She was worrying about when the labor pains would start, not about the routine flight her husband, LT William C. "Catfish" Davis, thirty-three, and CAPT Steven A. "Axle" Hazelrigg, forty-two, chief test pilot of the Strike Directorate, were flying that morning in an old A-6 bomber.

Hazelrigg was in the left seat, flying the bomber away from Pax River and south toward the Northern Neck of Virginia. A divorced and loving father of two daughters, Hazelrigg was widely admired within the Strike Directorate as a leader and an aviator. He was fun loving off duty—had even dared to bring his ski boat with him when he reported to Pensacola as a flight student—and on duty led by example rather than intimidation.

Catfish Davis was sitting on the right side, in the bombardier-navigator's seat. He was an old hand in the A-6. He had bombed Lebanon from one A-6 in 1983 and ejected from another in 1984, miraculously landing safely in the predawn dark on the flight deck of the USS *John F. Kennedy*. Catfish was a dedicated aviator who had been selected to work on the hush-hush A-12 stealth-bomber program at Pax but never forgot that he had a loving wife at home.

Axle and Catfish were up in the sky in the A-6 because they were testing a new bomb for the plane. The two graduates of TPS were resuming tests of the new dummy bomb they had taken aloft before. They were going along at 500 knots at 5,000 feet, setting up to test how the weapon would withstand the bomber's pitching maneuvers.

Steve Hazelrigg went into the up-and-down, nose-to-tail maneuver called a "sinusoidal stick pump" test to see if the bomb rode all right—if it stayed attached in stressful maneuvers. Suddenly, something broke between the control stick and the horizontal stabilizer on the tail. It could have been a section of rod, a crank—any one of scores of pieces in the control line leading from the stick to the elevator. The leading edge of the horizontal stabilizer slanted upward into the oncoming air, forcing the tail to ride up over a hill of air. This pushed the tail of the bomber up and its nose down. Hazelrigg pulled back on the stick to bring the plane back up to level flight. Nothing happened. The plane stayed in its straight-down dive. Catfish felt the bomber go into a sickening left roll during the dive.

The feeling was like having an elevator break away from its overhead cable and plunge toward the basement at 500 miles per hour. You would find yourself up against the ceiling of the elevator. The lap and shoulder harnesses held Axle and Catfish in their seats. But they were being pushed upward toward the canopy at a force 6.8 times their own weight.

"Pull!" Catfish told Axle, not realizing the pilot had already tried. The horizontal stabilizer was stuck with its full leading edge up. The plane was out of control. The excruciating gravitational force made it difficult for either flier to reach the ejection handles under his seat or behind his head. Somehow Catfish reached down and got his hand around the lower handle. The A-6 was diving at 550 knots. The plane was only 3,500 feet above the ground. Catfish was being pushed up against the canopy roof with more negative Gs than the ejection system was designed to overcome. But it worked. Catfish was shot through the roof one tenth of a second before negative Gs would have incapacitated him. Steve Hazelrigg either did not want to eject, perhaps figuring he could regain control of the bomber, or was so stricken by the negative Gs that he could not reach either of his ejection handles. The A-6 is not rigged so that Catfish could have ejected Axle along with himself— a flaw that infuriates those who fly the bomber. Axle rode the plane down to its head-first crash into the earth. Pilot and plane disintegrated in a farm field near Burgess, Virginia.

Catfish probably never heard the "gotcha" snap of his parachute's opening. He was grievously injured and would never remember exactly what happened immediately before and after his ejection, even under hypnosis. His parachute snagged a treetop, apparently providing a braked rather than sudden stop. An unimpeded smash into the earth probably would have killed him because of his many injuries. He hung suspended in his chute with just the balls of his feet touching the ground. He was conscious but too weakened by his many injuries to extricate himself from his harness.

Hazelrigg and Davis had been in constant electronic contact with engineers at Pax River. The engineers were studying the telemetry coming from the bomber as it went through its maneuvers. Suddenly, the telemetry revealed an unprogrammed dive. Then electronic contact was broken. The engineers sounded the alarm. Salty Dog 505 had gone off the radar scope, and one Emergency Locator Transmitter (ELT) had begun beeping.

LCDR Bill Warlick, an old friend of Catfish's from TPS Class 92 and now a test pilot at the Force Directorate, was aloft in a P-3 antisubmarine plane when he heard the call. Warlick pushed the throttles all the way forward and headed south toward the emergency beacon. Twenty-five miles later he saw the dreaded site, a smoking hole made by the main part of a crashing aircraft. Airplane wreckage was scattered across a field, in backyards, and in the road of the farming community. "It became very difficult for me to concentrate and keep the 100,000-pound airplane I am piloting out of the trees," Warlick recalled.

LCDR David Tibbs and Marine Maj Paul Croisetiere, pilot and copilot of the rescue helicopter dispatched from Pax River, landed in a field near where telemetry and the emergency beacon placed the bomber. Navy petty officers Billy Guzman and Walt Maffei jumped out of the helicopter and began frantically searching the wreckage and woods for the aviator whose beacon was working. Warlick continued to circle over the crash site in the P-3. One of the searchers radioed that he had found human remains, confirming at least one "Class Alpha," meaning one person dead.

"The lump in my throat at hearing this made it difficult to talk," Warlick said. "I selfishly and unashamedly prayed for it not to be Catfish."

A second search-and-rescue helicopter arrived and concentrated on pinpointing the beacon. Its crew spotted a parachute hanging in a tree. The helo landed in a field 75 yards away. One of its crewmen raced to the chute and discovered Catfish. He radioed that it was Phil Davis, then corrected himself—Bill Davis.

"I say a quiet thanks, and, though not in keeping with the test-pilot image," recalled Warlick, "wipe away a few tears of relief. I tell the air-crewman to pass on that 'Billy Bob says you better make it, Catfish!' The aircrewman says he passed the message and got a forced smile from Bill. We pass all the information we have to the Strike Directorate duty office. They had, understandably, been hounding us for updates the entire time we were on the scene. At one point we essentially told them to knock off all transmissions because they were hampering our search-and-rescue efforts."

A Virginia State Police helicopter, equipped with the kind of life-saving gear that saved Sean Brennan, landed in the field. Catfish was put inside that better-equipped helicopter and taken to the Medical College of Virginia Hospital in Richmond.

"I do remember saying, 'Pull!' and reaching like hell for the lower ejection handle," Catfish said afterward. "I don't remember pulling the handle. I ejected at approximately 500 knots, 3,500 feet, 180 degrees inverted, and minus 4 Gs." The bomber had nosed all the way over until it was upside down. "The ejection was extremely violent. My helmet and oxygen mask were sucked off my head and were later found with my mask still attached on both sides. I broke my lower left tibia, my right hand and shoulder blade; shattered my left humerus; cut my right ear; and had two symmetrical black eyes—probably from the massive negative Gs. I now have an Ace hardware store, three plates and about two dozen screws, in my left arm."

Navy leaders are schooled against raising false hopes or false alarms when it comes to such "mishaps." But in this case Lori Davis found herself on the painful middle ground. Her niece, Arica Gough, answered the doorbell of the Davis family quarters on the base. Lori Davis was resting in the bedroom. The doctors had said she might give birth to their second child this day. Arica told her that the three men at the door wanted to talk to her. Lori's internal alarm went off as soon as she saw a Navy chaplain standing with two of her husband's friends from the Strike Directorate, LT Ken Smolana and LT Dee Mewbourne.

"We have something to tell you," the chaplain began, "and we want you to hear it from us before you hear it from anybody else." He told her that her husband's plane had crashed and that only one man had ejected from it. The visitors said they did not know whether it was her husband or the pilot who had ejected. They said they would wait in the apartment with her until they received the call informing them of who had survived, if anybody.

"Oh, no!" Lori shrieked, covering her face with her hands. The stricken wife went into the bedroom with her nineteen-month-old daughter, Spencer; held her tight; and cried. No waiting wife wants to wish that it be the other man, not her husband, who dies. But no human is strong enough to resist praying that her husband will be the one spared if somebody in the cockpit has to die and somebody has to live.

The longest twenty minutes of her life passed before the phone rang. The Navy official at the other end told the visitors that Lori's husband was the one who had survived.

Once the word was out around Pax River that Catfish was alive but seriously hurt, the strongest sorority and fraternity in the world mobilized. Navy wives filled up Lori's home with help and love. They knew the chaplain could knock on their doors next. And then they would need this kind of support. Knowing they would get it made Navy life special to these women whose husbands have airplanes for mistresses.

The wives organized a schedule of baby-sitting and meal-cooking and house-tending that any executive would envy. Little Spencer was all taken care of; Lori's suitcase was packed; she was in the backseat of a car with Ken and Becky Smolana on her way to Richmond to see Bill— a name she liked better than Catfish.

In Richmond, the Davises were further blessed. Old college friends, Jeff and Julie Marshall, lived there. Better still, Jeff Marshall was a cardiologist at the hospital where Catfish was lying in a drugged state. Catfish must have put the hospital and Marshall together because he kept telling hospital attendants, "Call Jeff!" Jeff heard about this agitated aviator, learned it was his old friend, and introduced himself to Lori shortly after she arrived. Jeff and Julie Marshall insisted that she stay with them until it came time to go to the hospital to have her baby, which the doctors had predicted would arrive the day of Bill's accident.

Jeff Marshall, son of a former A-6 pilot, made sure the hospital was ready to care for Lori as soon as she went into labor. She did so two days after arriving in Richmond, giving birth at 9:50 P.M. on 17 August 1990 to 7-pound, 10-ounce William Taylor Davis. Jeff Marshall went into Catfish's room that night and said he had a job for him to perform. Catfish was soon on a gurney, rolling toward the maternity ward. A nurse put a pair of scissors in his left hand. Only his thumb and forefinger peeped out from his bandages. The nurse helped him put them through the scissors and told him to squeeze—to cut the umbilical cord linking Lori to his son.

It was twenty-three days before Catfish was strong enough to sit in a wheelchair. Even so, he told everybody he was going back to flying. Nobody dared say that after two ejections it was time to listen to what somebody up there was telling him and stay on the ground.

Back at their second-floor apartment at Pax River, some strong man always appeared as if by magic to carry him up and downstairs. CAPT Raymond A. Dudderar, skipper of the Strike Directorate, was pulling strings to help the Davises. Housing bureaucrats felt his blowtorch and agreed to give the Davises the Warlicks' first-floor apartment when they moved. The Warlicks vacated ten days early to help matters.

With the way cleared for the Davises' move to the Warlicks' first-floor apartment a quarter mile away, the Dudderar Moving and Storage Company swung into action, with seemingly everybody at Strike turning out to carry everything from couches to teaspoons. The Davises found themselves completely moved in two hours. They never asked for the help. They did not have to.

"George," Catfish, my old friend from the *Kennedy* wrote me after he had healed, "even though we are all flying different aircraft and going in a thousand different directions at Pax, we can bind into a pretty tight, supportive group. Before our accident, I didn't think that was possible. We got so much support from the whole community all around Pax River. It seemed everywhere I went on base and almost everywhere out in town, people knew who I was and did everything they could to assist us."

Every fatal crash releases geysers of personal emotion—anger, depression, fear, grief. A fatal crash often releases geysers of official emotion as well—including blind retribution. The crash of CDR Keith Crawford unleashed such blind retribution that was so painful it drove an outstanding naval officer to commit suicide.

Everybody thought test pilot Keith Crawford had a great idea when he laid it out in the fall of 1986. It would definitely save millions of dollars and might also save the lives of Navy pilots on the Blue Angels aerobatics team.

Crawford, thirty-nine, was one of the best and brightest in the Navy's post-Vietnam generation: brilliant, creative, dedicated. A graduate of Ohio State with bachelor's and master's degrees in aerospace engineering, Crawford breezed through Test Pilot School with Class 73 in 1978, winning both the Outstanding Student Award and the award for writing the best evaluation reports.

After working in the Systems Directorate at Pax River and serving as an instructor with the Empire Test Pilot School in Britain, Crawford assumed a number of management posts at the Strike Directorate. A former A-5 Vigilante pilot, he became project manager for the T-45 trainer and the F/A-18 fighter and attack plane. Steven A. Kapinos, a civilian aeronautical engineer at Strike, was Crawford's deputy from 1983 onward and became his close friend. Kapinos provided this word portrait of Keith Crawford:

"All fighter and attack pilots consider themselves the best, and some of them have egos to go with it. Although Keith was a superstar, he wasn't like that. You'd never guess he was a naval aviator because he was really down to earth. He was so extremely sharp he seldom needed the help of the people around him, but he always made everybody feel part of the team. He was better at this than anyone I ever worked with. He was not an ass-kicking kind of guy. He was leadership by example.

"Keith never forgot anything. We would be at some meeting and I would be digging through my notes for some detail and Keith would always know it. When he gave briefs, he would look at the slides five minutes beforehand and give the whole brief without ever looking at them again.

"But by no means was he a workaholic. Nothing was a rush. I sometimes thought he missed his calling because he could write so well. He could blow some smoke. If I said we needed a point paper, he would write it the first time with no spelling errors, no punctuation errors, ideas well organized. He would pull the paper off the printer, and I knew we would never have to change it.

"He was sort of like a Brit, with this dry sense of humor. He liked the Brits, and they liked Keith. I could see the sparkle in his eyes when the Brits came up with something simple, cheap, and effective. I thought he was more comfortable with the Brits than with Americans.

"Socially, he was a pretty quiet guy. He would attend office functions and give the farewell speeches, but he and his wife, Mary, preferred quiet time [at home with their two sons, Matthew and Michael]. They were very close with their kids." His wife recalled that when Keith made commander in 1986, he did not bother to get his picture taken in his commander's hat.

"I remember once when we were traveling through Britain, Mary gave Keith a book on power dressing. He was never into that. He didn't wear expensive suits. He drove a Volkswagen Rabbit diesel and liked to talk about all the mileage it got.

"On trips we'd go out to dinner and then come back to the hotel. We might have a drink, and then Keith would go up to the room to read or watch television. He was the cleanest guy I've ever seen. . . ."

Perhaps it was the British influence that prompted Crawford to look for a simple solution to the problem the Blue Angels were having with the F/A-18. When flying the A-4 and earlier exhibition aircraft, Blue Angel pilots purposely kept the plane out of trim so that there would always be tension on the stick. They did not want any delay in response when they were flying wing to wing and duplicating one another's moves every inch of the way. They wanted the stick engaged with the flight controls at all times, the same as having the steering wheel of your car already pulling on the wheels when you start your turn. But the F/A-18 was so smart that its computers would not allow the airplane to be set in an out-of-trim mode.

McDonnell Douglas wanted "millions of dollars" to change the software to give the F/A-18 the constant stick pressure the Blue Angels sought, Kapinos recalled. Crawford suggested a simple solution: attach one end of a sturdy spring to the airplane's stick and the other end to something solid in the cockpit. The computers would not be the wiser, and the Blue Angels would have the steady pressure they desired. No one could see anything wrong with Crawford's idea. Charles Hall, a metalsmith at the Range Directorate at Pax River, fashioned the spring in September 1986.

As Kapinos recalled, "Keith's course was: 'This is a great idea; let's make it happen; but can we get Mac Air [McDonnell Douglas] to give a thumbs up, to say this is safe to do?'" Standard Navy practice is for test pilots and engineers to identify deficiencies and request the manufacturer to correct them, not to do it themselves. But McDonnell Douglas eventually told the Navy it would be safe to install the spring on the F/A-18, Kapinos said.

However, Naval Air Systems Command wanted test pilots to fly the F/A-18 with the spring before it was cleared for use in upcoming Blue Angels' air shows. So Marine Corps Maj Rick Shows, an aggressive test pilot in Strike's F/A-18 unit, repeatedly flew the plane with the spring installed. He experienced no problems with Crawford's ingenious work-around. But he asked other pilots not linked with the Blue Angels to try the spring.

CAPT George J. Webb, Jr., chief test pilot at Strike, was among those scheduled to duplicate the Blue Angels' maneuvers in the F/A-18 with the spring installed on the stick. Webb and others at Strike had been arguing with their superiors at Naval Air Systems Command over how low they could fly while testing the spring. Webb gave me this account:

"NavAir had originally said something like: 'OK. You can test this spring out, but the minimum altitude must be 25,000 feet.'

"I said, 'The Blue Angels really don't fly at 25,000 feet. We need to get this thing down lower. We need to feel some bumpy air, thermals, to see if this thing is going to be good.'"

Webb's critics say he was making decisions that the commander of the Strike Directorate, CAPT Lewis Warren Dunton III, should have made because Dunton would be accountable for them. Webb counters he was fulfilling his role as chief test pilot to break the bureaucratic log-jam. Webb kept pushing officials at NavAir.

"They said, 'OK. We'll give you 5,000 feet.' I said, '5,000 feet isn't going to do anything. What the hell is wrong with 2,500, 1,500 feet? That's our base, a minimum altitude of 1,500 feet.' They said, 'OK,' and gave us a clearance for 1,500 feet."

Webb said that he flew wing on Maj Rick Shows the morning of 22 October 1986 to test the spring. "We were basically maneuvering from 3,000 to 1,500 feet. Rick never went below 1,500 feet. In fact, I had my RAT [radio altimeter] readout set at 2,000, so when the beeper went off, that was to remind me to start testing at altitude."

The spring worked. But Rick Shows went up twice more that day with different test pilots on his wing to gather additional evidence that the spring was safe and practical. On the third and last test flight of the day, Keith Crawford climbed into an F/A-18 rigged with the spring he had invented. He followed Shows into the sky and did everything he did, just as a wingman is supposed to do.

At one point, however, Shows apparently lost track of where he was in the sky and went into a wingover at too low an altitude. Shows completed his wingover and returned to the upright position dangerously close to the water. Crawford, who was following him, hit the water in the middle of his wingover.

Webb said Shows saw Crawford crash into the bay, flew back to the base, landed and parked his F/A-18 near the entrance to the Strike hangar, leaped out of the cockpit, and rushed into Webb's office in great agitation and disarray, oxygen mask hanging at his side and his helmet still on. Shows and Webb then had this exchange, according to Webb:

Shows: "I just killed him."

Webb: "What are you talking about? You just killed who?"

Shows: "Keith."

CDR Dave Finney: "Did you notice something coming from your airplane when you got out?" Finney asked Shows after he burst into Webb's office.

Shows: "What the hell do you want?"

Finney: "He left the goddamn engines running." Finney left Webb's office. Shows kept walking around and around Webb's office, anguishing about what had just happened over the bay.

Shows: "I can't believe it. I can't believe it. I can't believe I did this."

Webb: "What did you see?"

Shows: "He was flying wing. All of a sudden I realized I was about to hit the water. I pulled. I saw him in my mirror, and he went into the water."

Webb: "We don't know he's dead yet."

Shows: "Did you call SAR [search and rescue] and everything else?"

Webb: "Yeah." (He knew from the base tracking station that a plane had hit the water but not whether the pilot had ejected.) "I figured maybe he punched out before he hit the water. Rick, you don't know if he's dead."

Shows: "Skipper, he's dead."

Webb: "Well, you don't know that. Sit down. Take your flight gear off."

Shows: "Here! I'm finished." He yanked his name tag with the wings imprinted on it off the Velcro patch on the left side of his flight suit. He threw the leather tag on Webb's desk. He was symbolically turning in his wings, declaring he was never going to fly again.

Webb: "Oh bullshit! Put it back! Cool it! Let's find out what the hell happened. Let's go through this by the book, just like we're supposed to do."

While this emotional exchange was raging in Webb's office on the second floor of the Strike hangar, a fisherman was motoring toward the spot where he had seen a plane crash into the bay. He reached the wreckage and saw a severely damaged body floating on the surface. Neither he nor the Navy's SAR helicopter, which came overhead shortly afterward, managed to recover Crawford's remains.

"I still to this day do not feel I did anything wrong," Webb said in justifying the pressure he had put on NavAir to allow low-altitude tests of the spring. "I don't see that there was anything wrong with having a 1,500-foot base. We're test pilots. When you say 1,500 feet, we're not supposed to go below it.

"We're also supposed to be testing the airplane like it's going to be flown, and the Blue Angels don't fly at 25,000 feet. They fly at 500 feet. If I had my way, I would have the test base at 500 feet. And I think my test pilots are good enough to adhere to that.

"The haze had increased, and Rick just lost situational awareness. The accident never should have happened. First, you've got all kinds of sensors to tell you where you are at. You've got a radar-altitude readout, and you've got a pressure-altitude readout. When I went up to fly the Blue Angel stuff with Rick flying lead, I was watching everything he was doing. Plus, being a single-seat guy—having flown a hell of a lot of formation in my life—I'm always conscious of where the lead is. Keith should have been looking. In my opinion as a pilot, they both screwed up."

Steve Kapinos, Crawford's friend and deputy, disagreed. He said he had randomly asked five pilots if they would have flown into the water under the same circumstances that Crawford found himself in. Three said yes; two said they would have been scanning to keep aware of their position. "My assessment," said Kapinos, "is that it would have killed all five of those pilots. Keith was nugget of the year on his first tour; he was a very extraordinary pilot. Rick Shows thought he was 1,000 feet higher than he was. I have listened to these guys for 16 years, and after every accident it's, 'He should have done this; he should have done that.' The bottom line is that both guys are human. Somebody made a mistake, and Keith paid the price."

CDR Mary Perri Crawford, who in 1992 commanded the Military Entrance Processing Station at Fort Hamilton, New York, was pressing on with her life, trying mightily to be both father and mother to the Crawfords' two sons. She—like Cathy Eastburg, Sandi Brennan, Lori Davis, and other aviators' wives—said she knew that testing airplanes was a dangerous business but accepted the risk because "Keith was doing what he wanted to do."

There had been several other accidents recently at Pax River, producing an official feeling that "heads would roll" if there was another one. The word had already gone out that RADM John K. Ready, commander of the Naval Air Test Center, intended to hammer the skipper of any command that had an accident. Although Crawford's crash occurred shortly after RADM John F. Calvert had relieved Ready, Calvert followed Ready's policy. Calvert in effect fired Chief Test Pilot Webb and Strike Director Lew Dunton from their posts in October

1986. Because the accident board had attributed the cause of the crash to pilot error, no charges were filed against Webb or Dunton, but their "punishment" was highly visible. Webb was transferred to the Public Works office at Pax River, and Dunton became chief of staff at the Test Center's headquarters.

Webb called his transfer to Public Works "a slap on the arm." Dunton regarded his forced move to headquarters as an unacceptable, unjust humiliation that left him no choice but to resign from the Navy he loved. Webb made a career comeback. Dunton, a Harvard graduate and the son of a retired rear admiral, slipped into depression shortly after reporting to the Test Center's headquarters in November 1986.

Recalled Marjorie Stephens Dunton, his wife: "Around January 1987 Lew decided he was going to have to get out of the Navy. He felt humiliated, embarrassed, absolutely devastated. He couldn't sleep, couldn't get interested in anything. He wasn't himself." Their eldest son, Lewis Warren Dunton IV, nicknamed "Four," was eight, and his brother, James Cable Dunton II, was five when depression overcame their usually spirited and interested father.

Come spring 1987 Lew Dunton seemed worse to his wife. By June he was spending his off-duty days in bed. The Reverend Thelma Smullen of the Church of Ascension in Lexington Park persuaded him to seek medical help. Dunton, after initially resisting, agreed and visited a doctor and psychologist at the base hospital.

"They realized how depressed he was and sent him to the Naval Hospital in Bethesda," Mrs. Dunton said. "He went against his will—was most unhappy about it. But when he got there he admitted he was contemplating suicide. They kept him at Bethesda for three weeks. They gave him 600 milligrams of Desyrel a day for the first two weeks.

"The third week they started taking him off it to see how he would react. Well, he knew how to play the game. He's a Harvard graduate. All he wanted was out of that place. And he's going to fool them because he went in there against his will.

"Knowing what I know now about depression—they should have kept him in the hospital. When someone has been depressed for almost a year, you don't cure him in two or three weeks. At the end of June Lew came home. He was going to retire at the end of June, but they had to move his retirement to August 1 to provide time for him to complete his physical and retirement processing.

"He took some leave after he came home to look for a job. That was another downer. He had several interviews. A gentleman from Texas was honest. He said, 'We're going to hire a younger guy we don't have to pay as much as you.' Lew was forty-seven. He felt useless. He thought age was against him. Here he had this Harvard degree, but it didn't help. In mid-July Westinghouse hired him, but he didn't know whether he would like it or not. He used to say, 'After flying, what is there?' He loved to fly, loved the Navy.

"He retired from the Navy on August 1, 1987. He wanted a private retirement ceremony—just get his papers from the admiral with only the family there. Lew didn't want any others.

"At 1 P.M. on August 24, 1987—I remember it was a Monday—Joe Hoag, the senior engineer at Strike, called Lew to ask when he would like to have his retirement luncheon. They set it for the next Wednesday.

"Later that same day I told Lew I was going to the commissary. He said fine. When I was getting ready to leave, the only thing he said to me was that if he wasn't there when I returned, he would be taking a walk. It was not out of the ordinary. He didn't act nervous or anything.

"I left at 2:30 and got back at 4:30. The boys had been at the Webbs' house while I was gone but had returned home before I did. They were downstairs watching TV when I started getting dinner together. I was standing at the kitchen sink, looking at the backyard through the bay window. I thought I saw something in the woods. I thought to myself, 'Gee, it looks like a towel or something.'

"I must have felt a little uneasy because I went upstairs and tried to look down into the woods from the bedroom. I couldn't tell. I called my oldest son upstairs and asked him: 'Four, can you see into the woods? What do you think it is?'

"'That's Daddy. I can see his belt buckle.'"

"With that, I went running out of the house. Both of the boys followed me. I was not in any condition to tell them to wait because I was so scared.

"There he was in the woods on his back. My neighbor told me later that she had heard this noise at 3 o'clock, so that's when we think it was. He had shot himself in the head with a .38. He was still breathing, but he was unconscious.

"He was very bloody. I didn't want to touch him. You don't know. Somebody is going to think you did it.

"Four and I went running into the house. He actually called 911 for me. They were there in less than two minutes.

"They took him by helicopter to the Trauma Center at Prince George's General Hospital. He died en route at 7:12 P.M. in the helicopter.

"Ann and George Webb took me by car up to the hospital. By the time we got up there the doctor walked in and started to say, 'Well, Mrs. Dunton, we did everything. . . .' I said, 'You're going to tell me he's dead.' I said it so the doctor didn't have to. He said, 'Yes.' I said, 'Well, obviously this is what he wanted.'"

Both widows—Mary Crawford and Margie Dunton—resolved to carry on, to make life for their two sons as normal and fulfilling as they could. Lieutenant Commander Crawford had the stronger support system since she was still in the Navy. She stayed put in the family's Springfield, Virginia, house and went on with her career. Margie Dunton had left the tight embrace of the Navy when her husband retired. She was a flight attendant with Eastern Airlines, but had no home to return to while she planned the next moves in her suddenly changed life.

"Our house had been sold that morning. Lew called the guy who had bought it and asked him if we could rent it from him a few months to see if he liked the job at Westinghouse. He wouldn't rent it to us. That may have been the final push. All of this was more than he could handle.

"I didn't know where to move. I rented a town house in 'Wildewood' in the town of California, Maryland, for eight months to give me time to figure out what to do. People were very supportive. Chaplain Mike Jones was very helpful. Admiral Calvert wasn't nasty, but a little bit insensitive. He told me to refrain from coming to the base for legal advice. I was just trying to find out what my benefits were going to be and was having trouble finding out until a friend, Rear Admiral John H. Fetterman, Jr., assisted the family with our Navy benefits.

"I visited my family in Dayton [Ohio] at Christmas. I thought I might move there. The weather was cold. I hadn't been there in twenty-five years. I had left there when I was eighteen. I returned to Pax River and decided to see how Jacksonville [Florida] looked."

Margie Dunton had met Lew in Jacksonville. They had bought a house in the suburb of Park West and lived there from 1976 to 1983 when Lew was executive officer and then skipper of VA-87, an A-7 light-attack squadron. Thanks to Kathleen Goad, a former Navy wife and real-estate agent in Jacksonville, Margie Dunton sold the house in Park West and bought a smaller, newer one in Orange Park, which she figured would be easier to maintain. Goad completed the paperwork on both transactions during Margie's twelve-day leave in Jacksonville. She moved to the Orange Park house in April 1988 so that the boys could enroll in school and make friends before the summer recess.

Asked by his first-grade teacher to stand up and introduce himself, Jimmy Dunton gave his name and said he had moved from Pax River "after my father committed suicide." The teacher was shocked and chagrined. But Margie Dunton recalled, "He felt much better. He had to get it off his chest."

I visited Margie Dunton in early 1992. She seemed to have herself and her life together, but it was obvious as she talked of Lew Dunton that he would always remain the bright light within her. Her boys were playing basketball in the driveway of the neat, comfortable, one-story home in Orange Park. The family seemed united in their determination to march on despite their heavy loss. After having been out of work for almost two years because of the collapse of her employer, Eastern Airlines, Margie had just landed a job in January 1992 that seemed suited to the efficient charm of a former flight attendant. She would be doing public relations for a bank. She had moved past the Navy life and was not looking back except to regret that the doctors had prematurely released Lew Dunton from the hospital. He was like a bird with broken wings and was not ready to fly on his own. Margie told me she often wondered what her life would have been like "if Lew hadn't been made a scapegoat for the Naval Aviation mishaps at Pax River."

One evening in April 1991 I came across another example of true grit in the women associated with the testing of airplanes. Class 5 from Test Pilot Training was celebrating its fortieth reunion in the River

Room of The Roost restaurant in Lexington Park, just outside Pax River's main gate. When Class 5 was young in 1950 and 1951, its fliers and their wives went to The Roost to tell each other lies, to drink gallons of beer and booze, to sing songs, to laugh. So this evening was a sentimental journey back to those days.

CAPT Robert W. "Duke" Windsor acted as master of ceremonies at the dinner. On 21 August 1956 he had become the fastest man in the world by flying an F8U-1 Crusader jet fighter 1,015.428 miles per hour over the 15-kilometer course at the Naval Ordnance Test Station, China Lake, California. After drinks had been drunk, dinner had been eaten, and everyone had mellowed, Windsor asked each member of the class to stand up and tell the group what he or she had been doing since the old days at Pax. Each person, in the Naval Air tradition, tried to be bright, upbeat, and brief. Sally Gear stood up and spoke in that same light vein, but her story was too powerful to take lightly. I felt a surge of emotion and suspected the others around felt the same thing.

Her husband, CDR Bud Gear, forty, crashed into the Atlantic Ocean one black night off the North Carolina coast on 9 January 1962 in his A-3J Vigilante, the earlier version of the plane Keith Crawford used to fly. She would never know why or how Bud died, but the night before his disappearance she had dreamed of his plane's going into the sea. She did know that she had to raise their six children, two ponies, a dog, and a cat by herself with a minimum amount of money and a maximum amount of work. Like Helen Ellyson before her and Mary Perri Crawford and Margie Stephens Dunton after her, she had fought the good fight in the true-grit fashion of Navy wives.

"I'm really proud of you all," Sally Gear told her old friends from Class 5. She laughed between every sentence of her story of struggle. "We grew older, and we had lots of jollies," the fulsome Sally Gear said. And you could tell from the way she spoke that there indeed had been light and laughter in the Gear home, just as there had been in the Ellyson home after Naval Aviator Number One had crashed.

Afterward I asked how she had managed to rear her children so successfully for eight years on the salary of a registered nurse and her husband's modest insurance payments until she remarried in 1970. "I told them, 'It's all out there for you. Scholarships, loans. But you're going to have to go after it.'"

And all of her children did just that, four of the six connecting to the Navy. This was the status of the Gear children as of June 1992:

Dr. Susan Gear Carter, forty-six, oncologist, married to Dr. James Carter, chief of medicine at Cleveland's Metropolitan Hospital.

Kim Gear Waddell, forty-four, married to CAPT James Barry Waddell, skipper of the F/A-18 retraining group at Cecil Field, Florida.

CDR Chip Gear, forty-two, instructor at the Naval War College at Newport, Rhode Island.

LCDR Danny Gear, thirty-seven, combination nuclear and electrical engineer assigned to the Aegis program in Crystal City, Virginia.

Dr. Joshua Gear, thirty-two, psychiatrist in Chicago.

LT Sali Gear, thirty-two, Joshua's twin sister, a Navy jet pilot married to LT Jim Liddy, a Navy SEAL. Sali Gear wears her dad's Navy wings on her dress uniform.

"When Sali won her wings," Mother Sally recalled, "she called me and said, 'Now I know how it was for Dad.'"

Retired Captain George C. Duncan was a walking legend in Naval Aviation long before Hollywood showed the Class 100 generation his fiery crash by including it in the movie *The Hunt for Red October.*

During World War II he had shot down thirteen and a half Japanese planes in the Pacific, almost qualifying as a triple ace. So nobody expected him to get hurt testing airplanes while no one was shooting at him. But he had his most serious accidents during test piloting. Everyone could laugh about one of them, but in the other he came terrifyingly close to being burned alive on the deck of a carrier.

Just before graduating from Test Pilot Training—the original name for TPS—with Class 3 in December 1949, Duncan tried to take off from Pax River in the underpowered Vought XF6U-1. He rolled down the runway at full power but could not get the beast to lift off the ground. He saw a truck driving along the road in front of him and managed to make the plane skip up off the ground high enough to clear the vehicle. But he still did not have enough power to climb. He hit the Patuxent River like a flat rock skipped across the water by a giant.

As he bounced across the waves, the plane's cockpit filled with water. When the plane finally stopped, Duncan managed to slide back the canopy and stand on the wing. The plane stayed afloat. He jumped off it.

The wind was blowing strongly toward shore. So he let the bulk of his parachute carry him toward land like a sail filled with wind. He was body surfing along when he heard the crash boat.

"Hang on, sir!" one of the two sailors standing on the deck of the crash boat yelled down to him. They were holding a long rope between them. "We've got you."

With that, each sailor hurled his end of the rope over to Duncan. Of course, the rope was then useless. The sailors got another rope, held onto it this time, and pulled the freezing aviator aboard.

"I was so cold," Duncan recalled.

Just as he was about to go below to warm up, he heard a helicopter approaching. It had come from Test Pilot Training. CDR Thomas F. Connolly, then director of the school, was aboard. The helicopter crew lowered a rescue sack to Duncan as he stood on the boat deck. Hauling him up to the helicopter door, the crew could not get him inside.

"God, but you're heavy," quipped Connolly, who reached out and pounded Duncan on the back.

They gave up on trying to get him through the door and flew to the base hospital. Duncan was standing above the skids and directed the chopper pilot to the landing, warning him of a car below.

Freeing himself from the rescue sack, Duncan started walking into the hospital. Corpsmen tried to put him on a gurney. He refused. He walked into the reception room, still freezing cold. Finally a Navy chief said, "Sign this, and I'll get you some brandy."

At graduation, Duncan apologized to CAPT Frederick M. Trapnell, commander of the Naval Air Test Center, for losing the plane.

"It couldn't happen to a better airplane," Trapnell said.

Duncan had a second crash—this one not at all funny—in July 1951 when he was a test pilot in the Carrier Suitability section of the Flight Test Division at Pax River. His mission was to conduct the first carrier landings and takeoffs with the Grumman F9F-5 Panther. He flew to Norfolk, where the test aircraft was hoisted aboard the carrier USS *Midway*. Once out to sea, Duncan was catapulted off the *Midway* and then trapped without incident.

Catapulted off a second time, Duncan flew the landing pattern around the carrier and tried to get into the groove leading to the number-three wire across the flight deck. He was lined up with the deck when he hit the air burble behind the carrier. The plane dipped.

"I remember pulling back on the stick," Duncan said afterward. "Then I saw the flames and closed my eyes. That's the last thing I remember until I felt them sewing up my head in sick bay."

Films show Duncan's plane cocking nose high just before it smashed into the round-down at the after edge of the flight deck. The jet split in half. The part from behind the cockpit forward hurtled down the deck, skidding and tumbling and finally coming to a fiery stop. The fuel tank behind Duncan's head had ignited when the plane whammed into the ramp, engulfing him in flame. The rest of the plane dropped down on the fantail and became a fireball.

The impact had torn off both the canopy and Duncan's helmet, but his harness held him in place until the cockpit wreckage came to a stop. Sailors managed to unstrap him and pull him out before the fire burned him up, although his hands and forearms were scorched and his ears were eaten up by the fire.

Miraculously, Duncan had suffered no serious injuries. He was back flying in six months, with hearing and ears restored.

When I interviewed George Duncan in April 1992, he was a vigorous seventy-five years old and twice a widower. But he was still intensely interested in the Navy and in aviation.

I asked him what was the key to survival as a test pilot.

"Knowing what your airplane can do and how to handle it," he replied.

Taking an airplane to the boat for its first landing is some of the riskiest flying test pilots do, as Duncan's fiery crash had demonstrated. To see this kind of testing close up, I went aboard the *Kennedy* to watch the first landings to be attempted with the Navy's new trainer, the T-45A Goshawk.

Goshawk Gets Wet

LCDR Barry "Puppy" Love stood on the windy landing signal officer's platform at the edge of the flight deck, scanning the sky for the flying peanut of an airplane that was due overhead by 1 P.M. As I stood beside him, I could see nothing in the sky above the USS *John F. Kennedy* except the gray bodies of the carrier's own warplanes. The expected first-time visitor with the standout trainer colors of orange and white fuselage was late for its date with naval history.

Love, a veteran landing signal officer, or LSO, with more than seven hundred carrier landings of his own, had flown from Pax River to the *Kennedy* and was ready to make a little aviation history with the overdue plane this fourth day of December 1991. He was to stand on the platform and study the approach of the Navy's T-45A Goshawk as it came in for its very first attempt to land on any carrier deck. If the pilot, CDR David "DJ" Venlet, strayed out of the groove, Love's job was to get him back into it before the plane crashed, or else to call off the landing attempt.

LSOs like Barry Love are nicknamed "Paddles" or "Wavers" from their World War II practice of waving paddles to guide pilots down from the sky. Wireless telephones, called handsets, have long since replaced the wooden paddles and now connect the LSO with the incoming pilot. Over these handsets, the LSOs give both advice and orders. This guidance is called "waving," from the days the LSOs waved paddles. Waving is a highly sought art. It can save lives, planes, and even whole ships.

The Navy thought so much of Barry Love's waving that it made him a professor for future wavers. He told me that the key to success is saying enough but not too much to the pilot staring death in the face as he or she hurtles toward the back end of a carrier at more than 130 miles per hour. The pilot in these traumatic seconds between landing on or crashing into the heaving flight deck does not need some LSO filling his ears with useless jabber.

"My secret weapon [for knowing when to talk and when not to] is my Mark 1 Mod 1 Eyeball," Love said. Every pilot wiggles around in the groove a little bit. "The big thing is to make sure he doesn't get too slow or cocked up where he could get into a stall regime. If he's slow, I'll tell him, so he has a chance to fix it himself." But if the incoming plane is real close to the carrier, Love is more likely to give orders than advice to the pilot. A pilot who hears any of these words is required to respond immediately: power, lineup, attitude, wave off.

"When I say power," Love continued, "I want a handful right now." The pilot receiving that order must immediately push up the throttles to increase the plane's speed and/or altitude.

"Lineup is very critical," the word meaning the pilot will miss the white line painted down the center of the angled flight deck. Planes are parked on both sides of the landing area on a carrier's flight deck, so the pilot who strays off dead center when slamming down could crash into a parked plane and touch off an inferno of burning fuel. Early in the approach, Love explained, "I may say, 'Check your lineup; you need to come right; you need to come left.' Those are advisories. But if I say, 'Come left for lineup,' that's mandatory."

Attitude is how the plane is angled against the oncoming air as it flies along. The nose must be low enough to prevent a stall but high enough to put the dangling tailhook in position to catch one of the four steel cables stretched across the flight deck. The LSO's single-word call of "Attitude!" is an order for the pilot to pull up the plane's nose.

"Wave off" is an order to break off the landing attempt completely. The pilot adds power and flies out of the landing groove and reenters the landing pattern for another try. Wave-off calls are made when the pilot has gotten out of the groove or when the flight deck is not ready to receive the plane because of a "fouled deck."

Every pilot, every LSO struggles to put the plane on the sweet spot between the number two and number three wires stretched across the deck. Sometimes the pilot will land on the sweet spot, only to have the tailhook bounce off the deck and skip right over the number three wire. If the hook does not snag the next and last wire down, number four, the pilot must roar off the deck for another landing attempt. This missed landing is called a bolter.

The scheduled first landing of the T-45A promised to be interesting because of all the early doubts about whether this converted British land-based plane could fly slow and steady enough to hit near the sweet spot on a carrier deck. Hundreds of changes, large and small, had been made on the Hawk to turn it into a seagoing Goshawk. One big change was adding what look like long pieces of curved molding to the top, leading edge of the wing. These pieces, called slats, are extended from the wing's leading edge for takeoffs and landings. Extending the slats increases the maximum lift of the wing. This enables the plane to be flown aboard the carrier at a slower speed without mushing out of control.

Although the slats had been tried over dry land back at Pax River, nobody knew whether they would work when the T-45A flew low over the water on the way in to the deck for a landing. The sea presents different conditions than those found over land. For one thing, the air swirling off of the fast-moving carrier's flight deck and into the face of the airplane in the groove is not smooth. It has been roiled up by the big tower sticking up from the starboard side of the ship, the island. The turbulent air forms up behind the carrier in a burble. Flying through the burble can bring surprises.

Also, takeoff cannot be simulated completely on land. Pax River does have a catapult on a runway laid out like a carrier deck. But a plane being launched from this catapult on land has some extra lift under its wings because of the cushion of air between the airplane and the ground, called ground effect. A plane being hurled off the front end of a carrier flies into open air sixty feet above the water, and all planes sink some afterward. What speed the T-45A had to be launched at to keep the amount of sink from being dangerous was one of the many questions the plane's sea trials on the *Kennedy* were supposed to answer—if the damn plane would ever show up this cold December day.

"Probably wouldn't let him out of Beaufort [South Carolina]," Love theorized, trying to explain the delayed arrival of the T-45A. "They've had storms along the coast, and that bird can't get wet." It was still too early—and too unforgivable—to even hint that the trouble-plagued, single-engine Navy trainer might have crashed somewhere out there in the Atlantic. The *Kennedy* was orbiting 140 miles off Jacksonville, Florida, as we waited.

Before the trainer had taken off from Pax River, technicians from McDonnell Douglas, builder of the navalized T-45A, had instrumented it as if it were a critical patient in the intensive-care unit of a hospital. Every vital sign—temperatures, weight, pressures, structural loads, engine inhaling of air, pitch, yaw, roll, speed—was being carefully monitored. Rather than risk having rain short-circuit the instrumentation monitors, the technicians, Love thought, had delayed the T-45A's takeoff until the weather along the coast improved.

We had little choice but to watch and wait. I never mind spending hour after hour on the LSO platform of an aircraft carrier during flight operations. It is like sitting on the player's bench at a football game or in front of the cymbals in a band. You are so close to the drama that you feel part of it. You hear, smell, see, taste, and feel almost everything about a carrier landing when you are standing on the LSO platform right beside the impact point.

The *Kennedy* was on a training cruise, not a deployment this day. This meant that female sailors were allowed to work on the carrier. I was taken aback when I first saw them. Female sailors were not part of the scene during the seven and a half months I had been aboard the *Kennedy* during its Mediterranean deployment in 1983–84. From a distance, their regulation light-blue dungaree shirts and dark-blue trousers made the female sailors difficult to distinguish from their male counterparts. One of the several LSOs who had joined Barry and me on the platform to wave in other planes, not the T-45A, fell to talking about the females' presence. One LSO had a harrowing tale to share about a female sailor who had not had enough time on the flight deck to fully appreciate its killing power.

"She walked in front of an engine that was turning and got sucked into the intake. A chief ran over and grabbed her by the legs and tried to pull her out. He couldn't do it. A second chief ran up and tackled him. Between the two of them, they got the girl out."

As the LSO paused, the formerly chatty platform fell silent. We were all forced to reflect on how close death always was on the flight deck beside us. Then the LSO restored the ready-room atmosphere by quipping: "She's a C-cup now!"

"Yeah!" Barry chipped in. "And the chiefs are being processed out for sexual harassment!"

Everybody laughed. It was a joke on the times we were in, not an antifemale remark.

An E-2C Hawkeye with the call sign "Waterbug" came in for a landing. "Another great cross-country call sign," observed one of the LSOs. He was referring to the times when aviators would be far from home on a "cross-country" and trying to impress the local ladies with their daring in the air. "'And what's your call sign?'" the LSO asked, mocking one of the hooters in a faraway bar. "'Waterbug? Waterbug! Oh. . . . Next!'"

An LSO with dark, metal braces all over his teeth studied the clouds that threatened to dump on us. "You know, if we get rain, it's apt to corrode my mouth shut."

Just as Barry and I were wondering whether it was getting too late in the day for the T-45A to try to get aboard to start its sea trials, we spotted two of the orange-and-white trainers overhead. CDR David "DJ" Venlet was flying lead, and Marine Capt Craig "Bowser" Bowers was flying on his wing. Venlet broke away from Bowers to enter the landing pattern. Bowers stayed high above the ship to remain clear of aircraft traffic. DJ whipped over the carrier. The T-45A looked gaudy in contrast to the hazy gray-and-white of the carrier planes. It struck me as a corporate jet that suddenly found itself in a Navy landing pattern. DJ turned sharply left out in front of the carrier at the "break," turned left again to parallel the length of the carrier in a downwind direction, turned left a third time to cross the *Kennedy*'s wake, and made his final left to line up with the flight deck. He was feeling for the groove leading to that sweet spot between the number two and number three wires.

Barry watched and listened intently. He was far from alone. On the *Kennedy* and back on shore, scores of Navy leaders, Navy and contractor engineers, politicians, technicians, and aviators' wives were also listening for how the besieged T-45A did on its first attempt to get down on a carrier deck. Hitting the back end of the carrier—called a ramp strike—would almost certainly kill DJ and the whole $7 billion T-45A program. The pressure was on DJ.

The thirty-seven-year-old DJ Venlet knew something about pressure. He had been the radar intercept officer in the backseat of an F-14 Tomcat from the USS *Nimitz* on 19 August 1981 when two SU-22 Fitter fighter bombers challenged his plane and a second F-14 over the Gulf of Sidra. DJ and CDR Hank Kleemann, the pilot and squadron skipper, suddenly found themselves going beak-to-beak with one of the SU-22s. The SU-22 shot an Atoll missile in the F-14's face. DJ saw a curl of smoke and a blur. The missile had missed. The opposing aircraft were past each other. Then the SU-22 pilot made a big mistake. He allowed the F-14 to get on his tail. Hank heard the "got 'em" hum through his earphones from the heat-seeking Sidewinder missile. The hum told him that the SU-22 was within killing range. Hank pushed the firing button. The Sidewinder shot from the F-14 and exploded into the SU-22. Hank and DJ saw the SU-22 pilot floating earthward in his parachute. The other F-14 shot down the second SU-22. The two F-14s raced back to the *Nimitz* to a heroes' welcome. "Think we woke the President up on that one?" DJ asked Hank as they flew through the Mediterranean sky.

Shortly after that shoot down, DJ made the leap from backseat radar intercept officer to front-seat pilot. The Navy had eased the eyesight requirements that had earlier prevented him from realizing his boyhood dream of becoming a carrier pilot. He won his flying wings in 1983, went to Test Pilot School in 1986, and now was the T-45A program manager at Pax River. DJ personified the new breed of test pilot: serious, dedicated, unassuming, conservative, careful, responsible, highly educated. Right now he was looking for that ball of orange light mounted on the port side of the flight deck, which would help him keep his plane in the groove as it bore down on the *Kennedy*.

"One One Hawk, ball," DJ called down to the ship. "One point eight."

He had just told Barry Love and everybody else on the *Kennedy* that he had spotted the ball and had 1,800 pounds of fuel in the tanks.

"Roger ball," Barry Love acknowledged.

The T-45A looked a little jumpy, a little nervous to me as it whooshed down. Barry Love did not see anything amiss. He did not say a word to DJ over the handset.

Roar! Bang! Scrape!

DJ and the T-45A were safely down on the *Kennedy*.

DJ had caught the number four wire. The number three had been pulled off the deck before he made his pass. "He almost boltered," Barry laughed. But the T-45A had trapped. It could now be called "wet," a carrier airplane. The former British landlubber was sitting in the middle of the ocean and would have to fly off the carrier to get itself back to dry land.

DJ followed the hand signals of the yellow-shirted sailor to reach his assigned parking space on the *Kennedy*'s flight deck. He parked the T-45A on the starboard side, just ahead of the island, climbed out of the cockpit, and walked matter-of-factly across the flight deck. There were no cheers or champagne. But Air Boss Mike Gass, who had orchestrated the coming and going of aircraft so that there would be an opening for the T-45A when it showed up overhead, had a big smile on his face.

The next question was how the T-45A would behave when it was catapulted off the front end of the *Kennedy*. Joseph S. Wascavage, thirty-three, the T-45A's deputy program manager at Pax River and chief civilian engineer on the project, was anxious about this. He was on the *Kennedy* along with platoons of government and contractor aeronautical and mechanical engineers, technicians, and mechanics, most of them from Pax River. The Navy wanted at least one expert on hand for every conceivable T-45A problem. So much tinkering had been done to the plane since Wascavage became one of its chief shepherds in November 1986 that there could be surprises the first time it was catapulted off a carrier.

By prearrangement with DJ, LT Wade "Torch" Knudson, twenty-nine, the lead test pilot for the T-45A at Pax, would take the first cat shot. He had been anxiously awaiting DJ's arrival so that he, too, could make a little Naval Aviation history before going home for Christmas. I asked Wade Knudson how he felt about being the first man to be hurled off the end of a flight deck in the single-engine T-45A, which had exhibited so many flaws in the past.

"The biggest thing we're worried about right now is over-rotation"—meaning the T-45A's nose could jump up unexpectedly without the pilot's touching the stick. This could be dangerous, perhaps causing a stall while the plane was only a few feet off the water. Tests back at Pax River had revealed that the line of push rods and bell cranks connected to the stick were not harmonized to prevent undesired motion. The stick would pull itself back when the catapult yanked the plane forward, causing the nose to pitch up suddenly.

"I don't think it's going to pitch up into a stall or anything," Wade told me, "but it may be too high of a pitch attitude." This would make the T-45A lose altitude in those crucial seconds between running out of catapult energy and getting lift from the engine's thrust. "Those are unknowns because this is the first catapult launch, and those things were never looked at."

With a smile, Torch Knudson said his wife, Kimberly Rylant, had asked whether this pre-Christmas experiment was necessary. "She told me: 'I have a bad feeling about this one.'" Then, switching from sensitive husband to dispassionate test pilot, Knudson said he was not worried that the T-45A would settle into the water after launch, where it would be run over by the 90,000-ton carrier.

"Nothing is going to happen instantaneously. Yeah, sixty feet is not very far between the deck and the water, but on the other hand it's certainly enough time to make a correction. They're going to be launching me at speeds 20 knots above what our predicted minimum is going to be." The predicted minimum is the slowest speed the T-45A could be catapulted off the flight deck without losing altitude and falling into the water for lack of lift. "I wouldn't say I'm apprehensive. I'm anxious. I'm ready to do it. There's always the unknown the first time, but it's just another big challenge to do."

I left Knudson in the ready room to climb the ladders leading to the small room high up in the carrier's towering island, where engineers and technicians were preparing to keep track of everything the T-45A did prior to, during, and after its launch. Hundreds of steps later, I found myself inside a small room of the admiral's bridge. It was crowded with an L-shaped row of four machines with rolling charts and automatic pens. Each machine was programmed to show eight of the vital signs of the patient out on the flight deck.

Stephen E. Cricchi, at only twenty-eight one of the senior engineers on the T-45A project at Pax and a graduate of TPS, explained that all the data being collected was not just for Knudson's sake. The Navy engineers would not only watch for danger signs to safeguard Knudson but also gather the data needed to tell launching crews and student aviators at what speeds the new plane could be safely launched and how it behaved after being catapulted off the bow.

"When you have twenty students in a room," Cricchi told me, "you want to be able to say: 'OK. When I launch you off the catapult, this is what's going to happen. You're going to feel a slight pressure on the stick coming back in your hand, so you want to guard against that.'

"You don't want to say, 'Well, depending on your fuel weight, and how the airplane is loaded, and how heavy you are as pilot, and whether you've got two guys in the airplane or one guy, you're going to feel some aft stick movement or some forward stick movement. So you just kind of be ready to make that call real-time as the airplane is going down the cat.'

"For a student doing his first cat launch off a ship, you want to be able to say, 'Here's what's going to happen. It's not going to be a big deal.'"

During Knudson's upcoming launch and subsequent flight, Cricchi said he would be studying the strip charts set up to receive information on such flying qualities as airspeed, pitch rate, angle of attack, altitude, force on the stick, and position of the stabilizer.

Bruce Feldman, thirty-one, would be the engineer studying the strip chart showing what the T-45A's engine was doing. Tests back at Pax River had raised concern about the engine's surging when it swallowed the steam from the carrier's catapult. An exit for some of the compressed air headed for the engine's fire box had been added. This bleed off of air reduced the destabilizing differences in temperature inside the engine. On land, this had cured the engine's worrisome coughing. At sea, the larger clouds of steam might cause the engine to cough again, meaning less or no thrust to keep the plane airborne after launch. Feldman said he was not worried about this. "If we had any concerns, we wouldn't be out here." The T-45A back at Pax had made thirty-five successful launches after being subjected to more steam than the trainer was expected to encounter on the *Kennedy*. One of the squiggles on Feldman's strip chart would show whether Knudson had opened the bleed valve before launch and closed it before landing. An airplane enthusiast, Feldman told me as we studied the high-tech monitors all around us, "If the strip charts weren't working, I'd be looking out the window, watching the action along with everybody else" not studying the monitors.

Robert J. Sowa, twenty-six, was the youngest engineer in the room and would be watching the strip chart showing the T-45A's roll, yaw, rudder position, sideslip, flap position, and fuel weight. The work of this University of Maryland graduate might sound tedious, but Bob Sowa just happens to be nuts about airplanes. He is endlessly fascinated by what they do and why they do it. He flies private planes in his spare time and delights in trying what he has learned at Pax River on the unsuspecting Cessnas he rents at St. Mary's County Airport north of the base. "I like to mimic some of the tests," he told me.

Dave Lawlin, thirty-three, a graduate of the Lincoln Technical Institute, was the wizard for the telemetry linking the T-45A on the carrier deck with this little room. He typified the Nintendo generation of young Americans who know far more than their parents about what electrical pulses can do in this new world. "Going out on a carrier," he said, "you really get to put into action what you know. You don't have anybody running up to you with a problem all the time. Out here you're pretty much on your own. Gives you the opportunity to find out what you know and what you don't know."

At forty-seven, Jack Wyngate was the old man in the T-45A's nerve center, not counting your aged guide. Already in his career, Wyngate said, he had seen the mechanical testing of aircraft go from the medical equivalent of stethoscope to electrocardiogram. "Being on the cutting end of technology keeps me young," Wyngate told me. He would keep checking the telemetry links between the T-45A and the engineers in this room during the launch.

If Cricchi, Feldman, Sowa, Lawlin, Wyngate, or anyone else detected anything wrong, he would alert Henry Melton or Cal Lea, the two engineers from the Carrier Suitability Section of the Strike Directorate on board. Melton, another intensive young man in a hurry, would warn the Air Boss in the Primary Flight tower atop the *Kennedy*'s island. The Air Boss could then halt the whole launching operation with one quick call or loudspeaker announcement to the flight-deck crew below him.

Even though winds were strong, Knudson and the Navy test team, after getting the green light from superiors back at Pax River, decided to go ahead with the first launch of the T-45A. I joined others on a stretch of open deck above the flight deck to watch the cat shot. Almost everyone had cameras poised. Big clouds of steam from the catapult kept engulfing the jet. I could get only glimpses of Knudson's helmeted head in the plastic bubble of a cockpit. I could tell, though, that he was proceeding down the checklist because the catapult crew outside the plane was continuing its own prelaunch preparations. I was getting a little nervous for Wade Knudson. I figured he must have some butterflies flying around in his gut. The gray water out in front of the T-45A looked cold and menacing. If the plane stalled out there in front of the speeding carrier, Knudson might have time to eject before hitting the water. But pilots hate to land anywhere near a carrier. They fear they will get sucked under the ship and be ground up by its giant propellers.

The launching officer touched the deck—the signal to release a big charge of steam against the catapult piston. I saw a cloud of steam rise up from under the T-45A. Then the little orange-and-white peanut was rushing down the flight deck. It shot off the cliff and sank a bit before its engine took over and got the plane into a climb. The Goshawk was up and away. Everything had worked! Knudson and the Navy's new trainer were safely airborne.

An elated Knudson went around the landing pattern, trapped safely, and then was launched again. He kept doing this until he had made ten arrested landings. These ten traps made him the first naval aviator to become officially qualified to fly the Navy's only new airplane of 1991 on and off a carrier, day or night. The next day DJ Venlet got nine more traps, making him the second naval aviator qualified for carrier operations in the T-45A. Then it was down to the tedious work of testing airplanes—what test pilots really do 99 percent of the time.

Under the sea-trial plan mapped out in exquisite detail by the Pax River test team long before DJ flew the T-45A aboard the *Kennedy*, the two test pilots would be catapulted again and again, each time at a slightly lower speed. The objective was to determine how slow the T-45A could be going when it went off the front end of a carrier without settling more than twenty feet, leaving forty feet between the plane and the water. Another part of the plan was to land again and again while the ship was angled to the wind to see how the T-45A handled crosswinds. The testers in the air and on the ship were trying to take all the surprises out of the Goshawk before the first student climbed into the cockpit to try to land the trainer on a carrier.

To understand what Knudson did day after day with the T-45A on the *Kennedy,* imagine yourself being catapulted off a carrier at a speed of 120 knots; taking mental notes on how the plane behaved in front of the carrier; going around and trapping; being shot off the bow again at a slightly slower speed, noting the deeper sink; and landing again. Knudson kept this up until his launching speed got down to 107 knots. The T-45A dropped five feet toward the water after launch at that speed.

When Knudson was not using the T-45A for those tests, DJ Venlet tested how responsive the plane was to big corrections as the plane flew at the flight deck at speeds of more than 100 miles per hour. DJ was flying like a clumsy, nervous student pilot would fly to determine how forgiving or how punishing this new trainer would be when coming in slow for a carrier landing.

After five days of such testing, the T-45A's tailhook skipped off a wire and into the plane's fuselage and tail pipe with such force that the plane was no longer safe to go into that controlled crash that is a carrier landing. The sea trials were suspended on 10 December 1991 after thirty-three launches and traps had been completed. The Pax River boys went home for Christmas, believing the T-45A would succeed. The carrier tests had revealed that the plane's wing rolled to the left once it left the catapult and was in the open air out in front of the carrier. Also, the nosewheel sometimes misbehaved when the plane was taxied around the deck. These were among the problems that would have to be corrected back home at Pax River.

What DJ and Knudson had done on the *Kennedy* is what test pilots really do when they are sent to sea to see what a new plane can and cannot do. It is eyedropper testing—a little bit at a time, just the way TPS teaches. Take it easy. Do not let the airplane get ahead of you. Inch into the unknown, do not plunge into it. Careful, tedious, dangerous work.

Is not this a boring way to fly—a boring way to make a living? I asked both test pilots.

"Being a test pilot is more tedious than I thought it was going to be," conceded Venlet. "There's much less glamour than I envisioned before I got into it. Not much exciting flying. There is very little envelope expansion [of a plane's stated capabilities] done by any pilots at Pax River." Expanding the envelope is left in most cases to the civilian test pilots employed by the airplane builders.

"So what are we doing [as Navy test pilots]? What we're doing is fairly important but not glamorous stuff. But it's been exciting for me to work on the T-45."

"It's really challenging flying," Knudson agreed. "It's nice to be the first to do something." He added what I had heard from many other test pilots—that it is refreshing to look at what the plane is doing wrong instead of what you are doing wrong.

"When you're a test pilot, it's not like the Training Command where everything you did was your fault. If you're off altitude, it's your fault. If you overshoot the turn or can't get the pipper on the target, it's all your fault." The test pilot is taught that "it's the airplane's fault, because in a perfect airplane everybody would be able to do those things all the time. There are certain characteristics of airplanes that cause them to be not so good in certain areas." Identifying those "certain areas" is fulfilling work, Knudson said, especially if somebody corrects the flaws the test pilots detect in always-imperfect airplanes.

Civilian engineer Wascavage had similar answers when I put the same questions to him. "Just knowing you're working on something that's going to be in the fleet for twenty years, that's going to be out there training a lot of people. To me, that's where the motivation is.

"I feel that the airplane now, with a few more corrections, is going to be a good airplane," Wascavage continued. "If you had asked me that same question in November 1988, after we flew our first Navy evaluation, I would have convinced my nephew who wants to join the Navy to fly to go into the Air Force."

Little did Joe Wascavage know that this first T-45A, Number 001, would continue to have problems after it left the *Kennedy* and would crash six months later because of one of its many nagging flaws.

Fixing one problem seemed to create another in the T-45A. Tinkering with the wing, the engine, the controls, and many other things on the supposedly simple trainer still left the Navy with a flawed plane as of June 1992.

On 3 June 1992 LT Owen P. "OP" Honors, a test pilot at the Strike Warfare Directorate who went through TPS with Class 98, took off in the T-45A for Edwards Air Force Base, California. His mission was to subject the plane to severe angles of attack—the angle the plane heads into the onrushing air—to see when and how severely its Rolls-Royce engine would stall. He would be verifying engine tests conducted by the contractor.

An engine stall in a single-engine airplane like the T-45A can be catastrophic. Beginning aviators, not seasoned fleet or test pilots, would be flying the T-45A most of the time. They would be less able to handle partial or total engine stalls. So it was crucial to have a reliable engine in the T-45A, especially when it came to teaching students how to handle spins.

A partial stall is like having three of the cylinders of a six-cylinder auto engine conk out while the auto is going uphill. The remaining three cylinders have to do more work and are subject to more wear and tear. If the T-45A engine stalled frequently, the engine would wear out much faster than desired.

After the sea trials on the *Kennedy,* the T-45A engine had been stalling to a worrisome extent. Test pilots and engineers began discussing informally the possibility of installing a different engine in the T-45A. But Honors's job was to continue the Navy's effort, in concert with the contractor, McDonnell Douglas, to identify the problems with the installed Rolls-Royce engine in hopes they could be corrected.

Inviting engine stalls by putting the T-45A in demanding angle-of-attack positions is dangerous work in a single-engine airplane. The more flat real estate under you—the more landing fields—the better, in case your one engine stalls. Edwards Air Force Base out in the California desert has miles and miles of safe landing areas. Pax River is a dot surrounded by water and houses in comparison. So Honors had been ordered to do his airframe-engine compatibility tests at the safer and well-instrumented Edwards.

Except for some bumpy air, Honors hopscotched west in the T-45A without incident. He overnighted at Lincoln, Nebraska, then flew on to Albuquerque, New Mexico, taking off from there on 4 June to fly the last leg into Edwards. A McDonnell Douglas crew flying a Learjet 35 followed Honors westward.

At 11:30 A.M. on 4 June, OP set up for what promised to be a routine landing. The weather was clear. His radio checks indicated everything was a go on the ground. Sitting in the front seat of the T-45A, which has great visibility, he saw what seemed like limitless runway in front of him compared with the matchbox landing deck atop an aircraft carrier.

Touching down on the Edwards runway, the T-45A suddenly pulled left, as if the wheel on the left side of the landing gear was locked and skidding rather than free and rolling. OP tried to keep the plane on the runway, but it kept skidding and rolling left and was soon in the soft sand alongside the paved runway.

"There was nothing I could do to bring it back," OP recalled. "I attempted to go around," pushing the throttle to full power to get the plane into the air again, "but it was in the heavier sand."

Too mired in sand to take off and too fast to stop, the T-45A was a runaway plane that might kill OP and people on the ground at any second. He saw a trailer dead ahead that appeared to have people standing on top of it. He stayed with the plane until he saw it would miss the trailer. Once it passed the trailer, the T-45A began to rock violently from side to side. OP feared it would turn over. This could turn the plane into a fireball while he was strapped inside it. OP pulled the ejection handle under his seat. Small charges broke up the cockpit's plastic roof while a larger charge kicked his butt with the force of 100 Gs.

"It sounded like a shotgun going off," he said of the twin explosions during ejection.

Before he could fully comprehend what had happened, he was 100 feet above the runway and floating toward earth in his parachute. The pilotless T-45A hurtled onward, smashing into a corner of the concrete foundation of an abandoned non-commissioned officers' club. Although totaled, the T-45A came to a stop without bursting into flame.

OP landed safely in the soft sand. He was unhurt except for a sore neck and the physical reminder that he had gotten a kick in the tail.

Two men ran out of the parked trailer and sprinted over to OP.

"Are you OK?" one of them asked the pilot.

"Yeah. I'm OK. Are you OK?"

They were. OP's next emotion was anger. He was angry with the plane for failing. It was obviously beyond repair, totaled. Some damn little thing had ruined it. Just what, he did not know. He wanted to go over and punch Number 001 as it sat there as a wreck 1,000 feet to the left of the runway.

The Edwards crash truck, which had little to do at this point, wheeled up and took OP aboard. After the normal hospital tests to make sure he was neither hurt nor contaminated by any foreign substances in his blood—he was not—the thirty-year-old test pilot flew home by commercial airliner to his wife, Paige, and daughter, Samantha, in Park Hall, Maryland.

Just another day at the office!

As of September 1992 the T-45A was still a plane beset with problems. The installed Rolls-Royce engine was not considered reliable enough to enable student aviators to spin the trainer. The Navy would have to buy a new engine for its troubled trainer. The T-45A had turned out to be no bargain.

More than ten years ago—on 19 November 1981—the Navy awarded a contract to the team of Douglas Aircraft Co. (part of McDonnell Douglas), the prime contractor, and British Aerospace, the subcontractor, a contract to convert the Royal Air Force Hawk, a land plane, into a Navy training plane, the T-45A Goshawk. Navy leaders theorized that converting an existing plane would be far cheaper than building a trainer from scratch. The "navalizing" was projected to cost $701.2 million in fiscal 1993 dollars. By the end of 1991 the Pentagon's estimate for this research, development, testing, and evaluation had increased to $782.3 million.

The T-45A was to replace the T-2 Buckeye and TA-4 Skyhawk then used for training. In 1984 the Navy estimated it would cost about $3 billion to procure three hundred T-45As, or $10 million for each trainer. In April 1992 the Pentagon updated that estimate in its Selected Acquisition Reports. The new estimate jumped up to $4,497,500,000 for 270 aircraft, or $16.7 million each in fiscal 1984 dollars—an unrealistically low estimate because it does not include inflation. Even so, the increase from $10 million to $16.7 million in fiscal 1984 dollars represents a jump of more than 50 percent.

More revealing is the Pentagon's "Procurement Programs" book—dated 29 January 1992—which discloses what aircraft will cost in dollars actually to be paid to the contractor, the fiscal 1993 dollars. That Pentagon book—known as P-1—shows the T-45A costing $23,064,583 per copy, not counting the past research and development costs, nor the expense of buying a new engine!

This simple trainer, supposedly an easy modification of an existing plane, at $23 million each is approaching the $33.7 million price tag for the highly sophisticated Air Force F-16 fighter bomber. Those prices are an apple-to-apple comparison, expressed in fiscal 1993 dollars.

Cost per pound is a reliable guide to whether a plane is overpriced. The T-45A's gross weight is 12,758 pounds, or about $1,800 per pound at the fiscal 1993 price of $23 million. The F-16's gross weight is 37,500 pounds, or about $900 per pound at the fiscal 1993 price of $33.7 million. The supposedly bargain-basement T-45A, a primitive airplane compared with the F-16 with its Mach-2 speed and heavy electronics, has turned out to cost twice as much per pound as the F-16!

Obviously, something went terribly wrong. When I asked VADM Richard M. Dunleavy, who was head of Naval Air until mid-1992, what had gone wrong with the T-45A, he said, "We didn't want that" plane. He and other admirals implied that former Navy Secretary John F. Lehman, Jr., forced the British plane on the Navy.

Lehman himself, in a separate interview in 1992, denied that he had forced the British Hawk on the Navy. He said his own choice was the French Alpha Jet entry because it had two engines compared to the British Hawk's one. "But I left the choice up to the source-selection board," he said.

The General Accounting Office released a report entitled, "T-45 Training System: Navy Should Reduce Risks Before Procuring More Aircraft," in December 1990. In it the GAO blasted the Navy for leaping before looking, declaring: "At the outset of development, the Navy adopted a T-45 acquisition strategy which reflected what proved to be an overly optimistic assessment of risk. . . ."

Continued the GAO report:

> Probably the greatest risk in the T-45 acquisition strategy was the high degree of concurrency [developing and producing the airplane at the same time] that allowed no opportunity for operational testing before the first production commitment.
>
> The T-45 entered production prematurely, without a stable aircraft design and before any Navy flight testing. The aircraft's ensuing performance problems disrupted the program schedule and caused development and procurement costs to increase.
>
> After testing showed the aircraft's problems, we believe the most prudent approach would have been to halt further production commitments until the Navy had achieved a stable design. That approach would also have been consistent with Department of Defense's policy of advancing systems on the basis of demonstrated achievement.
>
> However, the Navy and the Office of the Secretary of Defense proceeded with a new production commitment while design corrections

were being developed. As a result, the Navy now has production commitments for 36 aircraft but still does not have a stable design.

The program's situation can be attributed to an optimistic assessment of the technical challenge involved in adapting the Hawk design to the T-45A mission. That assessment led to the use of an acquisition strategy which minimized development, testing and government oversight and encouraged early commitments to concurrent production. . . .

The Navy and the Office of the Secretary of Defense also attempted to reduce risks by decreasing rate of production commitments. With the extended development phase that has resulted from the aircraft's deficiencies, however, even the reduced rate will result in a more highly concurrent program—with all of the risks that an overlap in development and production entails. . . .

What that GAO report says to me, among other things, is that the Navy largely ignored its own testing system in its rush to get the T-45A into production. Why should the taxpayers pay for a multimillion dollar test center at Pax River if the Navy hierarchy is going to bypass it? Why should test pilots risk their lives finding out what is wrong with airplanes like the S-3 and the T-45A if Navy leaders ignore those findings?

In the course of pondering these and other questions for more than a year, often in concert with Navy test pilots and engineers who are often frustrated in their pursuit of the best, I met an experienced test pilot who was willing to speak his mind in print in hopes of showing how the checks and balances have gotten out of whack within the Navy bureaucracy. His name is George J. Webb, Jr.—a rebel with a cause.

Rebel with a Cause

"We write reports; we write reports, but I don't know who the hell ever reads them," lamented CAPT George J. Webb, Jr., in making his case that everybody would be better off if decision makers listened to what military test pilots, who have hands-on experience with the aircraft in question and are not tied to contractors, are trying to tell them.

"If anybody ever reads our reports," said Webb of himself and his fellow test pilots, "nothing ever seems to be done about it."

Webb's credentials for being an expert witness on what's wrong with military test piloting today are impressive.

Born on 30 March 1943 in Jacksonville, Florida, to George J. and Martha Webb, the young Webb went to the U.S. Naval Academy, graduating in 1965. He had grown up with airplanes because his father had been an enlisted Navy pilot during World War II, was later commissioned, and retired as a commander. A big thrill for father and son came in 1966 when George J. Webb, Sr., pinned the Navy wings of gold on George J. Webb, Jr.

During the Vietnam War Webb flew hundreds of missions in an A-7A while with VA-86 on the USS *America* and USS *Coral Sea,* winning the Meritorious Service Medal, eighteen Air Medals, six Navy Commendation Medals with Combat V, and the Vietnamese Cross of

Gallantry. Like Boecker before him, the young Webb went from combat flying in Vietnam to test-pilot training at Pax River, graduating in 1971 from TPS with Class 57.

As a test pilot he evaluated aircraft for a wide spectrum of specialized sections at Pax River, including Service Test, Weapons Systems Test, Rotary Wing, and the Carrier Suitability Branch of Flight Test. At Carrier Suitability he became project officer on the Lockheed S-3 Viking antisubmarine aircraft in 1972—the same plane that ripped apart over Chesapeake Bay when LT Sean Brennan and LCDR Steve Eastburg were putting it through some stressful maneuvers on 29 April 1992. He was the first to fly the British Hawk, which would become the T-45, during a second tour at Pax River, which started in 1982. He was then head of Carrier Suitability within the Strike Aircraft Test Directorate and in a third tour from 1986 to 1988 served as chief test pilot of the entire directorate. In July 1992 Webb was winding up his naval career as assistant chief of staff for facilities with the commander of U.S. Naval Forces, Japan. The veteran test pilot as of that date had logged 1,626 carrier landings, more than any other naval aviator in history.

Before getting into the case histories, I asked Webb to describe his own test-pilot creed:

"We test pilots have to put ourselves in the position of the guy in the fleet who will be flying this airplane, as we evaluate our test results and write our reports.

"I say to myself, 'Would I want to be flying this airplane as it is for the rest of my life, knowing I'll sometimes be trying to get it aboard a carrier at night and in the rain?' If I answer, 'No,' then why should I expect some lieutenant junior grade to do it? The test pilot has to think about Joe Schmuckatelli, who might be in the bottom 30 percent of aviators, and ask himself: 'Can Joe fly it?'

"What I was taught in going through TPS was that the purpose of a test pilot is to get in there early, find out what's wrong with a plane and let them know before it really gets into final production so they can make these changes—get it built right."

Webb said serving as a test pilot and manager during the development of the Lockheed S-3 in 1972 dramatized for him that defense contractors worrying about cash flow and the bottom line do not share his creed.

"Lockheed didn't want to make any changes on the S-3," Webb said. "In fact, Lockheed did a whole lot of things back then to try to get me fired, to try to hire me—all sorts of stuff" because of the critical reports he wrote about the plane then in development.

"When I first took the plane out to the carrier, I told them [his Navy superiors and the Lockheed executives] this plane has major problems. I came back and wrote [in his report] that this plane is unsatisfactory for carrier use. And the shit hit the fan.

"I was called up to Washington. I found myself on the short end of a long, green table with a total of about eight or nine stars sitting around me wondering who the hell was I to try to ruin their careers. I essentially said: 'Admiral, if you want to land it on a damn carrier, be my guest. But I am not going to say that it's safe for anybody else to land it on a damn carrier.'

"This was in 1973 when we first took it aboard a carrier. Lockheed was trying to put out the word that Webb was anti–S-3. At the same time Lockheed offered me sixty-five thousand bucks a year to go to work for them. I said, 'OK. Write me a ten-year contract.' They said, 'We can't do that.' So I said, 'Well, then I can't come to work for you.' I figured I'd have to resign from the Navy. Lockheed would give me the $65,000 and then say, 'Beat feet!'

"Shortly after the first carrier tests with the S-3, and after I had written in my report that it was 'unsatisfactory for service use,' I got called up to the admiral's office at the Test Center at Pax. He had been hearing all sorts of things, both from Lockheed and NavAir's management, which added up to the charge that 'Webb was anti–S-3, too critical, biased,' and that I therefore should be removed from the test team.

"After I was told to report to the admiral's office, I immediately called Captain Wayne Bodensteiner, the Test Center antisubmarine-warfare–aircraft program manager, and Captain Ken Melin, head of the Board of Inspection and Survey, to tell them what was happening. I asked for their support. They gave it. They came with me when I reported to the admiral.

"The admiral asked me if I thought I was too biased to remain objective in my tests. I told the admiral what I'd seen during the tests so far. I also told him about the pressure being exerted on me from outside the Test Center to change my test. Bodensteiner and Melin backed me 100 percent and told the admiral they wanted me to stay on the program.

"After that discussion, the admiral became irate, to put it mildly, at the people who had been phoning him about me. He told me: 'You are my S-3 test pilot, and I will tell everybody that. For the rest of these tests, I want you to live with Lockheed and get this airplane fixed. If you have any problems, you let me know!'

"One day Melin said to me, 'George, you've written up all these Part I, double-star yellow sheets [deficiencies on the S-3]. I want you and I to go flying, and you show me those deficiencies.'

"Lockheed hears BIS is going up in their airplane. I'm not working for the Test Center at this point. I'm working for BIS. The BIS report goes to the Secretary of the Navy—the civilian side of the house.

"I took Captain Melin up flying, showed him all these deficiencies. He just kept shaking his head, shaking his head.

"We came back, landed, taxied in. All these Lockheed guys were standing around. The captain gets out of the airplane first; I get out second. I was a lieutenant commander. The Lockheed guys didn't talk to me too much. They asked Captain Melin, 'How'd you like it, Captain? Wasn't that the greatest damn airplane you ever saw?'

"He wouldn't say anything. He just kept walking across the tarmac. They kept asking him, 'What do you think, Captain. Wasn't that great?'

"He still wouldn't say anything. Finally he stops and says, 'Well, I was taking notes. George was flying the plane. But I had to stop taking notes about one-third of the way through the flight because I couldn't figure out whether piss poor was one word, two words, or hyphenated.'

"Their mouths just dropped open. That's when they must have said, 'Oh shit! Maybe we better start fixing some of these things because otherwise it ain't going to get through BIS trials.' [Captain Melin could have recommended to the Secretary of the Navy that the Navy refuse to accept the S-3 for production and deployment, perhaps killing Lockheed's multibillion-dollar program].

"That's when I was sent out to California [to work with Lockheed to correct the deficiencies in the S-3]. I spent about six weeks [in 1973] working in Burbank and in Rye Canyon, where they have their laboratory. I worked with aeronautical engineers and flight-control designers. We invented direct-lift control for the S-3 [to make the airplane easier and safer to land on an aircraft carrier's deck].

"The primary problem with the S-3 stemmed from the fact that it is a very clean airplane—very aerodynamically clean. It makes a great glider. And the engines: being big fans—22-to-1 bypass ratio—meant that they did not change power very quickly."

The condition is similar to pressing on the gas pedal of your car and having to wait a few seconds for your car to speed up.

Because the S-3 is so aerodynamically clean, test pilot Webb explained, the pilot coming in to land on a carrier does not have to use much power to maintain the proper glide slope. "You're way back in a very low power regime," Webb continued. "Very low RPM [revolutions per minute] on both engines.

"If all of a sudden you're starting a settle coming into the carrier, you add power" to regain altitude, but nothing happens because of the delay in getting the engines to respond. "Then you find yourself sitting there, looking at the ramp," the wall of steel below the deck of the carrier. Hitting the ramp means dying. "In fact I almost hit the ramp" when testing the S-3 on the carrier, Webb said. "The combination of a very clean airplane and very slow power response was a major problem."

Another major problem, Webb continued, was that the nose of the S-3 would pitch up when the pilot added power and pitch down when he reduced power because the engines were "well below" the plane's center of gravity. "So you were always out of trim with a power change in the airplane."

Webb said that Lockheed's designers did not know that the wind swirling off a carrier forms a burble of air at the stern that an incoming pilot has to fly through. Lockheed's simulator at Rye Canyon assumed horizontal winds behind the carrier. Webb helped design a burble model for the simulator. The Lockheed test pilots who flew the simulated S-3 through the burble said, "Holy Smokes! That's how it is?" Webb recalled.

"The test pilots Lockheed had were super guys, but they didn't have any carrier experience," Webb said. "That was another problem with the S-3." Lockheed was not accustomed to building carrier airplanes and did not understand the unique demands of flying on and off a carrier.

Theoretically, there is a never-to-be-crossed firebreak between military test pilots working for the Department of Defense and civilian test pilots working for the private contractor. Military test pilots are supposed to tell the contractors what is wrong with their airplane and stop there, not tell them how to fix it. But most civilian test pilots learned their trade while in a military uniform and still have an allegiance to the Army, Navy, Air Force, or Marine Corps. And in the real world of trying to make an airplane better, military and civilian test pilots often ignore the firebreak and work together. They suggest fixes to the manufacturer.

Webb said he worked with Lockheed's test pilots, engineers, and designers to make the S-3 more responsive and easier to handle so that a pilot would not lose control of the plane while flying the ball. One fix, Webb said, addressed the S-3's pitching problem. He said "thrust trim compensation" was built into the plane's controls so that whenever the pilot increased or decreased power, the elevators would automatically move down or up to neutralize the pitching. With that fix, a pilot trying to stay on a glide slope while coming in to trap "does not have to fight the pitch with power all the time."

An even bigger help, Webb continued, was how the S-3's spoilers were used to assist the carrier pilot. A spoiler is a flight control on top of the wing. The spoiler is hinged on the wing's leading edge, rising up to disrupt—or spoil—the airflow over the wing. This spoiling of the airflow reduces the lift generated by the wing. Although normally activated on only one wing at a time, as the stick is moved left or right, to assist the ailerons with controlling roll, the S-3's spoilers were re-rigged so that by pressing a button on the stick, the pilot could also make the spoilers on both wings rise up simultaneously. This allowed the pilot to reduce the lift and caused the plane to descend faster without the pilot's having to pull back on the throttles to reduce power. With this direct lift control, which was perfected by the Navy-Lockheed team of test pilots and engineers, the S-3 pilot does not have to throttle the engines back to the unsafe, low-revolutions-per-minute regime. In that regime, response is slow. A pilot only seconds away from slamming down on a carrier deck wants quick response when adding or decreasing power to stay in the safe glide slope.

The Navy's former S-3 test pilot said he suggested other improvements to the S-3's flight-control system in 1973. The whole package was called the FQIP Mod, for Flying Qualities Improvement Program Modification. "Ten years later, in 1983, they finally fixed the flight-control system the way it should have been done," Webb lamented. "But we put enough Band-Aids on the airplane—with the thrust-trim compensation, with direct lift control, auto-bolter trim, and all the other little modifications to the automatic-flight-control system—that the S-3 was safe enough for carrier pilots to fly.

"I feel good about the changes in the S-3 I helped bring into being. I think history has proved their worth. The S-3 has never had a carrier-landing accident," Webb said. "I just wish all of the deficiencies we found in the airplane had been fixed all at one time in 1973 rather than be stretched over ten years. But Lockheed was trying to put the minimum amount of fix into it. If they had just gone ahead and bit the bullet at the beginning of the S-3 program, they could have had even a better plane than they've got right now. There was nothing wrong with the basic airplane. It just needed some more things."

Webb stayed at Pax much longer than the typical two years for his first test-pilot tour, not leaving until 1974. "Captain Melin got my tour extended three times," Webb recalled. "He told me: 'George, you can leave the test center as soon as the ink on your signature is dry on the final BIS report.'" Webb's final report to the Board of Naval Inspection and Survey said the deficiencies found in the S-3A had been corrected to the point that it was satisfactory for its mission, clearing the way for the Navy to formally accept the plane. Webb returned to the fleet after this first tour at Pax River, becoming landing signal officer for Air Wing Six.

When Webb returned to Pax River to head the Carrier Suitability Department within the Strike Directorate in 1982, the Navy had decided to buy the British Aerospace Hawk training plane.

By 1983 Congressional committees and some Navy leaders were beginning to worry about whether the Hawk could be adapted to carrier use. CAPT Paul A. Polski, project manager of the Navy's Hawk program at the Naval Air Systems Command, was among the worriers. Webb said Polski directed him, as head of Strike's Carrier Suitability Department, to fly to England to see how the Hawk, designated the T-45A by the Navy, behaved in simulated carrier approaches.

Recalled Webb: "Primarily, Polski wanted me to tell him if the airplane needed speed brakes during the landing approach. As it was designed, the Hawk has a ventral speed brake [one that hangs down from the belly of the plane], which automatically retracts when the landing gear is lowered so it will not hit the ground during landing. But a Navy pilot trying to land on a carrier might need that brake all the way down to the deck. The tests were to determine if the T-45 needed to have fuselage speed brakes, which could be kept extended during a carrier approach to make it easier for the Navy pilot to control the plane."

When Webb arrived at Dunsfold, England, on 10 November 1983 and flew the Hawk for the first time, "I saw a lot of similarities to the S-3. It was a very clean airplane. I was very impressed with this airplane in a lot of ways as a pilot. The aerodynamics of the airplane as far as lift and drag were just amazing—really fantastic.

"But again, as in the S-3, I was worried about the power response of the airplane. It was so clean. The Hawk was built for the Royal Air Force. Royal Air Force pilots land their planes at idle. They don't care where they land on a runway. On a long runway they can be plus or minus 1,000 feet. Navy pilots have to pinpoint a spot on the runway and land on it. The Hawk wasn't designed for constant angle of attack" in making its approach to a landing. A carrier pilot must be able to fly the plane at a specific angle to the oncoming air—the angle of attack—during the approach run to the deck.

As Webb flew round and round the British airfield in the Hawk, simulating carrier approaches and landings, "I found the power response was very slow. The Hawk didn't pitch up or down with the power like the S-3. But you had very slow power response. With the speed brake out, that created more drag. I was up on the power with the speed brake out" so that he could change the thrust of the engine more quickly rather than waiting for it to spool up. This quicker engine response would make the T-45A easier to control in the life-or-death approach to the steel flight deck of a carrier.

"So as far as that part of my mission went [determining whether the Hawk needed speed brakes for carrier landings], yes, the airplane needed speed brakes. But as I was flying the Hawk, I also noted some other things to be concerned about," with the plane's lateral directional stability at the top of Webb's preliminary list.

Whenever an airplane moves off of straight and level flight, it moves on one of three axes. An airplane rotates around an axis like a wheel rotates around an axle. The lateral axis runs across the airplane from wing tip to wing tip. The longitudinal axis runs lengthwise from nose to tail. The vertical axis spears through the airplane from top to bottom. Flex your outstretched hand up and down around a line through your knuckles and you are "pitching," in aeronautical terms. Roll your hand from side to side so your thumb and pinkie take turns going up and down and you are "rolling." Twist your hand side to side around an imaginary spear right through the center of your palm and you are "yawing."

The elevator located on the tail of an airplane controls pitching. Moving the control stick in the cockpit backward and forward makes the elevator go up and down.

The ailerons—panels fitted into the trailing edges of the wings—control roll. To roll the airplane to the left, the pilot pushes the control stick to the left. This causes the left aileron to move upward, killing lift on the left wing at the same time that the right aileron moves downward to increase lift on the right wing—an arrangement Glenn Curtiss built into the first biplanes Spuds Ellyson and Jack Towers flew in the first years of Naval Aviation. Less lift on the left wing and more lift on the right wing creates an imbalance that causes the airplane to roll left as long as the pilot holds the stick over to the left.

To make the airplane yaw, the pilot pushes on the rudder pedals. Pushing on the left pedal moves the rudder to the left, making the nose swing—also called yaw—to the left. Pushing on the right pedal causes the plane to yaw right.

To change the direction in which the airplane is flying, the pilot usually uses the control stick to move the ailerons. This is faster and smoother than using the rudder alone. However, the aileron that dips down into the onrushing air creates drag on that wing, called "induced drag" because the pilot, not the metal body of the airplane, induced it. This induced drag causes the nose to swing off the desired course—called "adverse yaw" because it is in the opposite direction of the desired turn. Rolling left produces right yaw.

Webb said the Hawk's poor lateral directional stability produced too much adverse yaw for the plane to be safe to land on a carrier's deck. He said that when he returned to Pax River, "I told them: 'You better do something about this adverse yaw. You better do something about lateral directional stability. You better do something about the neutral speed stability and about weak static longitudinal stability.' It did not meet spec [Navy specifications for performance] on any one of those things, and the airplane was very uncomfortable to the pilot because of it. I said, 'Unless these are fixed, this thing will never be a carrier airplane.'

"I was thoroughly impressed with the Hawk for flying around in as an airplane. But I was not looking at it that way. I was looking at it from the standpoint of 'Can this airplane be landed on a carrier by a student aviator?' My first thought was, 'I wonder what the Alpha Jet was like. Was it this bad?'"

Despite his concerns about the suitability of the Hawk for carrier operations, Webb believed after his test flights in Dunsfold that the flaws could be corrected. But he also feared the fixes would be difficult and expensive, partly because the Hawk was a simple airplane in which the ailerons and other controls were worked by the pilot's own muscle, not by a hydraulic system that would have provided the equivalent of power steering. "One of the things that would correct the adverse-yaw problem," Webb said, "would be an aileron-rudder interconnect." With this system, when the pilot pushes the stick to the left to bank in that direction, the rudder automatically moves left to overcome the adverse yaw. This would have been easy to implement with hydraulic controls. But with the Hawk, a hydraulic system or at least part of one would have had to be added to hook the aileron and rudder together—meaning more expense, more weight.

Webb said that he pushed, pulled, pleaded, and yelled in a vain effort to have the deficiencies he had found in the Hawk corrected before McDonnell Douglas put it into production. He contended that if this had been done, everyone—the contractors, the Navy, and the student pilots who will train in the navalized version of the Hawk—would have been far better off.

The written record of the British Aerospace Hawk's evolution into the Navy's T-45A trainer confirms what Webb said. After testing the carrier-landing capability of the Hawk in Dunsfold, England, from 10 to 16 November 1983, Webb wrote a memorandum for RADM E. J. Hogan, Jr., commander of the Naval Air Test Center, to send to Naval Air Systems Command. Webb's draft described these shortcomings in the Hawk for its role as the Navy's future training plane:

> . . . Glide slope tracking [with speed brakes not extended] was difficult, and corrections from high, low and off speed conditions often resulted in numerous glide slope overshoots. Use of the ventral speed

brake improved glide slope tracking and made any necessary corrections easier to accomplish. . . . Aircraft attitude changes associated with speed corrections were very small and difficult to discern. The combined effect made it difficult for the pilot to recognize an underpowered, decelerating situation sufficiently early to make timely corrections. Consequently, student pilots will occasionally land hard or short of the runway during syllabus flights not monitored by an LSO. . . .

The aircraft exhibited very lightly damped Dutch roll characteristics [Dutch roll on an airplane is like the rocking of a canoe when it is hit sideways by a wave and is knocked off course as well. If the plane or canoe rocks only a little bit from a push of air or water but quickly stabilizes without being knocked way off course, the Dutch roll has been heavily damped—this is good. But if the plane or canoe takes a long time to stabilize, its Dutch roll has been only lightly damped—this is bad.], and the Dutch roll mode of motion could be easily excited in the normal turbulence experienced during FCLP [field carrier-landing practice] or carrier approach. This Dutch roll oscillation could seriously degrade line-up control and cause the student to spend too much time on directional control at the expense of glide scope control. Dutch roll characteristics were improved with the speed brake extended, but the student will [still] experience line-up problems in moderate turbulence. The adverse yaw characteristics further exacerbated the Dutch roll motion. During full deflection aileron rolls in configuration PA [power approach] with speed brakes in, up to 18 degrees of sideslip was observed. . . . The amount of sideslip generated during rolls was lessened with the speed brake extended but remained excessive. . . .

In March 1984 Hogan sent a memo to Naval Air Systems Command, concluding with the sentence that the Hawk "exhibited excellent potential as an intermediate/advanced jet trainer." Webb said potential was the magic word, signaling to any knowledgeable test pilot that the Hawk needed a lot of work before it was safe to send to the Training Command. His own list of deficiencies inserted in Hogan's letter shouted the warning loud and clear, Webb contended, but I fear only other test pilots who know the code words and what weight they should be accorded would understand the message.

An unsigned, undated memo from an unidentified Naval Air Test Center "program manager" to Naval Air Systems Command warned that there was not enough time in the Navy's T-45A schedule to correct the deficiencies discovered by Webb and others before McDonnell Douglas froze its design. The program manager suggested turning one of the existing British Hawks into a test bed so that Pax River could evaluate the fixes before the metal cutting for the T-45A began. Webb, in commenting on the memo, said of the program manager's test-bed proposal, reportedly made in 1984 and rejected: "This was a pretty smart idea, which, alas, never came to fruition."

The unidentified program manager expressed concern about the Navy's leaping before looking in these words:

> A three article FSED [full-scale engineering development] program will include only 50 aircraft test months which will be barely adequate to cover required testing. There is virtually no room in the test program for aircraft lay-up for design modifications or for iterative retesting in search of fixes to unexpected deficiencies. If major program milestones are to be met and Initial Operating Capability achieved on schedule in this success oriented program, the areas for potential deficiencies outlined in Table 1 must be investigated prior to FSED while aircraft design is fluid and time exists for thoughtful resolution of any problems discovered.
>
> . . . A flight test program of 10 hours would be sufficient to identify any significant deficiencies in the areas outlined in Table One and provide limited scope for iterative retesting of any problems discovered. . . .

Other documents on the paper trail include the first interim report issued in November 1988 on the Goshawk that McDonnell Douglas had built for the Navy. The report documents that many of the deficiencies that Webb and others had spotlighted five years earlier had been built right into the new airplane. This report—a DT 2 (a phase-two developmental-testing evaluation)—listed twenty-four Part I deficiencies, including "inadequate directional stability; excessive altitude loss due to poor engine performance; excessive adverse yaw at contractor's recommended approach speed; inadequate stall warning"; and poor control when building up to a stall.

Besides the twenty-four Part I deficiencies the test pilots listed, there were also twenty-nine Part II and ten Part III deficiencies.

"Within the scope of these tests," the DT 2 stated, "the T-45 exhibits limited potential for the undergraduate jet training mission but will be satisfactory upon correction of all Part One deficiencies. . . ."

Long before the General Accounting Office got into the act, Webb decried, "Somebody should have said: 'This guy Webb—whoever the hell he is—already says these things are wrong with Hawk. You haven't fixed them yet; so we're not going to let you go into production.'

"I know that, theoretically, buying an off-the-shelf airplane is going to be a lot less expensive than going through the whole design of a new airplane. But really, an Alpha Jet is not built to land on a carrier. The Hawk isn't built to land on a carrier. How much more money, time, and effort does it really take to design an airplane to land on a carrier than to take one not designed to land on a carrier and rebuild it so it does? Did we really save anything except international goodwill, which means nothing to the test pilots or the taxpayer?"

Webb said it is unrealistic to rely on program managers to cancel or suspend their own aircraft programs. "A program manager is given this program and is told, 'Make it succeed,'" Webb said. "If it does not succeed, the program manager does not succeed in the Navy. So the program manager is not really looking out for the fleet. The program manager is looking out for his ass. And that is not the way it ought to be.

"The Naval Air Test Center is looking out for the fleet. But when you're at the Test Center and talking to a program manager at Naval Air Systems Command, you're too often talking to a guy who is looking out for his butt, looking out for his dollars. He is only given X number of dollars for this program. And he wants to be ahead of schedule and under cost. So he doesn't want to spend any more money, and he wants things to go fast. That's how he makes flag rank."

Although the Navy's Board of Inspection and Survey was established to provide an assessment independent of program managers and other potential boosters of a project, a wide spectrum of test pilots told me that BIS is now called "The Paper Tiger" because its reports to the Secretary of the Navy seldom result in countermanding project managers. They assert that modern aircraft projects are so few and so big and so expensive that once the Secretary of the Navy approves a project, he is reluctant to delay or stop it no matter what BIS's reports say. When aircraft were cheaper, the Navy could afford to develop two competing models at once, compare them through elaborate flight-testing, and then put the best one into production. This is no longer done because planes cost too much. This means that canceling an existing plane could leave the Navy with none at all when other services are poised to grab any savings from cancellations. All this adds momentum to existing aircraft-development programs like the T-45A, flawed or not.

Webb said the current system for making sure the best possible aircraft get to the fleet is broken. He is among the evaluators who believe that test-pilot findings should be taken more seriously before projects gain too much momentum to stop.

He called for changing the present system to restore the checks and balances.

The Future

Test pilot Webb's call for change in the way the Navy decides which aircraft are worth buying came in 1992 when the entire American military was under orders to change.

With the Cold War over and the Warsaw Pact threat gone, President Bush and Congress demanded that the Navy and the other armed services restructure themselves by subtraction after the Reagan years of restructuring by addition.

This restructuring was highly visible at Pax River in 1992 and will become even more so in the future as the nation spends less money on defense and more on domestic programs.

On 4 March 1992, for example, the Navy held a stand-up ceremony at Pax River to mark the congressionally mandated absorption of the Naval Air Test Center into a new conglomerate called the Naval Air Warfare Center Aircraft Division. A group of aviators distressed over the passing of the fiercely and effectively independent Naval Air Test Center held a mock funeral and wake in the museum at Pax River a few nights before the stand-up ceremony. Rear Admiral McCain would have been proud of the mourners. He was the former Chief of the Bureau of Aeronautics who had warned against putting testing and development under the same roof. The new Naval Air Warfare Center at Pax does just that by bringing the Naval Air Development Center at Warminster, Pennsylvania, to Pax River.

I went to the stand-up for the Naval Air Warfare Center, already being called "Knock" from its initials, NAWC, and found myself musing over the ironies. Here we were, commemorating a new day for Pax River, in a place that signified how dim that day will be for test piloting specifically and Naval Air generally. The ceremony was held inside the Captain Steven A. Hazelrigg Memorial Flight Test Facility, a cavernous hangar. The hangar was all dressed up with flags but had no place to go. Defense Secretary Richard B. Cheney had canceled the A-12 attack plane for which the hangar had been built. Hazelrigg, for whom the hangar was named, was killed when the old A-6 bomber, which the A-12 was to replace, broke during a test flight on 15 August 1990.

On the day of the stand-up ceremony, there was only one brand-new airplane at Pax River for the Navy test pilots to test, the T-45A trainer. Less than a mile away from the Hazelrigg hangar, a new $5 million Test Pilot School was being built on a knoll in front of the existing school. Its future as a building was far more assured than the future of test pilots. Would the new school building be used for something else while the Navy test pilots who were scheduled to go there were sent to the Air Force test-pilot school at Edwards Air Force Base, California? With fewer aircraft being bought and Pentagon and congressional leaders insisting on "jointness" in military endeavors, would future Army, Navy, Air Force, and Marine Corps test pilots learn their trade at one place? Would the number of military test pilots be cut because of budget restraints and a lack of aircraft to test?

One of the Navy leaders studying those and other jointness questions was Rear Admiral Boecker, the same aviator who was blown out of the sky over Laos in 1965 and who welcomed Class 100 to Pax River in 1991 while commander of the Naval Air Test Center. In 1992 he was vice commander of Naval Air Systems Command.

By the summer of 1992, when this is being written, this uncertainty about the future of Naval Air and test piloting was taking its toll. Several Navy test pilots at Pax River, including some from Class 100, felt so under utilized that they were volunteering to return to the fleet ahead of schedule in hopes of finding more flying time and excitement.

Deepening the gloom at Pax River and every other Naval Air installation in 1992 was the far-ranging Defense Department investigation of sexual harassment by naval aviators at the 1991 Tailhook convention. This funereal atmosphere contrasted sharply with the upbeat, noisy, exciting, and dangerous golden years at the Naval Air Test Center in the 1960s. Back then, old-timers recalled, Navy and Marine Corps test pilots were evaluating more than a dozen new aircraft and helicopters, often flying two competing models against each other. Pax River and its environs rocked with sonic booms. Tales of what this or that new airplane did during its test flight that day electrified the local drinking spots. A sense of urgency energized Pax River because requests to test aircraft and weapons kept test pilots in the air. The testers were stressed but happy. They often took shortcuts. Airplane crashes and aviator deaths were frequent, but the future of Naval Air looked unlimited.

The new future of Naval Air and of some of its best and brightest, the test pilots, now depends not only on how much money becomes available but on how the Navy fits into the war plans for regional conflicts. Desert Storm was not reassuring in this regard. Naval Air took a backseat to the Air Force. If sea-based aircraft are deemphasized in the war plans for the next century, there will be fewer carriers built and fewer aircraft bought for their decks. This will mean fewer new aircraft for test pilots to test for the fleet.

Former Navy Secretary John F. Lehman, Jr., an effective advocate of Naval Air while in office from 1981 to 1987, is among those who believe that Desert Storm marked only the start of the decline of Naval Air. He predicted the Air Force with its newer, longer-range, stealthier aircraft will increasingly be assigned roles previously performed by Naval Air. He blames the downfall of Naval Air on the anti–Naval Air mind-set in the Pentagon and the failure of Navy leaders to buy carrier aircraft with enough range to hit targets far inland.

"There has been a very strong orthodoxy and bureaucracy in the Defense Department against letting the Navy have an offensive-strike capability," Lehman said in an interview in 1992.

"You can trace it person by person back to the fight over the Air Force B-36 bomber versus the aircraft carrier—the roles and mission debate that occurred after World War II.

"Some of the same people in the Pentagon's Program Analysis and Evaluation Office today were there fighting the same battle twenty years ago, and they learned it from guys who were there fighting it twenty years before them.

"It's the school of thought which argues for what was called KISS—Keep It Simple, Stupid. Members of that school are within the Office of the Secretary of Defense and within various private military reform groups. They have opposed such things as heavy divisions for the Army and all-weather planes for the Navy. They advocated the lightweight fighter, following the lead of the Soviets with the MiG-21. They wanted the Navy out of the strike mission, on the ground that this should be done by the Air Force, the service with strategic bombers."

Lehman said he was up against that philosophy whenever Pentagon executives sat down to apportion the total defense budget among the Navy, Army, Air Force, and Marine Corps. If the Navy was denied the offensive, deep-strike role for its aircraft, there would be no money allocated to buying bombers for that mission. As Lehman saw it, every budget was a battle for the survival of Naval Air and its personnel, including test pilots and testing centers like Pax River.

He cited the fight over the Navy's long-range A-6 bomber as an example of the continual struggle to keep the Navy in the deep-strike business.

"The Office of the Secretary of Defense opposed offensive-strike aircraft in the Navy for as long as I have been associated with the issue, which is twenty-five years.

"When I was Secretary of the Navy, the Defense Secretary's Office of Program Analysis and Evaluation tried to cancel the A-6 because there was a fundamental, deep philosophy opposed to Navy carriers having that offensive-strike capability."

However, Lehman said, he and his allies managed not only to save the A-6E, which was flying when he became secretary, but persuaded the Reagan administration to buy a much-improved version of the bomber called the A-6F, another Navy plane that Defense Secretary Cheney canceled shortly after taking office in 1991.

Lehman, in revealing the master plan he had for Naval Air while he was Navy Secretary, said he intended to rush ahead with the A-6F while keeping its successor, the A-12, on the back burner. He said he wanted to let the Air Force work out the bugs in its B-2 flying-wing bomber before the Navy bought a downsized version of it, the A-12.

"We did not want to get concurrent with the B-2," he recalled, "and pay for the same mistakes the B-2 made. We said, 'Let's keep it in advanced development under a cost-plus contract so we can adapt the

Air Force's technologies to the carrier environment. When all the kinks are worked out, we can go into full-scale development.'" He said 1997 was the target date for starting full-scale development of the A-12.

But the Office of the Secretary of Defense and its Office of Defense Research and Engineering, he lamented, "were strongly in favor of the stealth technology. They ordered us against our recommendation to fully fund what became known as the A-12. In 1983 we were ordered to go into full-scale development and skip prototypes so we could have an initial operating capability in 1992.

"That was when Paul Thayer was there. [Paul W. Thayer had been a member of Class 1 at Test Pilot School, which graduated in 1948, and served as Deputy Secretary of Defense from 12 January 1983 until 4 January 1984.] They killed the A-6F. Then [William Howard] Taft came in to replace Thayer. Taft agreed to fund the A-6F as long as we proceeded with full funding of the A-12 with an initial operational capability of 1992. So that's when we accelerated the A-12, on the order of the Office of the Secretary of Defense. Cap [Defense Secretary Caspar W. Weinberger] was not in the loop.

"So when I left as Secretary of the Navy, the development of the A-6F under a fixed-price contract"—one that froze the total price at the signing of the contract (meaning the contractor would have to pay for any increases)—"was in good shape, ready to go into production. After I left, the A-6F was canceled by the Office of the Secretary of Defense. The A-12 was taken to contract. Its contract wasn't signed until nearly a year after I left.

"To me, the most incredible thing is the double standard that is still so rife in the Office of the Secretary of Defense. Here you had both the ATA [Advanced Tactical Aircraft, which became the A-12] and the Air Force ATF [Advanced Tactical Fighter] starting at the same time back in 1983. Both were given $3 billion as the target, nonrecurring cost for the development of those planes.

"The Navy made every effort, given that schedule, to contain the cost under a fixed-price contract. The Navy tried to keep out all the upgrades—the bells and whistles. The cost would have gone up to maybe as high as $6.5 billion under the worst case. In constant dollars that would be a $2 billion overrun. The Secretary of Defense canceled it. The Air Force is now going up to $18 billion on the ATF, and it's being held up as a successful program. So there's a double standard there. The Navy is without an airplane because they were going to go all the way to $6.5 billion. The Air Force has theirs because they're going to $18 billion. It's crazy!"

Turning to how the cancellation of the A-12 will affect all of Naval Air, including test pilots who evaluate planes before they go on carriers and whenever they are modified, Lehman said the lack of a deep-strike capability will make carriers increasingly irrelevant. He predicted the Navy's deployable carrier force will shrink from the currently projected twelve to "seven or eight" by the year 2000.

Since each carrier goes to sea with about eighty-five aircraft, the loss of five carriers—from twelve to seven—would mean 425 fewer aircraft to buy, test, and deploy. The Navy in July 1992 was planning to build a new F/A-18 fighter and attack aircraft—designated the F/A-18E and F—in hopes of obtaining the deep-strike range offered by the aging A-6 bomber. Critics of this approach, including the House Armed Services Committee, contended that the F/A-18E and F would draw so much money away from the A-12 that the latter plane would never get built.

Lehman agreed with that danger, declaring that without the A-6F or A-12 to provide the deep-strike capability, "carriers will appear less and less" in the nation's war plans. "And as carriers become less important" to the theater commanders, he continued, "the carriers won't be able to compete in the arena at budget crunch time. That's the way carriers will fade out of the picture.

"The mission that has carried the carrier," he said, "has been the deep-strike mission. And it is that that they have pissed away."

Although test pilots will always have modifications of existing aircraft to test, the danger, as Lehman saw it, was that they would become dispirited if they concluded they were no longer on the cutting edge of technology.

"You can keep morale high at places like the Naval Air Test Center and Edwards Air Force Base if the aviators feel they are part of a winning organization, that they're part of building the future and testing things that are going to make the fleet keep its edge," Lehman contended.

"The danger is that a lot of young naval aviators worry about whether they're headed toward second-class status, whether they're going to become a Coast Guard kind of operation instead of being the cutting edge of aviation and national defense. That's the big threat to morale.

"Naval Aviation is going through a particular crisis of confidence because the Bush Administration has been the most anti–Naval Aviation of any administration since Truman's. I'm sure nobody planned it that way. But that's what the lieutenant at Pax River sees. Twelve Naval Aviation programs have been canceled by the Bush administration and not one Air Force program. The appearance from the deck plates is that the Bush administration has basically decided to really downgrade Naval Aviation. I'm not optimistic" about the future of Naval Air.

VADM Richard M. Dunleavy, Assistant Chief of Naval Operations for Air Warfare until mid-1992, chose to be more optimistic about the future of Naval Air and its test pilots.

Naval Aviation will have a deterrent role, he said, even if there are no shooting wars to fight. The threat will be "Third World countries with first-class weapons, the proliferation of weapons around the world," as Dunleavy saw the future. "We'll put out more fires than anybody will ever give us credit for, just by being there."

But how much of a future can there be for Navy test pilots in the coming era, with a slashed aircraft-procurement budget and a shrunken fleet?

Dunleavy said no matter how few new aircraft will be bought, "you'll always need a good cadre of test pilots and engineers" to determine how the changes in existing aircraft affect their performance and flying qualities. Also, he said, tomorrow's test pilots and engineers will have to test and evaluate the new systems and weapons under development.

ADM Frank B. Kelso II, Chief of Naval Operations in 1992, agreed that the end of the Warsaw Pact threat does not mean the end of Naval Aviation. Downsizing, he said, will require constant testing of aircraft, weapons, and systems to keep the nation's qualitative edge. He added that only the Navy can control the seas for the United States.

"I believe there will be a role for Naval Aviation in the future because if you want to control the ocean surface," Kelso said, "you've got to be able to control the surface above it. Unless we have airfields nearby, the only way to do it is with a carrier. So I think there are a lot of scenarios in the world where we are going to continue to need Naval Aviation."

Whether the outlook is really pessimistic like Lehman's or optimistic like Kelso's, it seemed to be clear in the summer of 1992 that the transcendent challenge for military leaders was to do more with less without dispiriting their best and brightest in the process.

As a long-time student of military affairs who had the opportunity to spend more than a year studying and listening to many of the best and brightest within the test-pilot community, I concluded the following changes would help meet that challenge.

Test-Pilot Training

RECOMMENDATION

To make test-pilot training more relevant to the military aircraft, weapons, and systems that the United States will be using in the next century, commission an outside panel to identify the mismatches between what test pilots and engineers are taught today and what they will be evaluating in the year 2000.

After an outside panel of experts identifies the mismatches, determine the best ways to correct them. It seems to me that the smaller cadre of pilots and engineers to be trained as evaluators for the future would learn more by moving from one specialized center of excellence to another rather than spending a whole year at either Pax River or Edwards Air Force Base.

Pax River, Edwards Air Force Base, private industry, and, for rotary-wing evaluation, the Army helicopter center at Fort Rucker, Alabama, might each become a center of excellence for specialized instruction and flying. Small classes would rotate continually through the centers, perhaps staying three or four months at each center.

Sitting in a classroom at Pax River, listening to lectures on how lasers and radar technology will be applied in the future, I wondered why for such courses the military does not send its future test pilots to an aerospace firm that is actually working on those systems. The students could then see and feel the high-tech gear as well as hear what it was designed to do from the very people who designed it. Certainly the aerospace industry would welcome the business and the chance to explain itself to tomorrow's evaluators.

As one who flew in the Army's Apache helicopter at Fort Rucker, I cannot believe this giant training area with all its instructors and helicopters could not be effectively used to teach future rotary test pilots from all the services. The students would also learn about the special requirements of special operations from people who actually undertake them. Before reporting to Rucker, the students would have completed courses at an aerospace firm that makes modern systems and weapons for helicopters. At Rucker, they would learn how the American military intends to employ those weapons in the future. Their instruction flights at Rucker—or perhaps at a test center like White Sands, New Mexico—would be designed to show them how to evaluate aircraft, systems, and weapons for their intended use.

While keeping families housed under this mobile system of instruction might sound like a problem, it need not be. The pilots and engineers would live with their families where they were to work after finishing Test Pilot School. The students would travel unaccompanied, just as during a regular Navy deployment, to take the specialized courses away from home. As it is now, families do not see much of the students at Test Pilot School anyway because of all the studying and flying.

One benefit of breaking the course into specialized parts at different centers would be to give more emphasis to the weapons and systems that will win future air battles, at the same time deemphasizing aircraft flying qualities and performance, which are not advancing so rapidly.

Test-Pilot Boards

RECOMMENDATION

Establish a system for convening temporary boards of former military test pilots still on active duty to review the findings of working test pilots and engineers at each milestone of an aircraft's development.

If test pilots who fly an airplane to evaluate it and engineers who sift through the data collected aloft are not expert witnesses on whether a project should go forward or be nipped in the bud, who is?

The saga of the T-45A illustrates that the present system does not work, that program managers and other leaders are unwilling to say, "Cancel!"; "Fix!"; or even "Delay!"

To help throw more light on problems before they are built into an aircraft, the test-pilot board would study the reports of working test pilots and perhaps call the test pilots themselves as witnesses. The whole idea is to get the truth from knowledgeable untouchables unconnected with the project being reviewed.

A test-pilot board would write a blunt report in plain language, explaining its conclusions. The board would say straight out whether an aircraft, system, or weapon is worth buying and what the contractor should be required to do to fix it—if it is worth fixing at all.

Besides going to the Secretary of the Navy and Chief of Naval Operations, the reports of the test-pilot boards would go to the relevant congressional committees and be available to the press. This distribution would address test pilot Webb's complaint that test-pilot reports are being ignored or buried in the Navy's bureaucracy.

The test-pilot boards would not become another bureaucracy. They would be individuals called away from their regular jobs to perform a service for a short time, like civilians called to jury duty. After the members of the test-pilot board met and made their recommendations, they would return to their regular jobs—again, like jurors.

I believe such oversight from people who really understand what test pilots and engineers are saying would reestablish some of the credibility lost inside and outside the Navy and raise the morale of the evaluators. Recall that Melvyn R. Paisley, the Navy's former research-and-development chief, pleaded guilty in federal court in 1991 to taking bribes from contractors in exchange for throwing them Navy business.

"If the Secretary of the Navy or his people are bought," said Webb to cite an example of why test pilots are disillusioned, "what the hell difference does it make to have a BIS [Board of Inspection and Survey]?" BIS, through its direct line to the Secretary of the Navy, is supposed to ensure that program managers in Naval Air Systems Command or other executives do not railroad through pet projects of questionable value.

Outside the Navy, Congress needs reassurance, in the wake of the A-12 and T-45A cost overruns and the F/A-18's disappointing range, that additional oversight by hands-on experts with no vested interests has been imposed.

Safety

RECOMMENDATION

Computerize the key data needed to write safe flight plans to avoid catastrophic surprises like the breaking of the S-3's tail during rudder sweeps on 29 April 1992 at Pax River.

With today's computerized reference systems, it takes only a matter of seconds for anyone with access to them to get printouts of material in the data bank. For example, if you feed such key words as Bush and Navy into the computerized data bank, almost everything written about President Bush's Navy career can be retrieved. If the engineers and test pilots who planned the near-fatal test flight of Steve Eastburg and Sean Brennan had been able to retrieve all the data on similar S-3 tests from a computerized data bank, they might have been forewarned of the dangers and avoided them.

RECOMMENDATION

Equip a rescue helicopter with the latest lifesaving equipment and man it with a highly trained medic who knows how to treat burns and other conditions common to aircraft accidents.

Two aviators' lives were saved in less than two years at Pax River by helicopters equipped with modern medical gear and trained personnel. But neither rescue helicopter was a Navy one.

On 15 August 1990 a Virginia police helicopter rushed a critically injured LT William C. Davis from a field in Burgess, Virginia, where he had landed by parachute after a violent ejection, to the Medical College of Virginia Hospital in Richmond. He lived.

On 29 April 1992 a Maryland police helicopter rushed a critically burned LT Sean Brennan from Deal Island, Maryland, to the burn center at Francis Scott Key Medical Center in Baltimore. He lived, after having received sophisticated medical treatment aboard the helicopter. Maryland Trooper Collins told me afterward that he was shocked at the lack of lifesaving equipment and trained medical personnel in the Navy helicopter that would have otherwise flown Brennan across the Chesapeake Bay to the base hospital at Pax River.

The next time a Navy airplane from Pax River crashes, there may not be a police medical helicopter available. The Navy should not ask its people to take that risk. A Navy rescue helicopter with the latest lifesaving equipment and at least one highly trained medic should be on call at Pax River whenever Navy planes are being tested in the area.

If test pilots are willing to risk their lives to find out what is right or wrong with an airplane, the least the rest of us on the ground can do is to make sure we give them everything they need to increase their chances of surviving crashes.

Women in Combat

RECOMMENDATION

Open the Navy the rest of the way to women, including giving female aviators billets in aircraft-carrier squadrons during wartime as well as peacetime.

Granting women full equality is not only the right thing to do but the best way to neutralize some of the poison Marine and Navy aviators threw in the Navy's well by assaulting women at the Tailhook convention at the Las Vegas Hilton Hotel 5–7 September 1991.

The failure of Navy leaders to respond quickly and severely once they were informed of the attacks further damaged the reputation of Naval Air. Marine and Navy officers from lieutenant to rear admiral were guilty of malfeasance and/or nonfeasance at Tailhook. Their behavior confirms that there is indeed a cultural problem within the Navy when it comes to recognizing and respecting women's rights.

Those who counter that aviators at Tailhook were just having fun the traditional way should read the sworn statement LT Paula A. Coughlin gave to the Naval Investigative Service after she was assaulted in the fully lighted hallway of the Las Vegas Hilton by fellow officers the night of 7 September 1991.

Even more disturbing, her sworn statement documents that RADM John W. Snyder, Jr., who had replaced Boecker as commander of the Naval Air Test Center before the Tailhook convention, failed to act on the sexual assault and harassment of Coughlin, his own military aide, despite her repeated requests for redress. While reading the following excerpts from Coughlin's sworn statement, imagine this is happening to your own daughter, wife, or sister:

> There were approximately six to eight of the young men on each side of the hallway and two in the center of the hallway, each with their backs to me. . . .

I advanced down the hallway and continued to look for a familiar face but saw none. As I arrived at the location of the two men in the center of the hallway, I attempted to pass the one on the right side.

As I passed the individual, the man intentionally bumped into me with his right hip. The bump was sufficient to cause me to stop, turn around and address the man, saying, "Excuse me."

The man who bumped into me was approximately six feet two, dark skin with short dark hair, being perhaps Hispanic or a light skin black. As I excused myself, I observed that he had nice appearing white teeth, no glasses and a crew collar type T shirt which appeared to be a faded burnt orange.

I also noted that as I excused myself the man was standing with his shoulders back, chest out and smiling in a challenging way as I made eye contact with him. I did not perceive any danger at this time.

A blond haired man either standing next to the man that bumped me or leaning against the wall yelled in a loud voice twice, "Admiral's aide! Admiral's aide!"

I was astonished at not only the loudness of the announcement, but startled that the man knew who I was.

As I turned to look at the man, the man who originally bumped into me grabbed me by the buttocks with such force that it lifted me off the ground and ahead a step. [Coughlin is 5 feet 4 inches tall and weighs 120 pounds.]

As this happened I wiggled from his grip, turned around and asked the man, "What the fuck do you think you are doing?"

As I did this, I was grabbed by the buttocks again by someone behind me. And as I wheeled to identify the individual, I again addressed another individual by asking him the same.

Each time I turned to face a new assault on my person, I would receive several others from various individuals.

The group not only grabbed my buttocks, but my breasts as well.

Shortly after the assault began, the man with the dark complexion moved in immediately behind me with his body pressed against mine. He was bumping me, pushing me forward down the passageway where the group on either side was pinching and then pulling at my clothing.

The man [with the dark complexion] then put both his arms over the top of my shoulders and then put both his hands down the front of my tanktop and inside my bra where he grabbed my breasts.

I dropped to a forward crouch position and placed my hands on the wrists of my attacker in an attempt to remove his hands. The man was off balance leaning forward over me. I then turned my head to the left and sank my teeth into the fleshy part of the man's left forearm, biting hard. I noted no jewelry or watch.

I thought I drew blood, as I tasted something in my mouth that I suspected was either blood or sweat. As this occurred, the man struggled and removed his left arm, to which I turned and bit the man on the right hand at the area between the base of the thumb and base of the index finger. The attacker then removed his right hand as well.

As I was attempting to regain my balance, someone in front of me reached under my skirt and grabbed the crotch of my panties. There was no penetration or, in fact, any touching of my skin. This individual seemed to be attempting to remove my panties by pulling on them. It was a quick in and out attempt.

As I continued to try to regain my balance, I kicked one of my attackers with my right leg but didn't think I caused any damage. At this point, I felt as though the group was trying to rape me. I was terrified and had no idea what was going to happen next.

As I made it back to a standing position, I observed an open door on my right. The distance was approximately two steps. And as I took the first step, I saw that on each side of the doorway was one of the group involved in my assault.

As I began the second step, one of the men took a step to the left, and the other a step to the right. And both blocked my entrance into the room and smiled at me.

The room behind them was dark, like a barroom, and [I] was unable to determine if anyone was in there. Both of these individuals were wearing crew type T shirts, light colored, with the one on the left having a pocket on his left breast.

The group was still grabbing my buttocks, breasts and attempting to remove my clothing.

Then I noticed a member of the group with his back to me and walking away from the group. I asked him for help. I reached out and tapped him on the right hip, pleading for the man to just let me get in front of him.

The man stopped, turned to the right and pivoted to a position directly in front of me. With this action, the man raised both hands and put one on each of my breasts.

I broke from the man's grip and ran past him on the right side. This man was apparently older than the rest of the group, perhaps 30 years; five feet ten to five feet eleven; blond hair. He was wearing a faded red polo shirt and jeans. I covered my chest, breaking his grip, and ducked down and went forward three steps to the next open door.

During the entire assault, I could hear the group proclaiming, "Admiral's aide! Admiral's aide!" I did not hear anyone call my name or make any sexual comments regarding my anatomy. The only other sounds I could hear were the sounds of the group music in the background.

I suffered no bruises, abrasions, cuts or any other injury exclusive of a minor injury to my knee.

I was appalled not only by the brutality of the incident, but the fact that the group did that to me knowing I was both a fellow officer and an admiral's aide.

At this point in the evening [11:45 P.M.] the only alcohol I had consumed was two glasses of champagne that I had with LT Scott Wilson [at 5:30 P.M.] toasting the news of his wife's pregnancy, a vodka screwdriver [at 7:30 P.M.] waiting for Admiral Snyder [her boss] to show up for dinner, a glass of red wine with dinner and two sips of beer while changing clothes in my room [at 11:30 P.M.]. I was not intoxicated.

After I broke from the group, I ran into the next room and sat on a chair in the dark. . . .

Coughlin managed to compose herself, cautiously left the darkened room and gained the elevators. Riding down the elevator to the lobby of the Hilton, she encountered two of the many women who had been assaulted while caught in the gauntlet on the third floor.

As Coughlin told the Naval Investigative Service,

Both were extremely upset, one almost in tears and the other extremely angry. The angry woman stated that they had been invited to a party by some Navy pilots and never expected to be manhandled. I recall one woman saying, "Those guys are a bunch of animals."

After the elevator arrived at the lobby, I parted company with the two women and did not see them again. I walked towards the main lobby. I was in total disbelief and in shock from what had taken place. . . .

Coughlin told Admiral Snyder the next morning at breakfast what had happened to her in the hotel hallway the night before. He took no immediate action. Snyder could have gathered all the aviators in a banquet room that very morning and had his aide identify the assailants. Coughlin said her chief assailant was a Marine captain. He could have been identified by the bite marks. If Snyder had acted promptly and aggressively, he might have kept the poison from spreading all through the Navy in the ensuing months and enabled the Navy to discipline the guilty. The long delay in responding allowed the poison to wash over the innocent as well as the guilty officers in Marine and Naval Air. In failing to act promptly, Snyder not only failed his own military aide, he failed his Navy.

These other excerpts from Coughlin's sworn statement indicate that Snyder just did not get it—did not comprehend why his aide was so upset:

> The following Sunday morning, 8 September 1991, I called Admiral Snyder at 0815 to meet him for breakfast. While on the phone, Admiral Snyder asked, "How was the third deck?" I told him that it stunk, "I was practically gangbanged by a group of fucking F-18 pilots, but we'll talk about that later." He said something to the effect of, "I went down to the third deck; had one margarita, said hello to a few friends and then left." He commented that it was too wild down there, and he didn't like to hang out there, or something to that effect. We arranged to meet at the lobby and have breakfast. . . .
>
> I told Admiral Snyder [at breakfast], "The guys I ran into were completely out of control. It was really bad. These guys started grabbing at me and grabbing my rear. They were so out of line. Just completely out of line, and they knew I was an admiral's aide. They started yelling, 'admiral's aide.'" I told him, "I just walked down the hall and these guys went to town on me. It was really bad."
>
> Snyder was shaking his head and said basically, "That's what you have got to expect when you go up to the third deck with a bunch of drunk aviators." I told him again that these guys were completely out of line; I had to kick and fight and bite to get out of there; that I bit the crap out of one guy; that it was really, really bad.
>
> His remarks next turned to something about Tailhook always being out of hand on the third deck. And the conversation turned to the filming of "Topgun." . . .
>
> I was incredulous that Admiral Snyder said those things and never asked if I was okay or if I was hurt. I told Admiral Snyder that I thought the fighter bubbas here at Tailhook really are disgusting and what happened to me was too far out of line.

Coughlin swore in her statement that she complained to Snyder again on 13 September 1991 and for a third time on 16 September 1991 about what had happened to her at Tailhook. He still took no action, she said. In her statement she said she went into his office at Pax River on 17 September 1991 and declared:

> "Sir, I don't think you understand how bad that thing was in Tail-hook. It was the worst thing that has ever happened to me." I do not recall any specific comment that he made except something very vague like, "Yeah, those guys get really wild."

Coughlin said she complained to other officers in Snyder's office about Tailhook. Overhearing her, Snyder said, according to Coughlin:

> "That's what you get when you go to a hotel party with a bunch of drunk aviators."
> At that point, I lost my temper and yelled at him, "You better watch what you say!"

Snyder left the office on a trip. Coughlin said she then went into the office of CAPT Robert Parkinson, Snyder's chief of staff at Pax River, and declared:

> "That's it. I quit. I will not work for a man who tells me that's what I get. . . . Admiral Snyder just doesn't understand how bad it was and doesn't care enough to ask about his aide getting abused."
> Parkinson was extremely alarmed and spoke with me at length. He stated that we have a bigger problem than me quitting my job with Admiral Snyder. He said we needed to do something about this [sexual abuse at Tailhook]. . . .
> [Parkinson telephoned Snyder the morning after his meeting with Coughlin to tell the admiral that] the most important issue here was that I had been sexually harassed and it had gone this long unreported. He was very adamant about the fact that not acting on this was in fact condoning the behavior, and Admiral Snyder and I needed to talk about the specifics so that we could take action immediately.

Coughlin said Parkinson repeated those sentiments to Snyder during a meeting the three officers had on 19 September 1991 when Snyder returned to Pax River.

At this point, almost two weeks after the assault on his military aide, Snyder agreed to write VADM Richard M. Dunleavy, Assistant Chief of Naval Operations for Air Warfare, to describe the assaults and demand corrective action.

Three weeks after she had been assaulted, Coughlin was still furious. At first, she said in her statement,

> I didn't want a witchhunt, and then I changed my mind and said, "Yes, I do want a witchhunt. I want to know who did this to me and let everyone know you can't get away with that type behavior."

Fearful that the assault "would be swept under the carpet," Coughlin on 29 September 1991 wrote a letter to Dunleavy, detailing what had happened to her at Tailhook. Snyder hand-carried the letter to Dunleavy the next day, along with one of his own.

Once informed of Coughlin's complaints and Snyder's failure to act on them promptly, Navy leaders relieved Snyder as commander of the Naval Air Test Center. The Tailhook assaults were revealed in a general way in the press. Coughlin personalized them in June 1992 by telling newspapers and television stations what had happened to her in the hallway of the Hilton.

Tailhook exploded into the worst sexual-abuse scandal in the history of Naval Air. Navy Secretary H. Lawrence Garrett III, who attended the Tailhook convention, resigned. President Bush called Coughlin to the family quarters of the White House to extend his personal apology for the behavior of Marine and Navy aviators.

"I wanted to let you know how angry I am," Coughlin recalls Bush, a former naval aviator, told her. "I have a thirty-year-old daughter who is getting married tomorrow. I know how your father must feel. I should have let Barbara come in here."

Mrs. Bush entered the room at that point and told Coughlin, "I can't help but think this is a symptom of an attitude."

Mrs. Bush had cut to the heart of the problem as far as Coughlin, the gutsy lifeguard from Virginia Beach, was concerned.

"I know this is improper for the Commander in Chief to do with one of the troops," President Bush said at the end of the warm meeting with Coughlin, "but I just wanted to give you a hug." He did so, making Coughlin feel she had a Commander in Chief who cared what happened to her.

At this juncture, it seems to me the only obstacle for opening Marine and Naval Air all the way to women is what Mrs. Bush called "attitude."

Coughlin in the fall of 1992 when this book went to press was trying to shove that attitude aside and concentrate on learning to fly the Navy's CH-53 helicopter at Norfolk. But it was proving impossible to escape

Tailhook and its aftermath, to seal it away as a compartment in her mind.

For one thing, Coughlin had to travel all around the country to help identify assailants for Navy and Defense Department investigators. This interrupted her training.

Also, this task made it impossible for her to be regarded as one of the guys, an aviator who happened to be a woman rather than a woman who happened to be an aviator. She could sense bristling whenever she walked into a room full of aviators.

"I'm the biggest, ugliest reminder there is" of the Tailhook embarrassment, she told me in late 1992 in describing the Typhoid Mary reception she was receiving from many aviators.

"I am now the Navy's sexual-harassment poster child. But I wasn't harassed. I was assaulted.

"Sometimes some guy stops me in the hall of the Pentagon and tells me, 'That takes a lot of guts,'" to blow the whistle on officers who assaulted her. "I don't hear that from people I work with. But I have to keep an attitude that going to work is key to my survival even though there are days I hate going to work. To be a nonperson in a squadron is not a pleasant thing. I've aged fifty years in the last two years."

Despite the personal anguish and professional distractions, Coughlin hoped in the fall of 1992 to continue her flying career by being assigned to Sigonella Naval Air Station, Sicily, as a CH-53 helicopter pilot. ADM Frank B. Kelso II, Chief of Naval Operations, publicly thanked Coughlin in 1992 for reporting the Tailhook abuses and promised that her career would not be impeded by her whistle-blowing. ADM Jeremy M. Boorda, while the three-star Chief of Naval Personnel in 1991, told Coughlin: "We're going to make things right. You did the right thing."

The Navy and Defense Department moved on several fronts in the wake of Coughlin's disclosures in an attempt to reduce sexual assaults and harassment. Criminal investigations and sensitivity classes for officers on women's rights were part of the broad corrective effort.

The Naval Inspector General conducted the first investigation, sending Naval Investigative Service investigators all over the country, including TPS, to interview Tailhook attendees and victims. Said the Naval Inspector General in his 29 April 1992 report:

> U. S. Naval Investigative Service reports 26 victims of varying degrees of sexual assaults. More than half were female officers. There are an addi-

tional unknown number of female victims of the gauntlet who strongly protested their treatment but left without being identified.

Most victims went to the third floor not knowing what to expect. They were either invited to squadron hospitality suites or were on the third floor to meet friends. The gauntlet consisted of a varying number of males lining a narrow portion of the third floor hallway outside the suites. The character of the gauntlet, which existed over all three nights of the symposium [5 through 7 September 1991] changed with its participants. The gauntlet ebbed and flowed as participants came and went. On different occasions, it was organized to the point where participants were alerted to females specifically targeted or allowed to pass by call signals, "decks awash" or "decks afoul."

When women attempted to walk down the hall, they were encircled and sexually molested to varying degrees. The attacks ranged from being patted on the buttocks to having other portions of their anatomy groped and grabbed.

The gauntlet has existed for at least the last two years, and most likely back to 1986. Some of the women who recognized the gauntlet for what it was, reportedly went through it voluntarily. However, a significant number of women openly objected to their treatment, and, when they protested to their attackers and the other men surrounding them, their protests were ignored and their means of escape blocked. Often expressed emotions of victims were helplessness and the absolute loss of control over their safety. They feared that anything could happen to them and they were helpless to prevent it. The attacks not only varied in degree of severity but in duration. . . .

Closing ranks and obfuscation were the predominant responses to the questions posed by the Naval Investigative Service and Naval Inspector General inquiries. Interviews with Tailhook Association committee members produced similar results. While they admitted to being present on the third floor corridor and suites throughout the evenings, they observed little which they would classify as untoward conduct requiring their intervention. This was even after a committee member admitted observing women's slacks and underpants thrown through the air in the third floor corridor, and accompanying hotel security assisting a partially nude female minor off the floor. In general, like the majority of personnel interviewed, committee members did not identify attendees in the third floor corridor or suites. . . .

As reflected by the interviews, Naval Inspector General found that the conduct in several Navy and Marine Corps hospitality suites created an atmosphere demeaning to women. Attendees interviewed revealed the presence of scantily clad female bartenders; the hiring by duty officers of strippers who generally ended up nude and participated in simulated sexual acts with members of the audience; the showing of pornographic films; the practice of shaving women's legs and other body parts; women encouraged to expose their breasts in exchange for tee shirts; obscene drink dispensers.

Other activities in and around the third floor included male streakers, male and female mooning and males exposing themselves to women. In one incident, where three individuals were pressing their buttocks against an upper story window, the window was forced out and crashed onto the crowded patio area, slightly injuring at least one woman. In another instance, a duty officer removed an obviously extremely intoxicated minor out of his squadron's suite into the hallway where she apparently lost consciousness and was passed up [the] gauntlet where she was partially disrobed. . . .

The hotel suffered $23,000 in damages, of which $18,000 was due to spilled drinks and cigarette burns in third floor suites and on corridor carpeting. These damages were paid for by the Tailhook Association or from funds collected by the various squadrons.

Alcoholic beverages were also served in at least one identified contractor hospitality suite to one flag officer and other senior Naval officers despite long standing specific Standards of Conduct prohibitions against accepting entertainment in contractor hospitality suites.

The activities which took place in the corridor and suites, if not tacitly approved, were allowed to continue by the leadership of the aviation community and Tailhook Association. Further, the conduct in the corridor was merely reflective of the atmosphere that was created by the activities in a number of the suites.

As reflected by interviews, there is still little understanding of the nature, severity and number of assaults which occurred involving the female civilians and officers. A common thread running through the overwhelming majority of interviews concerning Tailhook '91 was: "What's the big deal?" Those interviewed demonstrated no understanding that the activities in the suites fostered an atmosphere of sexual harassment and that the actions which occurred in the corridor constituted at a minimum sexual harassment, and, in many cases, criminal sexual assault.

It is Naval Inspector General's opinion that the atmosphere in the suites condoned, if not encouraged, the gang mentality which eventually led to the sexual assaults. Further, despite Secretary of the Navy guidance concerning sexual harassment and the deglamorization of alcohol, the atmosphere which permeated the third floor promoted the abuse of women and the excessive use of alcohol. While there is no question that the excessive use of alcohol contributed to the misbehavior of individuals, there is every indication that nearly all participants made conscious decisions and were aware of their actions. . . .

Individual comments in interviews and numerous letters to the editor reflect a belief that because of the risks associated with carrier aviation, the conduct of Tailhook '91 should be tolerated. A number of female officers assaulted expressed hesitancy about reporting their experiences because of their belief that the ensuing investigation and publicity would be detrimental to their careers. In one instance, a Tailhook Committee member harassed and berated an officer victim for reporting her assault by the gauntlet, an assault which he witnessed but did nothing to stop.

A review of the tapes of the Flag Officer Panel [which included questions about why male aviators could not freely express their opposition to female aviators' being admitted to all-male aircraft squadrons] at the symposium noted the very negative reaction to a question about the possible future presence of women in the tactical air community. Tactical air leadership failed to strongly counter the openly demonstrated unwillingness of the community to accept women.

The Naval Inspector General report submitted a list of conclusions, including these:

The results of interviews showed a marked absence of moral courage and personal integrity. This was evidenced by interviewees' unwillingness to accept responsibility, either for their own actions or for the actions of others in their command for what transpired during their floor social activities. Apparently, there is a sense in the tactical air community that what happened on the third floor was acceptable social conduct and that allegations concerning their conduct had been blown out of proportion.

The inappropriate sexual behavior in the Navy and Marine Corps squadron and unit sponsored suites at Tailhook '91 had been accepted, tolerated and condoned over the years, making it now the norm for Tailhook gatherings. This is in contrast to most of the rest of the Navy which has modified its behavior in response to changing social standards.

There is an apparent lack of awareness of sensitivity to sexual harassment and to the treatment of women in the tactical air community.

There is a long standing, continued abuse and glamorization of alcohol within the aviation community.

The Naval Inspector General's report did not satisfy anyone, least of all the Senate Armed Services Committee. Committee members were outraged that the Navy confirmed what Coughlin had reported about Tailhook but found few of the culprits, did not investigate the activities of Garrett and other top Navy officials at Tailhook, and deleted from its report testimony from a Navy captain that he accompanied Garrett to several of the hospitality suites at the Las Vegas Hilton, contradicting Garrett's assertions that he did not go into them. The Armed Services Committee put a hold on approving Navy promotions until it received better answers from the Navy about Tailhook.

In response to the scalding criticism of the Naval Inspector General's investigation, Garrett on 18 June 1992 requested that the Defense Department's civilian Inspector General review the Navy's inquiry and go beyond it if warranted. On 24 September 1992, Acting Navy Secretary Sean O'Keefe released the report by Derek J. Vander Schaaf, the Pentagon's deputy Inspector General, on the Navy's investigation.

Vander Schaaf, who has a reputation for merciless fairness, assailed the Navy investigation as inadequate and unprofessional. O'Keefe, in releasing Vander Schaaf's searing assessment, vowed the Navy would reform with regard to respecting women's rights.

"I need to emphasize a very important message," he told a packed news conference at the Pentagon's studio. "We get it. We know that the larger issue is a cultural problem which has allowed demeaning behavior and attitudes towards women to exist within the Navy Department. . . . Our senior leadership is totally committed to confronting this problem and demonstrating that sexual harassment will not be tolerated. Those who don't get the message will be driven from our ranks."

In a letter to O'Keefe, Vander Schaaf used these words to charge shallowness, bureaucratic bungling, and shielding of Navy higher-ups during the Navy's own Tailhook investigation:

> The scope of the investigations should have been expanded beyond the assaults to encompass other violations of law and regulation as they became apparent and should have addressed individual accountability for the leadership failure that created an atmosphere in which the assaults and other misconduct took place. . . .
>
> Inadequacies in the investigations were due to the collective management failures and personal failures on the part of the Under Secretary [of the Navy J. Daniel Howard], the Naval Inspector General [RADM George W. Davis VI], Navy Judge Advocate General [RADM John E. Gordon] and the commander of the Naval Investigative Service [RADM Duvall "Mac" Williams, Jr.].

In our view the deficiencies in the investigations were the result of an attempt to limit the exposure of the Navy and senior officials to criticism regarding Tailhook 91.

In documenting those conclusions, the Vander Schaaf report included these specific findings:

Finding

Under Secretary Howard "with oral direction" told the Inspector General to limit his inquiry to "the details of the Navy 'business relationship' with the Tailhook Association" and refused the Inspector General's request to conduct an "all-up" investigation.

Elaboration

Naval Inspector General Davis recommended to Howard that Davis

form a large team to examine comprehensively three areas of concern to him: first, whether the Navy had a cultural problem that contributed to the assaults at Tailhook; second, whether the chain of command took appropriate action when notified of assaults by Navy victims; and third, whether there were noncriminal violations arising from Tailhook 91 that should be referred to the chain of command. The Naval Inspector General told us that the Under Secretary told him that the Naval Inspector General did not have the resources to conduct an investigation of that nature. The Under Secretary advised the Naval Inspector General to let the Naval Investigative Service take the lead and conduct all interviews, which the Naval Inspector General could then review, performing whatever follow up was necessary. According to the Naval Inspector General, he told the Under Secretary that if that was to be the procedure, the Under Secretary should task the Naval Investigative Service specifically with investigating the misconduct issues because that was not an area Naval Investigative Service normally investigated. The tasking was never given. The Under Secretary told us he does not remember such a conversation with the Naval Inspector General. The Secretary of the Navy delegated to the Under Secretary the responsibility to oversee the conduct of the investigations.

Finding

The Naval Investigative Service failed to interview senior officers about Tailhook, concentrating on junior officers, and turned a blind eye to crimes other than assault, such as indecent exposure and conduct unbecoming an officer.

Elaboration

We believe thoroughness demanded the senior officers present be interviewed. The other weakness is that, as evidence of non-assaultive criminal activity, such as indecent exposure or conduct unbecoming an officer, developed, the Naval Investigative Service investigative scope was not expanded to encompass it. . . . Important information was not pursued.

Finding

The major flaw in the Naval Inspector General investigation is that, with very few exceptions, he failed to interview senior officials who attended Tailhook 91 and failed to assign any individual responsibility for the misconduct that occurred there.

Elaboration

Naval Inspector General Davis "told us that he believed" if he questioned senior Navy officials his investigation would be regarded as a

witch hunt that would detract from fixing the cultural problem identified in the reports. He stated he believed that would hurt the Navy rather than help it.

In a very telling comment, the Naval Inspector General told us: "Once we determined we had a cultural problem, then it was our contention—in that group around the table, the Under and all these people—that the corporate 'we' had allowed this to take place. And to interview squadron [commanding officers], to ask them why they allowed that to happen, didn't make any difference because the whole system allowed it to happen. And frankly, I think a Navy captain who had seen that over four or five years, had seen the Rhino room with a dildo hanging on the wall, is not going to walk in there in 1991 and change anything."

While it is easy to be sympathetic to the attitude—that the Navy had allowed that kind of activity to go on for so many years the attendees had become enculturated to it, could not be expected to change it and therefore should not be held responsible for it—it [the Naval Inspector's rationale] must ultimately be rejected.

For what the Naval Inspector General failed to understand is that the time for attributing misconduct of that nature to a cultural problem had long since passed. At least a year prior to Tailhook 91, the Navy established a zero tolerance policy with respect to sexual harassment and sexual misconduct. . . .

Finding

Under Secretary Howard and Navy Judge Advocate General Gordon "were uncertain as to their respective roles and responsibilities."

Elaboration

Most significantly, the Under Secretary told us that he believed his role was to be an information gatherer only and that he was not supposed to direct, control or coordinate the investigations. The Under Secretary stated the following: "I felt hamstrung, trapped, blocked in every place that I tried to exert any influence at all. I was very dissatisfied, very frustrated. And there's a civilian control of the military issue here. . . . When a non-lawyer [which Howard was], a non-legal trained person tries to interfere in this process, you face roadblocks all over the place. People tell you, no, you can't do that; no, you can't do this. And they cite you line and verse. . . . If I was trying to figure out who the real master in this situation was, I knew it wasn't me."

Others, including the Secretary of the Navy, believed that the Under Secretary was, in fact, supposed to be controlling and coordinating the efforts of the Naval Inspector General and the Commander, Naval Investigative Service.

Additionally, the role of the Navy Judge Advocate General was unclear. When asked why the Navy Judge Advocate General was present during the meetings, the Under Secretary told us: "God, I don't know." When we asked the Navy Judge Advocate General who was providing legal advice to the Under Secretary, he responded, "I guess I was."

Finding

Under Secretary Howard failed to develop "a comprehensive investigative plan" under which the activities of the Naval Investigative Service and Navy Inspector General were coordinated.

Elaboration

We believe an investigative plan would have helped overcome a poor working relationship between the two agencies. From the outset, there was a gross lack of cooperation between the Commander of the Naval Investigative Service and the Naval Inspector General.

Finding

Under Secretary Howard's

assertion that he was merely an information gatherer is not acceptable. As the second highest civilian official in the Department of the Navy, we view his failure to provide effective leadership and direction to the Naval Inspector General and the Commander, Naval Investigative Service, an abrogation of responsibility. The Under Secretary's failure to exercise leadership to ensure the overall adequacy of the Navy investigations into Tailhook was a key failure in the matter.

Finding

RADM Williams as commander of the Naval Investigative Service "demonstrated an attitude that should have caused an examination of his suitability to conduct the investigation."

Elaboration

Williams told several Navy associates that "men simply do not want women in the military" and "made comments to the effect that a lot of female Navy pilots are go-go dancers, topless dancers or hookers."

Barbara Spyridon Pope, Assistant Secretary of the Navy for Manpower and Reserve Affairs, "was outraged by the commander's comments and believed it raised an issue about his suitability to conduct the investigation."

When a female investigator told Williams that LT Coughlin had screamed at the Marine aviator assaulting her in the hallway of the Las Vegas Hilton, "What the fuck do you think you are doing?" Williams replied, according to the investigator quoted in the Vander Schaaf report:

" 'Any woman that would use the F word on a regular basis would welcome this activity.' "

"I remember this so vividly because I am a woman, and I have been known to use the F word on more than an occasional basis. So I personally found it offensive because personally I would never welcome that type of activity that [the victim] received up on the third floor. . . ."

We were told by several witnesses that the Commander of the Naval

Investigative Service commented on his concern that conducting the investigation could ruin the Naval Investigative Service relationship with the naval aviation community. That provides a more believable explanation for the commander's failure to interview senior officers

rather than his own excuse that he did not believe Secretary Garrett or any of the admirals at Tailhook had relevant information to his inquiry.

One of Williams' investigators quoted him as saying that his agency did not have "a fart's chance in a whirlwind" to conduct a successful investigation. The Regional Director of the Naval Investigative Service for the National Capital Region "stated that he was under constant pressure from Naval Investigative Service headquarters, specifically RADM Williams, to close the investigation.

> We believe the Commander's overriding goal, and the motivation for his actions, was to keep the investigation within narrow limits and to dissuade the investigators from pursuing issues that might lead them to question the conduct of senior officials at Tailhook 91.

Finding

"Senior Naval Investigative Service officials showed poor judgment, if not professional incompetence," by failing to include in the agency's report the statements from witnesses who said they saw Navy Secretary Garrett visiting hospitality suites at the Las Vegas Hilton. Although Garrett denied having visited those suites, "we believe the statements contradicting the Secretary's affidavit cast doubt on the Secretary's credibility regarding his activities on the third floor."

At the end of the thirty-two–page Vander Schaaf report, the Pentagon's deputy inspector general urged an overhaul of the Navy's investigatory capability. Vander Schaaf's recommendations included these:

"Consider whether" Under Secretary Howard, Judge Advocate General Gordon, Naval Inspector General Davis, and Naval Investigative Service Commander Williams "should continue in their current leadership roles within the Department of the Navy.

"Consider appropriate disciplinary action with respect to" Gordon and Williams "for their failure to fulfill their professional responsibilities in the Navy's Tailhook investigation.

"Consider whether any organizational changes or procedural modifications would improve the investigative process within the Department of the Navy and coordinate any changes with the Office of Inspector General, Department of Defense."

O'Keefe announced at his 24 September 1992 news conference that he would replace Williams, who opted to retire, with a civilian as head of the Naval Investigative Service; that he was replacing the one-star Davis with a three-star officer in the Naval Inspector General job; and that Judge Advocate General Gordon "has requested retirement, and I have granted that request." Gordon issued a statement after O'Keefe's press conference, saying he had "no supervisory authority" over the Naval Investigative Service and denied that his retirement was requested by the Navy Acting Secretary.

As for Under Secretary Howard, who was the closest thing to the captain when the Navy's investigatory ship went aground, O'Keefe said he had decided to keep Howard in the Navy's second-highest job. O'Keefe said Howard had been "relegated to the task of being a referee because he relied upon those with professional expertise in investigative matters. These professionals failed him."

The most significant message for me in the whole Tailhook mess, including the investigation that outdid the Three Stooges for bumbling incompetence, is that the Navy has a deep-seated cultural problem when it comes to granting professional equality for women. No President, no presidential commission, no Pentagon inspector general, no Navy secretary, no admiral, no captain, no congressional committee can change that culture by instant orders or laws. This cultural intolerance is similar to racial intolerance. It is a seeping poison that must be neutralized wherever and whenever it shows up. Constant education, punishment for the bigots, and rewards for the enlightened must be part of a never-ending campaign to give full rights—in the head, in the heart, and in the rule book—to the women who decided to answer their country's call and serve in the American military.

Despite the supportive words President Bush and Admiral Kelso uttered to whistle-blower Coughlin and all the promises of Acting Navy Secretary O'Keefe about reform, the fact that Bush and Defense Secretary Richard B. Cheney—after Congress opened the door all the way to U.S. military women in 1991—slammed it shut for a year by appointing yet another commission to study the question demonstrated that they still don't get it.

I asked Lori Melling, Class 100's point woman for full equality for female aviators, whether the fallout from the Tailhook explosions would advance her cause. "If anything," she said of Tailhook, "it's been a distraction. The bottom line is being treated as an equal. A lot of guys are still fighting it. Things are going to get better eventually. But I'm probably too senior now to get into a fleet squadron. But if I can help open things up for my daughter, great."

Melling was among those women who were buoyed by the message recently delivered by RADM Barton D. Strong to all hands at the newly organized Naval Air Warfare Center Aircraft Division, which encompasses the former Naval Air Test Center, at Pax River. He told everyone in a series of sensitivity sessions in the base movie theater that women were in tactical air to stay and anybody who could not accept them as professional equals could pack up and leave.

LT Coughlin said the professional acceptance she received from fellow Navy and Marine aviators during her pre-Tailhook days at Pax River "spoiled me." Getting back to that professionalism and holding onto it is a worthy goal for the second fifty years at Pax River, which begins on 1 April 1993.

Summing Up

Despite budget woes, T-45A problems, Tailhook, and other high waves slapping against the Navy of 1992, it still has thousands of men and women pursuing excellence day after day for the good of the service, for the good of the country. Navy test pilots and engineers are at the forefront of these pursuers of excellence. I close with a salute to all those who are pressing on, regardless.

Acknowledgments

No one could write a book like this without a lot of help from a lot of people.

I am indebted to officers at the top of the Navy; to administrators, teachers, flight instructors, parariggers, and students at the U.S. Naval Test Pilot School; to friends who read the manuscript, and to editors at the Naval Institute Press who improved it.

Within the Navy's information directorate, I am particularly grateful to RADM Brent Baker, Chief of Navy Information, for supporting the project; to CAPT James P. Mitchell of that office for his skillful liaison efforts; and to Lola Hilton and her public-information staff at Patuxent River for on-the-scene assistance.

At the top of the Naval Air Test Center at Pax River, I am indebted to RADM Don Boecker and his wife, Gay, for their help and friendship, and to Boecker's deputy in 1991, CAPT Robert Parkinson.

At the U.S. Naval Test Pilot School, Director Thomas J. Bernsen proved to be far more than just officially cooperative. He shared his insights and friendship in a warming way, which meant more to me than he can know.

Marine LtCol Robert A. Price, Bernsen's deputy during Class 100's school year and now director of TPS, also extended the hand of friendship, even to taking me fishing. So he, too, must be on this short list.

Robert B. Richards, chief academic instructor, and William B. Rhodes, technical director, always made time to talk to me, as did individual teachers. I must include the name of John J. McCue, Jr., aerodynamics instructor, if for no other reason than that his constant and good-natured needling of this invader from the press kept me buoyed spiritually even when his lectures were sinking me intellectually.

All the instructors I flew with were great, so I am not going to pick out a few to name. I thank you all for your patience and clarity as you explained what we were doing in the skies over Patuxent.

Before you can fly in Navy jets, you have to wriggle into all kinds of flight and survival gear. Among the unsung heroes here were parariggers Terry Delay, Tina Dial, Tom Cranford, Joe Hautzenroder, Tim Jeffas, and John Snyder. They are a can-do bunch who never seem to think anything is too much trouble.

And, of course, I would never get my phone calls to TPS answered or any more flights scheduled if I did not throw a deserved and sincere salute to the women who really run the place: Sandy Dyson in the front office, Debby Lewis and Tammy Harry in flight operations, and Joyce Ridgell and Karen Jensen in the faculty beehive.

Ed Stokel, a St. Mary's County historian, was both helpful and joyful company as he filled me in on life at the Naval Air Test Center when it was raw and rip-roaring.

Once the first draft of the manuscript was written, Burt Hoffman, former national editor of *The Washington Star,* was kind enough to give it a skillful read through the eyes of a civilian. RADM Gary F. Wheatley, skipper of the USS *John F. Kennedy* while I was aboard to write *Supercarrier* and an experienced test pilot who taught at TPS, followed up by focusing the eyes of the expert on what I had written. Former foreign correspondent and editor Charles S. Foltz, a neighbor, also made valuable suggestions, and Lois G. Parker gave a big assist in proofreading.

At the Naval Institute Press, Thomas F. Epley, editorial director, was unflagging in his enthusiasm for the book. And Anthony F. Chiffolo in editing the manuscript displayed the kind of perfectionist skill and care that any test pilot would envy.

Lastly, on the home front, I thank my wife, Joan Gibbons Wilson, for tolerating the disruption of book writing one more time and never complaining about the long absences nor the compost of papers that kept piling up in the house.

Index

About the Author

George C. Wilson has been a student of military affairs from the ground up for more than twenty-five years, first as a reporter for *Aviation Week & Space Technology* magazine and most recently as national military correspondent for *The Washington Post*. *Flying the Edge* is his fifth book. It is based on a year spent at U.S. Naval Test Pilot School in Patuxent River, Maryland, flying with test pilots to see and feel how they are trained. Wilson's other books include *Supercarrier*, which chronicled life as he saw and lived it while on a seven-and-a-half-month deployment on the USS *John F. Kennedy*, the first correspondent to complete a deployment on a carrier, and *Mud Soldiers*, a year-long study—most of it conducted in the field—of an Army rifle company.

THE NAVAL INSTITUTE PRESS

FLYING THE EDGE

The Making of Navy Test Pilots

Designed by Pamela Lewis Schnitter

Set in Simoncini Garamond in Adobe Post Script
on a Macintosh IIci and output
by BG Composition, Baltimore, Maryland

Printed on 60-lb. Glatfelter offset eggshell white
and 70-lb. Glatfelter Glatco gloss smooth white
and bound in Holliston Roxite B and DSI Papan
by The Maple-Vail Book Manufacturing Group
York, Pennsylvania